Dimensions of Native America: the Contact Zone

Co-Curators:

Jehanne Teilhet-Fisk
Professor of Art History

Robin Franklin Nigh

*For Moira
with wonderful
memories of our
adventures in education
love,
JeL*

Organized by the Museum of Fine Arts of the School of Visual Arts & Dance at Florida State University with grant assistance from the Florida Arts Council—Visual Arts, Interdisciplinary, and Arts in Education Programs; the *Communiversity* Partnership of the Cultural Services Grant Program of Tallahassee-Leon County; the Congress of Graduate Students of Florida State University; and Private Benefactors.

Museum of Fine Arts
School of Visual Arts & Dance, Florida State University
Tallahassee, Florida
February 13-March 31, 1998

Appleton Museum of Art
Ocala, Florida
April 14-May 31, 1998

Project Support and Organization:

Guest Curated for Florida State University Museum of Fine Arts by Jehanne Teilhet-Fisk, Department of Art History, and Robin Franklin Nigh, Museum Special Projects / Art in State Buildings Coordinator; Grantwriter / Administrator—Allys Palladino-Craig; Fiscal Officer—Julienne T. Mason; Joint Projects /Appleton and Florida State Museums—Jean Young; Registrar and Coordinator of Education Programs—Viki D. Thompson Wylder; Chief Preparator—Mark Fletcher.

Florida Department of State
Sandra B. Mortham
Secretary of State
Florida Arts Council
Division of Cultural Affairs

This program is sponsored in part by the State of Florida, Department of State, Division of Cultural Affairs, and the Florida Arts Council.

Publication:

Editor of Research & Content: Dr. Jehanne Teilhet-Fisk, Department of Art History, Florida State University. *Catalogue Research:* Hilary Scothorn, MA, 1996, Native American Art History, University of New Mexico. *Special Advisor:* Dr. J. Anthony Paredes, Department of Anthropology, Florida State University.

Publication Funding: This catalogue was published by the Museum Press with funding generated from private contributions and public grant funds raised to support programming. Portions of Museum programming in the 1997-1998 calendar are generously underwritten by support from granting agencies noted under Benefactors. Other Museum funding derives from the School of Visual Arts & Dance, J. L. Draper, Dean; fund-raising by the Museum on behalf of its programming includes the gratefully-acknowledged support of the Membership.

Museum Press:

Editor / Publisher: A. Palladino-Craig
Book Designer and Senior Editorial Assistant: Julienne T. Mason
Editorial Intern: Jeanette Balchunis
Cover Design: Anna McCambridge, Creative Director / Graphic Design, Architects Design Group, Winter Park, Florida.
Printer: Progressive Printing Company, Inc., Jacksonville, Florida.

Editorial Note on Variations in Usage:

Language is a landscape in transition: the variant spellings in words such as *tepee / tipi* or *kachina / katsina* and many other common and proper nouns in this text reveal the evolution of transcription. At present, multiple usages are employed—both historical spellings and more contemporary reflections; total standardization for the sake of this publication would be undesirable since it would force alteration of spellings in the titles of historical artworks or in quoted passages from other sources. Indeed, there is no consensus, only plurality of usage in texts today, a situation which this publication mirrors. Variations in the citations of dimensions of works of art likewise reflect information available at press time; some omissions were unavoidable because sources could provide images, but did not have access to all vital statistics. We trust that these minor inconsistencies in treatment will not impede the Reader's enjoyment of the concepts and analyses presented.

Cover:

Front Cover ■ Portion of a ledger drawing by Howling Wolf (Cheyenne), created at Fort Marion, St. Augustine, Florida, *c.* 1875-1877. Collection of Sara W. Reeves and I.S.K. Reeves V. Collection no. P-1240. (Photo: Northwest Document Conservation Center, Andover, Massachusetts)

Back Cover, left to right:
■ Pop Chalee, *Black Forest*, n.d., Taos painting, 49.5 x 64.8 cm. Collection of the School of American Research, Santa Fe, New Mexico.
■ Young Man's Big Shirt, Seminole, *c.* 1925, patchwork, length 36 inches. Collection of Sara W. Reeves and I.S.K. Reeves V. (Photo: Beverly Brosius)
■ Man's Turban with Beaded Fobs, Seminole, *c.* 1890, wool, 5 1/2 high and 15 inches in diameter. Historical Society of Martin County, The Elliot Museum, Stuart, Florida.
■ Plains Indian child in "fancy dress" at Taos Powwow, New Mexico, 1990. (Photo: J. Teilhet-Fisk)

Table of Contents

Benefactors and Lenders

Benefactors

Architects Design Group, Inc., Winter Park, Florida
Art Students League of Florida State University
Congress of Graduate Students of Florida State University
The Florida Arts Council: Visual Arts, Interdisciplinary, and Arts in Education Programs
Florida State University Department of Art Visiting Artist Program
Tallahassee Cultural Resources Commission, *Communiversity* Partnership
Dr. Jehanne Teilhet-Fisk, Tallahassee, Florida
Shoney's Inn and Suites of Tallahassee, Florida
Women's Studies, Florida State University, Dr. Jean Bryant, Director

Lenders

American Museum of Natural History, New York
A:shiwi Publishing, Zuni, New Mexico
Buffalo Bill Historical Center, Cody, Wyoming
Butler Institute of American Art, Youngstown, Ohio
Florida Museum of Natural History, Gainesville, Florida
Sandy Green, Glenn Green Galleries, Santa Fe, New Mexico
Historical Society of Martin County, The Elliot Museum, Stuart, Florida
Indian Temple Mound Museum, Ft. Walton Beach, Florida
International Folk Art Foundation, Museum of International Folk Art, Santa Fe, New Mexico
Lauren Rogers Museum of Art, Laurel, Mississippi
Collection of George Longfish
Collection of Mary Lyon
Museum of Northern Arizona, Flagstaff, Arizona
Collection of J. Anthony Paredes
The Philbrook Museum of Art, Tulsa, Oklahoma
Collection of Sara W. Reeves and I.S.K. Reeves V
Collection of Robin and Robert Rhodes
School of American Research, Santa Fe, New Mexico
Star / Fire Collection—Sandra Starr-Tanner
Steinbaum Krauss Gallery, New York
Whitney Museum of American Art, New York
&
Private Collectors and The Artists

Acknowledgements

Professor Jehanne Teilhet-Fisk, co-curator of this exhibition, never thinks small; by temperament and topic, she addresses a large audience. The Museum is deeply indebted to her curatorial leadership and to the team she pulled together for this important event. Team members include co-curator Robin Franklin Nigh, research assistant Hilary L. Scothorn, and fifteen enthusiastic student authors; the Advisory Board was comprised of prominent spokesmen for issues addressed in this exhibition. Those distinguished advisors include: Joe Quetone, Director of the Florida Governor's Council on Indian Affairs; Blue Sau-Pa Pahdocony, President, Four Horses Native American Productions; Special Advisor J. Anthony Paredes, Professor of Anthropology; Lance Lane, President, and Leandra Scott, Vice President, Native American Student Association (Fall 1997); and John Chaves, Attorney-at-Law.

The Museum has a tradition of working with exceptional guest curators whose ideas rivet the attention of the community; we may proudly note other museum projects in past seasons that have involved students of the university in key professional positions—as curators, authors, designers, education program specialists, and support staff. The strength of the university-wide Certificate Program in Museum Studies has been built upon just such investments of interdisciplinary time and expertise by the university faculty. The Museum enjoys its role of making projects happen: writing grants, negotiating loans, editing and publishing texts, and training student participants in the mysteries of museum work.

Before the Reader turns the pages of this outstanding effort by so many dedicated participants, a few particular acknowledgements are in order. Our Benefactors have been pledged to the academic excellence of this project, and the support of three separate panels at the Florida Arts Council and the *Communiversity* Partnership of the Tallahassee Cultural Resources Commission were vital components. Art History graduate students Kelly Barnes, Kevin Sandridge, Hilary L. Scothorn, and, of course, Robin F. Nigh successfully presented a petition for funding to the Florida State University Congress of Graduate Students. Among a prestigious list of Lenders, three collectors deserve special gratitude for overall contributions—Sara W. Reeves and I.S.K. Reeves V, and Sandra Starr-Tanner. Through his wise *Preface*, our great and good friend J. Anthony Paredes has again been a supporter of this Museum's programming. Our visitors' experiences will have been immeasurably enriched by the artists who will be on hand for the exhibition—James Luna, Sara Bates, Hulleah Tsinhnahjinnie, and by those who have guided us both spiritually and in practical ways—Joe Quetone and Blue Sau-Pa Pahdocony.

To the staff who have brought this project to completion, my personal gratitude: Robin Franklin Nigh, as co-curator and chief architect of loans, negotiated for permission to borrow every artwork, and most photo rights, on behalf of the Museum, as well as contributing her own lively essay; the hand of Julienne T. Mason, as designer par excellence, is apparent on each page of this catalogue, and she has benefited the project even more greatly by what is, perhaps, *not* apparent, i.e. her innate understanding of the rigors of academic press; Viki D. Thompson Wylder and her volunteer corps, including Alyssa Whittle and Mary Spadafora, have created educational materials which will serve the full spectrum of age groups from kindergarten through high school, including adult community groups and touring senior and handicapped-student groups; Jean Young has acted as trouble-shooter, a role she handles with élan for joint programs of this Museum and the Appleton Museum of Art in Ocala; the capable Mark Fletcher will work with graduate assistants Bill Woolf and Ya-Mei Su in implementing the design of the exhibition; Kevin Sandridge and Harry Bleattler continue to oversee community visitation; and Jeanette Balchunis was an inspired editorial assistant.

It is with great pleasure that we join Professor Jehanne Teilhet-Fisk in acknowledging the hard work and commitment of so many talented individuals in bringing *Dimensions of Native America: the Contact Zone* to the public. The two museums under the aegis of the School of Visual Arts and Dance, and our Dean Jerry L. Draper, look forward to welcoming our visitors and visiting artists on this superlative occasion.

Allys Palladino-Craig
Director

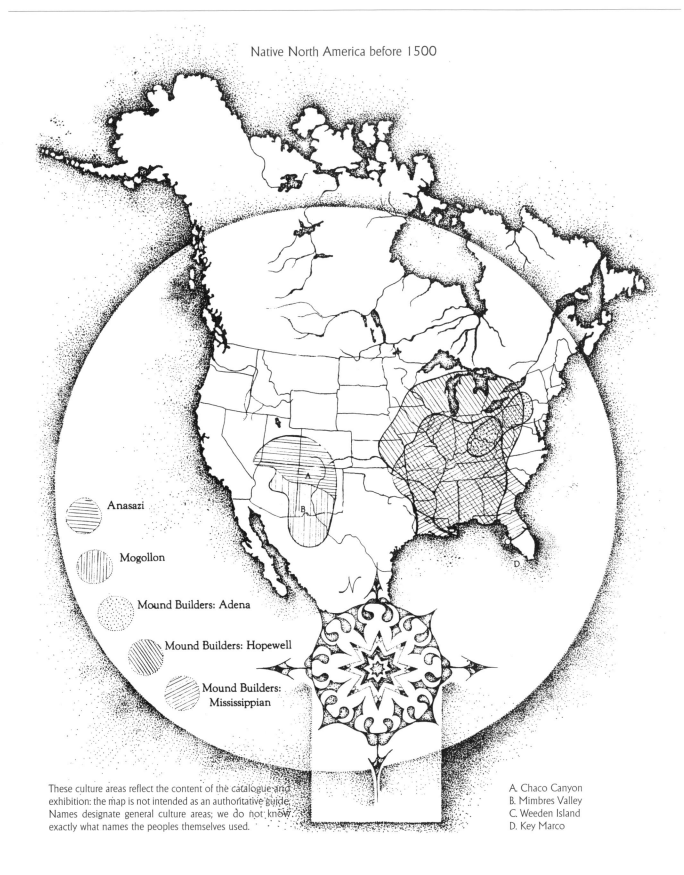

Native North America before 1500

Anasazi

Mogollon

Mound Builders: Adena

Mound Builders: Hopewell

Mound Builders: Mississippian

These culture areas reflect the content of the catalogue and exhibition: the map is not intended as an authoritative guide. Names designate general culture areas; we do not know exactly what names the peoples themselves used.

A. Chaco Canyon
B. Mimbres Valley
C. Weeden Island
D. Key Marco

Compiled by Kata Faust from the following sources—*North America before Columbus*, Map, Washington, D.C.: National Geographic Society, 1979. Carl Waldman, *Atlas of the North American Indian*, New York: Facts on File, Inc, 1985.

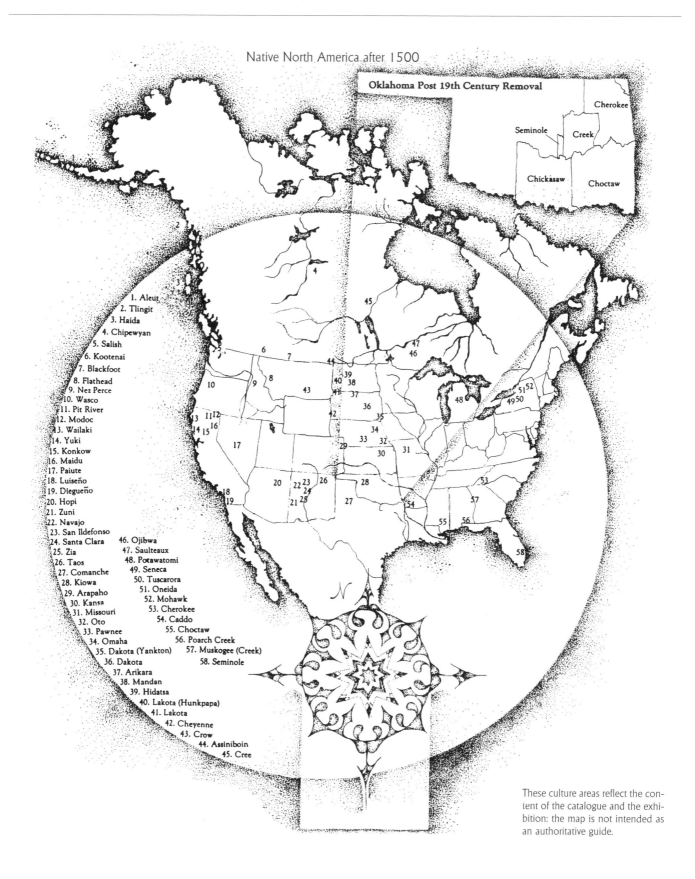

Native North America after 1500

Oklahoma Post 19th Century Removal

Cherokee

Seminole   Creek

Chickasaw   Choctaw

1. Aleut
2. Tlingit
3. Haida
4. Chipewyan
5. Salish
6. Kootenai
7. Blackfoot
8. Flathead
9. Nez Perce
10. Wasco
11. Pit River
12. Modoc
13. Wailaki
14. Yuki
15. Konkow
16. Maidu
17. Paiute
18. Luiseño
19. Diegueño
20. Hopi
21. Zuni
22. Navajo
23. San Ildefonso
24. Santa Clara
25. Zia
26. Taos
27. Comanche
28. Kiowa
29. Arapaho
30. Kansa
31. Missouri
32. Oto
33. Pawnee
34. Omaha
35. Dakota (Yankton)
36. Dakota
37. Arikara
38. Mandan
39. Hidatsa
40. Lakota (Hunkpapa)
41. Lakota
42. Cheyenne
43. Crow
44. Assiniboin
45. Cree

46. Ojibwa
47. Saulteaux
48. Potawatomi
49. Seneca
50. Tuscarora
51. Oneida
52. Mohawk
53. Cherokee
54. Caddo
55. Choctaw
56. Poarch Creek
57. Muskogee (Creek)
58. Seminole

These culture areas reflect the content of the catalogue and the exhibition: the map is not intended as an authoritative guide.

Compiled by Kata Faust from the following sources—*Indians of North America*, Map, Washington, D.C.: National Geographic Society, 1979. Harold E. Driver, *Indians of North America*, Chicago: University of Chicago Press, 1969. Carl Waldman, *Atlas of the North American Indian*, New York: Facts on File, Inc., 1985. Carl Waldman, *Encyclopedia of Native American Tribes*, China: Facts on File, Inc., 1988.

Fritz Scholder (Luiseño), *Indians Forever*, poster, 21 1/2 x 13 3/4 inches, c. 1968.
Collection of J. Anthony Paredes.

Preface

Dr. J. Anthony Paredes
Professor of Anthropology, Florida State University

When the organizers of *Dimensions of Native America: the Contact Zone*, Dr. Jehanne Teilhet-Fisk and Ms. Robin Franklin Nigh, asked me to write this preface, I was very pleased. But, I half-way expected it. Having taught North American ethnology at Florida State University for many years, plus long-time research and service programs with the Poarch Creek Indians of Alabama and others, like it or not, I had become FSU's local expert on Indian cultures. Being an "Indian expert" is a reputation any academic must wear with great caution and self-effacement if he is to be credible with real live Indian people. Nonetheless, I was confident enough in my expertise that I cockily thought to myself that I could give a flip-through of the text for the catalogue and quickly knock off a few sage comments on the changing nature of American Indian art. After a careful reading of the catalogue text, it was clear that this would be no easy task.

I finally collected my thoughts around three reactions I had to this guide for viewers. In the paragraphs that follow, I will not have much to say about the individual essays or the objects they frame. Much of what I have to say is from personal experiences that I hope will be read as allegories of larger messages. Those reactions were, first, a kind of audacity-induced humility; second, a sense of *déjà vu*; third, a wounded sense of historical responsibility to defend the overlooked accomplishments of others who preceded me.

Humility. The scope of *Dimensions of Native America* is simply overpowering. Here is an attempt to bring together a sampling of hundreds of traditions of Native America many times more diverse than the various cultural traditions of Native Europe. Likewise, the time-range covered in the exhibition is an audacious undertaking: from the eras of Anasazi and Mississippian cultures, centuries before the arrival of Europeans and Africans, to what's happening in the 1990s.

Despite what I judge to be a very innovative sampling of the palette of hues of representations of Native Americans, by themselves and by others, much is left out. Huge chunks of North America are barely represented, if at all, in this exhibition—e.g., the Arctic and the Northeast. There are vast epochs of life in the "Contact Zone" barely noticed—e.g., the protracted involvement of native peoples in the military and economic struggles among the European nations themselves to gain control of the Americas. There are many art forms not represented at all, both ancient—e.g., rock painting and featherwork—and modern—e.g., Eskimo stone sculpture or Cherokee wood sculpture. This is but a tiny, tiny sampling of what is left out, yet it is a reminder of just how audacious is any undertaking that attempts to deal with the complexity of the whole of Native America over so much time.

As Professor Teilhet-Fisk explains in her Introduction, one general category of objects left out of this exhibition is that of works whose very exhibition would be sacrilegious and, thereby, profoundly offensive to many Indians and sensible non-Indians alike (as I write this, it is late December and Christmas music is playing on the radio; imagine, if you can, a gallery show of costumes made for a Sunday School Christmas pageant at the local Baptist church—it's not quite the same, but you'll get the idea). Perhaps this can be taken as a reminder of just how provincial our western notion of "art for art's sake" really is. In most cultures—and in western culture for a very long time—art was inextricably woven into the fabric of work, social life, and religion. "Galleryizing" objects as art is not only decontextualization but also expropriation. Whether an ancient exotic pot or a wry jab at non-Indians by a modern American Indian painter, merely the act of displaying the piece in an art gallery is to "domesticate" and "westernize" it, is to place it into a niche meaningful for the elite and would-be elite of Euroamerican culture.

Having said all that, I was put in my place by the daunting task of being the "content" monitor for the historical and ethnographic accuracy of the catalogue essays. After a lifetime of study of American Indian cultures and history (and a participant in some of it), I thought I had a fairly detailed knowledge of American Indian cultures. Even so, and despite the limited range of regions, genres, and time-periods of Native America that I have noted, reviewing the drafts of these essays put me to a very severe test. From the nuances of Navajo inheritance customs to the history of contemporary ceramic traditions among Choctaws and Cherokees to the gender of participants in Pueblo public dance rituals, I found myself going back to the sources to check on specific points of information lodged at best in vague recollections of books read and lectures heard decades ago.

No matter how much one might think he knows about his subject, being reminded of what one does *not* know is healthily humbling. No doubt some historical and ethnographic errors in this catalogue have still gone unnoticed. For this, I apologize.

Déjà vu. At the grand opening of the Maxwell Museum of Anthropology at the University of New Mexico in the early 1960s, when I was a graduate student there, a huge exhibition of Navajo rugs marked the occasion. There were rugs everywhere; the place looked like an Oriental bazaar. At the time, I thought I had seen and learned as much as one could possibly want to know about different types of Navajo weaving. In 1995, when visiting a new museum in Albuquerque's Old Town, I was surrounded again with Navajo weavings. This time, however, there was a whole new startling style, unimagined in the 1960s: the "pictorials." Here in 1997, and in that 1995 Albuquerque show, I could not help but be transported back to that overpowering display of Navajo weaving at the Maxwell. Despite the differentness of the pictorials, there was a sameness in the seriousness with which the aficionados scrutinized the "Navajo weaver's art." American Indian art is as much about change as it is about tradition.

As the students who contributed to this exhibition show us, "real" Indian art is not frozen in time nor in the images by which non-Indian artists would represent native peoples and their cultures. It seems almost strange that this lesson has to be learned anew so many times. Reflecting on the way in which this exhibition attempts to educate us about the dynamism of American Indian art, I was transported in my mind back to a particular set of bookshelves beneath a window in my high school library. There, in the mid-1950s, after having already immersed myself in the minutiae of "traditional" Indian culture (found in everything from the Boy Scout Indian lore merit badge manual to the dry prose of late-nineeenth and early-twentieth century Bureau of American Ethnology reports), in an article in *National Geographic* I discovered contemporary Indian painting by the likes of Richard West, Oscar Howe, and Woodrow Crumbo. I came back to it again and again. Somehow I was transfixed by those flat, boldly outlined, often horizon-less, soft-colored paintings. They were just so different. Yet they, too, were somehow "authentically" Indian.

Detail of *Braided Rug* fabricated c. 1968 of plastic bags by Rose Sargent (Red Lake Chippewa [Ojibwa]), Minnesota. Collection of J. Anthony Paredes. (Photo: Mark Fletcher)

In the late 1960s, while employed at Bemidji State College, in Minnesota, I organized a small exhibition of contemporary Chippewa (Ojibwa) arts and crafts. The show had plenty of basketry, beadwork and such. It had, too, some beautiful modern powwow costumes—most notably some gorgeously beaded black velvet pieces. Also included were some paintings by a contemporary Chippewa artist, the renowned Patrick DesJarlait; there was something eerily ordinary about stopping by the neat but very modest frame house of one of Mr. DesJarlait's reservation relatives to pick up a loan of some of his famed paintings, paintings that hung without fanfare on his relative's livingroom wall among her inexpensive furnishings.

The exhibition also included such items as a carefully carpentered wooden birdhouse made by one of my elderly Chippewa friends and some charming crepe-paper flowers attached to a

spray of "stems" cleverly crafted from a tin can by a paritially disabled man who once had worked in a tourist souvenir "totem pole factory" in a nearby town. As *Indian* arts and crafts, these things were quite unsettling to some of my colleagues. I recall, however, that the item that most upset them was a braided rug made from plastic bread bags and "baggies." In that rug lies much historical symbolism. The typological ancestor of my "bread-bag rug" is the braided rag rug and before that the braided marsh-rush rug. Because of the possible (probable?) European origins of this type of rug, they were included, it seemed to me, as almost an afterthought in Carrie Lyford's book *Ojibwa Crafts* (1943), a book written as part of John Collier's enlightened efforts to encourage Native American arts and crafts during his administration of the Bureau of Indian Affairs in the 1930s and '40s. To those who would question the "authenticity" of some of the works displayed in *Dimensions of Native America*, I would respond to them as I did to my colleagues in long-away Minnesota, "If an Indian made it, it must be Indian." In the modern world, "*real* Indians" are not to be found in the romantic paintings of white (or Indian) artists nor in the mystical yearnings of New Agers but in the everyday life of remote camps, rural villages, reservation settlements and border towns, city neighborhoods, and the suburbs of North America.

Forgotten History. Part of the "new" multicultural scholarship in many fields is the rediscovery of the achievements and accomplishments of American Indians (and others) and bringing this "forgotten history" to public attention. We anthropologists never forgot. Now, it seems sometimes, there is a concerted effort to "forget" us anthropologists. An earlier draft of the text for this catalogue was predicated on the assumption that *Dimensions of Native America* would be the first FSU campus exhibition to address aspects of Native American art and culture. Not so. In 1993, Teresa Harris organized an exhibition of American Indian baskets in the Museum of Fine Arts as part of her undergraduate honors thesis in anthropology. True enough, Ms. Harris's exhibition was a small, unifocal (only basketry) "permanent collection" exhibition drawn from resources of the Department of Anthropology's Mary D. Lewis Collection—rather than a large, grant-supported, catalogue-documented exhibition. More to the point are the earlier, pioneering, and then widely-acclaimed efforts of Hale G. Smith at Florida State University.

Professor Smith was the founder and long-time head of the Department of Anthropology at Florida State University and directed the University Museum of his day. Although the Museum is now defunct, in the 1950s and the early '60s, the Museum was to North Florida the single shining point of light for the exhibition of the arts of indigenous peoples, including American Indians. In 1952, for example, the anthropology museum mounted a major exhibition entitled "Northwest Coast Indian Art" comprised of works on loan from the National Museum of Canada at Ottawa (all of this is documented in a scrapbook in the anthropology department—it was way before my time).

Hale Smith was one of the organizers and once-President of the Southeastern Museum Association. Apparently, he was an extremely innovative designer of exhibitions who developed dramatic lighting techniques and off-beat ways of positioning objects that are now routinely used in museum display, according to George Milton and Richard Puckett. Mr. Milton is a still-working Tallahassee painter who was Museum curator and instructor of courses in museology until his retirement in the early 1980s. Puckett is now director of Tallahassee's LeMoyne Art Foundation, Inc., but in his student days at FSU he worked with Smith and Milton on those early eye-catching exhibitions in the anthropology museum.

Ironically, during his student days (1953-57), Puckett was also half of an acrobatic duo known as the "Flying Seminoles." They performed, among other places, at FSU football games decked out in stylized Plains Indian costumes. The Flying Seminoles were the precursors for "Sammy Seminole," played by a series of students in the men's gymnastics and the circus programs until 1968. The threads of history are often woven together in unexpected and ideologically inconvenient ways: someone who helped build a new appreciation for American Indian art and culture in North Florida was also a "Flying Seminole" who fired up fans on gamedays in simpler times gone by, just as the mounted warrior ("Spirit of the Seminoles") does today.

Nowadays, it has become chic in certain circles to bash anthropology for imposing its own definitions on the lives and lifeways of American Indians. My profession comes in for a fair number of knocks in this exhibition. Yes, it is true that anthropologists seemed awfully depersonalized in their documentation and reporting of the beliefs and customs of native peoples. And, true enough, in the past anthropology seemed more obsessed with the differences than with the similarities among us humans. But, our objective has been and continues to be one quite different from that of the artist or mainstream humanist: we are concerned with gaining an empirical, objective understanding of human nature in all its many manifestations over time and space, no matter how unflattering such a scientific understanding might be. By a scientific understanding of human nature, as with such an understanding of any part of nature, we might avoid the pitfalls of magical thinking and rationally approach the problems of human adaptation to this planet of which we are an ever more prominent part of the ecosystem.

Contrariwise, the arts and humanities can give us an emotional understanding of our common humanity in which anthropology plays, perhaps at best, only a supporting role. Through exhibitions such as *Dimensions of Native America*, we can be awakened by visual jolts to emotional complacency and our jaun-

diced eyes brightened to new perspectives, This is not to say, however, that it's all a matter of point-of-view or multiple voices or "deconstructions" or "narrative constructions of negotiated reality" or whatever are the currently popular locutions of postmodernism gone amok. To crib from a controversial automobile bumper sticker, "shit does happen." Smallpox kills, people fight, crops dry up, a few people get more than their share of life's goodies and many more get much less; firmly-held beliefs turn out to be simply false. All of us humans together face a new "contact zone" in the world order of multi-national corporations and fragmenting states slipping deep into cyberspace. Here, more than ever, we must avoid the temptation to shrink from uncomfortable truths—whether they are emotional truths or rational truths, scientific truths or artistic truths. And, we must be careful not to retreat into feel-good philosophies and mere mysticism making us ripe for technological totalitarianism. Too often, as we gaze upon the "Native American Experience," we focus only on the aesthetic and spiritual dimensions and lose sight of the "practical" Indian—past or present—who labors, manipulates, plans, and experiments with technologies at hand to carry out the fundamental, mundane tasks of meeting the needs of physical survival and comfort.

By the time I joined the FSU anthropology faculty in 1969, its Museum had been reduced—for want of funding—to a single large display case just outside the then-new departmental office in the Bellamy Building. (I am one of the last anthropologists recruited by Hale Smith still on the faculty.) When I arrived, that lone case contained an eclectic assortment of objects from a variety of North American Indian "culture areas;" most of the items were beautiful in their craftsmanship even if not truly "art" by European standards. Only after staring at the exhibit several times did I notice that in an obscure corner of the floor of the exhibit case without any accompanying explanatory label was a perfectly formed "buffalo chip," a disk of dried bison dung. This was Hale Smith's cagey reminder that, ultimately, art is built upon the material foundations of any cultural system and of life itself.

To ignore the technological and economic dimensions of Native America—or any portion of our species—is no less dehumanizing than is ignoring the religious and artistic. Both my anthropological self and my (would-be) artistic self are confident that viewing and reading about *Dimensions of Native America: the Contact Zone* can lead the gallery visitor to a deeper understanding of the intersection of those dimensions over time and space, internally and externally, now and for the future. As Luiseño artist Fritz Scholder's poster declares "Indians Forever."

Introduction to the Contact Zone

Dr. Jehanne Teilhet-Fisk
Professor of Art History, Florida State University
Co-Curator and Editor of Research and Content

The collision and reconciliation of meanings and interpretations found in the arts of and by Native Americans is the theme that dominates *Dimensions of Native America: the Contact Zone*. Arts change through cultural drift or through a form of acculturation or contact with a foreign culture.[1] This exhibition focuses on the Native American arts that changed as a result of contact with Euroamericans through acculturation or assimilation. At the same time, Euroamerican art also changed through contact with Native American cultures. The exhibition is concerned with those acculturated art forms made by both Native Americans and Euroamericans that deliberately converge with and often appropriate each other's cultural properties. New concepts of technology in making art, new media, new subject matter, new styles, and new or different canons of aesthetics that were absent in a pre-contact situation for the Native and non-Native are now integrated into the visual and performing arts. By focusing on the acculturated arts, this exhibition will provide our multi-cultural community with a framework for better understanding and appreciating how these arts express fertile new ideas that are integrated into the matrix of tribe, culture or society. A further objective is to question the accuracy and intentions of the Western artists (particularly from the nineteenth and early twentieth centuries) who appropriated cultural property from the different American Indian tribes, making visual constructions of them in alignment with the prevailing objectives of the dominant culture at that time. These arts can then be compared with the visual constructions made by contemporary North American Indian and non-Indian artists (of the late twentieth century) whose internationally recognized works address in avant garde terms what it means to construct ethnic identities and cultural experiences that can and have led to misrepresentations of cultural truths and stereotypes.

This exhibition is the effort of a group of enthusiastic undergraduates and graduates who took in the spring of 1996 my art history course on the arts and cultures of the Southwest (the Pueblo and Navajo / Diné peoples). Since Florida State University has identified with and valorized the achievements of the Florida Seminole Tribe, the group felt it fitting for FSU students to organize and develop a campus exhibition addressing aspects of past and present American Indian art and culture.

Working under extraordinary time constraints and limited funding, these six undergraduates and eleven graduates never wavered in their commitment to this project. All of the students felt the need to see the arts and visit the cultural areas they were writing about. They traveled on their own resources to see muse-

ums, historical sites and private collections; to meet with artists (among the Florida Seminoles, Choctaw, Navajo / Diné, Zuni and Hopi); and to attend Powwows, Festivals, Santa Fe Indian Market and the Native American Art Studies Association meeting in Berkeley, California. This enterprise was carried out on top of normal student academic loads with cheerful sacrifices of weekends and holidays. I have great respect, admiration and affection for each student. Together they worked as a cohesive group and I know they will all go on to make major contributions in the fields of art history and museum studies or whatever they chose as their life's work. I would like to give a special "thank you" to Hilary L Scothorn who was a tremendous resource with her profound knowledge of American Indian arts and culture.

The title of the exhibition was carefully chosen by the students after hours of deliberation. Robin F. Nigh, a Ph.D. candidate in Art History and the indispensable co-curator of this exhibition finally proposed "Dimensions of Native America." She knew that "The Dimensions of" part of the title came from a 1970s exhibition that I mounted with a group of my undergraduate students from the University of California, San Diego campus. We called this exhibition on African and African-American art *Dimensions of Black*. The idea was to give college students a unique learning experience while enhancing, through the universal language of art, the community's understanding and appreciation for the art of African and African American cultures. In 1973, another group of my students assembled an exhibition on the arts of Polynesia, as a fitting tribute to Polynesians and the indigenous people from the state of Hawai'i and American Samoa. We also wished to acknowledge the many Polynesians who migrated to the United States and helped contribute to our great country. This exhibition was called *Dimensions of Polynesia*.

The rest of the title also requires explanation. We spent hours debating the various meanings of Indian, American Indian and Native American within the context of our exhibition. The early seventeenth-century Europeans who encountered the diverse indigenous tribal cultures on the North American continent referred to them as "Indians" or "American Indians." These generic headings are misnomers perpetuated by Christopher Columbus' mistaken idea that he had arrived in the Indies and was greeted by Indians. In recent years, well-meaning scholars have attempted to counter the original misconception about the native peoples of the Americas by promoting the use of "Native American." According to FSU anthropologist Anthony Paredes, however, while the phrase "Native American" has wide currency, the phrase has fallen into disrepute in some tribal circles. "Native American", as a census category to include Eskimos, Aleuts, as well as American Indians remains generally acceptable. Also, "Native American" seems to fit well in some sociological contexts and is even the language used in one important piece of federal legislation, but for the most part "American Indian" is the phrase preferred nowadays by most tribal people in most contexts. Nonetheless, in the spirit of the continuing dialogue addressing the inequities of colonialism, authors of the essays in this catalogue freely alternate between uses of the terms "Native American" and "American Indian" and their derivatives.

The term "contact zone" was first coined by Mary Louise Pratt in her book *Imperial Eyes. Travel Writing and Transculturation,* 1992.[2] We chose this term over *acculturation, hybridity* and *confluence* because it stresses the notion that the concept of colonial "contact" can also be applied to certain art forms in a way that celebrates their ingenuity, rather than their being looked upon as inferior products or degenerate forms. The term *contact* is used in the study of linguistics and "refers to improvised languages that develop among speakers of different Native languages who need to communicate with each other consistently, usually in context of trade."[3] "Contact zone" art can serve in a manner similar to "contact" language, since this kind of art acts as a form of visual communication where the end product results from contact between native and alien peoples. Pratt's definition also focuses on the space of these encounters: "the space of colonial encounters, the space in which peoples geographically and historically separated come into contact with each other and establish ongoing relations, usually involving conditions of coercion, radical inequality, and intractable conflict."[4] This notion of the contact space is also addressed by Lucy Lippard when she writes that we should fix our gaze, when writing about art made by those with different cultural backgrounds, "on the area in between—that fertile, liminal ground where new meanings germinate and where common experiences in different contexts can provoke new bonds."[5] Pratt reinforces Lippard by suggesting that "a 'contact' perspective emphasizes how subjects [or, in our case, art forms] are constituted in and by their relations to each other." Other terms Pratt uses are also applicable to our exhibition: "anti-conquest" refers "to the strategies of representation whereby European bourgeois subjects seek to secure their innocence in the same moment as they assert European hegemony."[6] This is admittedly an "unfriendly label" of, in our situation, the male or female Euroamerican artist who constructs a less than accurate portrayal of American Indians. Typically, their Euroamerican constructions visually shaped, reinforced and monitored the prevailing or dominant attitudes towards the indigenous people as interpreted at that time by Euroamericans and their nineteenth and twentieth century descendants.

The exhibition's Native American Advisory Board, headed by Joe Quetone (Kiowa), Executive Director, Florida Governor's Council on Indian Affairs, and Blue Sau-Pa Pahdocony (Comanche), President of Four Horses Native American Productions, was introduced to us by Dr. Anthony Paredes. This Board was most instrumental to the success of the project in donating their knowledge,

advice and guidance. When our concept of the exhibition was first presented to our Advisory Board, there was the polite, but implicit question as to who our audience was to be and who were we to write about Native American art. Our response was simple and naive: we were a concerned body of students and one faculty member who wanted to do something for our multi-cultural community, FSU, and Tallahassee, the Capital of Florida, so we and the community could learn more about the acculturated arts made by Native Americans and the constructions of American Indians as depicted by Euroamerican artists. As young art historians and future educators with limited writing experiences, the students felt that they could meet the challenge. Some compromises have been made in response to our Advisory Board. In compliance with the Board's wishes, our exhibit does not have any Native American objects that are held sacred and, consequently, unviewable. One of the best ways to avoid sacred art forms was to omit those acculturated arts that were made for indigenous ritual uses, such as the sacred Hopi or Zuni *katsina tihu* images and exhibit only those that were made as fine art commodities for sale in the global art market. "Kachinoids" are made by the Navajo; they are not on display since these acculturated art forms were never integrated into their culture. The acculturated Native American art forms that we selected are ingenious continuations of the traditional or neo-traditional arts, even though the media, style, process, subject matter, market, function or even the gender of the maker may have changed dramatically. These acculturated arts express new ideas that became integrated into the matrix of tribe or culture and, thereby, guarantee some form of authenticity in ethno-aesthetics, form, style or transactional function. These arts, used, traded or purchased by the indigenous culture and / or outsiders, such as the art-buying public (dealers, collectors and museums) or the wealthy tourist, range from miniaturized Haida argillite souvenirs that were reintegrated back into the culture to exciting new forms of contemporary fine art. Many of these acculturated arts now command a new respect as their soaring auction prices at Sotheby's and Christie's attest; in fact, some pieces could not be shown in this exhibition because of their escalating values.

We try to recognize the tribal affiliations of the Native artists in this exhibition, but there is some confusion in the literature. We also try, where possible, to keep a Native voice in the exhibition, while knowing that we cannot please everyone, nor can we presume to speak for any Native people. But, as art historians, we can address the exhibited acculturated objects that were made as artful commodities and/or intentional artifications of the artifact. The pieces in this exhibition were chosen because they serve both the Native as well as the non-Native communities as aesthetic forms and carriers of indigenous cultural values.

The collecting and displaying of Native American works as formal objects of art isolated from their original context, and hung in Western museums which have their own agendas and aesthetics, will always be a point of contention. Within the last decade, many articles, books, symposia and Native artists have addressed the adverse problems one faces in trying to make a broad range of Native American or Polynesian-American arts meaningful within the limiting confines of an alien museum space.[7] Most recently, James Clifford has devoted a chapter, "Museums as Contact Zones" in *Routes, Travel and Translation in the Late Twentieth Century,* 1997, to discuss the Portland, Oregon, museum's Northwest Coast Indian Collection and the display of American Indian identity as culture and art.[8] Works by contemporary artists like James Luna (Luiseño) have also confronted the issues. Luna's 1987 "Artifact Piece" appropriated the ethnographic mode of scientifically encasing representations of "Indian" culture as artifacts into a contemporary installation where he became the artifact.

Granted that there are major restrictions placed on museums (such as, for example, security compounded by insurance concerns which leads to placing objects under locked cases in less than optimal viewing spaces, addressing the fragility of the work and its proper temperature control and lighting), the means and methods of displaying the arts from the "concept zone" is not an easy task. Criticism is easy, finding correct solutions is difficult. Nevertheless, we have made every effort for the viewer to see and admire the aesthetic and contextual merits of these acculturated products of the contact zone from an informed, revisionist framework. The Native American Board came to terms with the museum imposed constraints and our Euroamerican interpretation of art, but felt that, if given the opportunity, they might display American Indian art in a different manner. Joe Quetone and Blue Sau-Pa Pahdocony were given the opportunity to arrange the arts they selected in a space that was in accord with their sense of aesthetic socializaton.

The catalogue and exhibition are divided into separate themes and approximate time sequences in order to enhance the viewer's understanding of the different dimensions of knowing another's culture. There are hundreds of Native American tribes or peoples who create impressive examples of art that were and are products of the contact zone. Rather than focusing on a generalized survey of Native art and culture, we chose instead to address current issues that are in the forefront of contemporary Native art and art making. Therefore, the issues selected determined the choice of tribal groups. Each paper is an example of a particular dimension of contact with Native America. We begin the zone of contact art with: 1) The Artification of the Indigenous Artifact; 2) Blurred Boundaries: Contact, Confluence and Hybridity; 3) Misconceptions: The American Indian; 4) Photographs Don't Lie? 5) Contemporary Native and non-Native Arts in the Contact Zone of a Fine Arts Museum; 6) Regional and Pan-Indian Arts.

It is our hope that the broad range of subject matter, media and aesthetic forms will invest the public with a new appreciation for and understanding of the many dimensions of the Native and non-Native arts that are a product of the contact zone.

I. The Artification of the Indigenous Artifact

This section addresses the changes in an indigenous art form that emerge from contact with foreign cultures. The artifact may lose its contextual meaning or functional validity when it enters the contact zone in response to a Euroamerican art market. The objects, such as Zuni Ollas, can change to address new needs,

tastes and a market economy brought about by contact with the Spanish, Mexicans and Euroamericans while retaining their inherent sense of ethno-aesthetics, formal standards and cultural value as important transactional markers of tribal identity, nationalism and/or ethnic pride. In this situation the indigenous process and medium (clay, wood or weaving materials) usually remain constant.

Highlighted in this section are: 1) The ingenious Puebloan ceramics made in New Mexico as a result of contact with the Spanish from the sixteenth to the end of the 19th centuries; 2) the revival of reproducing the techniques and designs found on ceramic wares belonging to ancient North American Indian cultures (*c.* 400 to 1500), and the more recent interest in replicating sacred objects for museum displays; 3) the sacred Hopi Kachina Tihu artifact has undergone an artification process that allows it to be made for sale in the contact zone; 4) basketry is one of the oldest (portable) forms of surviving indigenous art, and the Choctaw, Florida Seminole and especially the Hopi, still use these arts as neo-traditional forms within their cultures, though many are sold to non-Indians as fine art and tourist forms so that change resulting from contact is mainly seen in the functionality of these pieces and/or the new shapes and colors.

II. Blurred Boundaries: Contact, Confluence and Hybridity

Here the viewer looks at artistic works created by American Indian artisans and artists that have, again, commingled in contact with alien (i.e. [post-Spanish] Mexican, Spanish, Chinese, African, American) systems of art. But now dramatic changes have occured with the introduction of new processes (introduced techniques and tools), media, shapes, or colors that are reintegrated for use within their own cultures and the contact culture. This section covers a broad range of subject matter and addresses the way certain acculturated artworks can retain their ethno-aesthetic sensibility in one form such as silver jewelry or horse headstalls made for the Native owner while the silver jewelry made for the contact zone captures an extraordinary understanding of Anglo aesthetic preference. Contact zone art works can retain cultural truths and ethnic identity while shifting transactional meanings, uses, former "copyrighted styles" that designate a specific tribe or aesthetic systems to fit the new needs of American Indians, and non-Indian consumers.

Showcased works are the: 1) Haida argillite pipes, platters, bowls and minaturized crestpoles (popularly called totempoles); 2) Zuni and Navajo / Diné silver jewelry; 3) appliqué quilting and patchwork from the northern Plains, and from the Poarch Band of Creeks, the Hopi, the Navajo / Diné, and the Florida Seminoles; 4) Navajo / Diné pictorial weavings; 5) Plains ledger-drawings mainly from Ft. Marion in Florida; 6) and Southwest watercolorists from the "Studio School Tradition" with an emphasis on revisiting the alleged "Bambi-art style."

III. Misconceptions: The American Indian

By the seventeenth century, the American continent saw Spain in present day Florida and New Mexico, France in the North and the English (Swedes and Dutch) on the Atlantic Coast. Contact with the various aboriginal tribes of the so-called New World were depicted in paintings, engravings and sculpted forms. The constructed images of these indigenous Americans commanded the interest of Europeans and Americans for centuries. Early folk images, made by lesser known or anonymous craftsmen were constructed to function as useful objects—such as weathervanes, ships' figureheads, and iconic images that signalled the services of a tobacconist. These objects were often placed outside, in prominent common spaces that interfaced with the public, thereby serving to visually reinforce the prevailing attitudes towards American Indians. One has to remember that unlike fine art, the folk arts interacted at a more intimate level with the public. Folk images of "cigar-store Indians," dragged or rolled onto the sidewalks and streets, were literally embraced as icons of the Noble Savage or stereotypes of pan-Indianism.

How American Indians were represented as "cigar-store Indians" or displayed in museums and at World's Fairs during the nineteenth and twentieth centuries has created a dialogue within several fields. Engaged in this important discourse are issues that question the role of museums, the philosophy of anthropology, the methodology of archaeology , as well as the proper means of studying the art history of Native Americans and the acculturated arts. This dialogue is central to the portion of the exhibition which focuses on the works and field methods of Western artists who deliberately appropriated American Indian art forms, cultures and identities in an interpretative manner that was perceived as being authentic. Like many of the folk images and fine paintings, an array of "Indian" museum displays (such as Ishi at Berkeley), Wild West Shows and the reconstructions in Worlds' Fairs, were also being used to promulgate the aspirations and ideals, even when well intended, of the dominant Euroamerican culture.

This section critiques how staged displays and Western artists have contributed to our misunderstanding of indigenous American cultures. Here meaning and interpretation collide with post-colonial theory and revisionist truths as seen in: 1) the Euroamerican construction of Chief Osceola, the Seminole culture and Florida State University; and, 2) the works of Western artists, such as Joseph Henry Sharp, Karl Bodmer, George Catlin, Frederic Remington and others who essentialized their conception of the Indians' identity as being authentic and who, in their time, were recognized for the veracity of their works. Were they cultural brokers, artist-ethnographers, myth makers or merely self-servers?

John L. Cromwell, Cigar-store figure of a Mohawk chief, c. 1855, 73 1/2 inches h. The raised hand of this figure is missing its original tomahawk. Courtesy of Museum of Tobacco Art and History, Nashville, Tennessee.

IV. Photographs Don't Lie?

Photography was a popular medium of documentation in the late nineteenth and early twentieth centuries. The reading of these allegedly authentic portrayals of the American Indian is fraught with issues of how one interprets, with the dislocation of time and contextual space, visual meaning, truth of the photographer's account and artistic approach, and the desires of the purchasing Euroamerican market.[9] Photographic constructions of American Indians as the "Vanishing American," "Noble Savage," "Romanticized Native," or "Real Indian" are seen through the works of Gertrude Käsebier and Edward S. Curtis. These works are juxtaposed with photographs by Hulleah Tsinhnahjinnie (Creek / Seminole / Diné), whose innovative use of the medium and collage makes strong commentary on the ways American Indians have been constructed through photography, film and television. With elegant beauty and skill, Shelley Niro (Iroquois) adroitly manipulates and overlays her photographs with culturally-embedded media that lead to fertile new ideas about the contact zone.

V. Contemporary Native and Non-Native Artists in the Contact Zone of a Fine Arts Museum

This is one of the most important parts of the show and catalogue. Here, the complex issues of cultural property, cultural ownership and the construction of ethnic identities that confront contemporary Native and non-Native artists are addressed. Where does the non-Native artist position him/herself in comparison with the Native artist and how do both come to terms with their content, media and style while working to be recognized by their peers and the agenda set in the competitive, global art world? Internationally-recognized contemporary American Indian artists such as James Luna (Luiseño), Jaune Quick-to-See Smith (Confederated Salish and Kootenai Nation), Hulleah Tsinhnahjinnie (Creek / Seminole / Diné), Marcus Amerman (Choctaw), Colleen Cutschall (Oglala Lakota), Richard Glazer Danay (Mohawk), Shelley Niro (Iroquois), Sara Bates (Cherokee) and others in this exhibition, have taken command over their cultural propeties, and transcended "tradition" and critique with cutting edge techniques, quiet passion, outrage, and irony, the acculturated arts in the contact zone. These are not derivative forms of acculturated art but powerful new expressions of a multicultural America. As revisionists they seek to redress (in avant garde terms: installations, performance, written texts, sculptures, photographs, paintings and drawings) what it means to be contemporary artists and indigenous peoples living in the late twentieth century. Contemporary Western artists, such as Elaine Reichek and Mark Tansey join hands in the contact zone with their interest in and integration of American Indian art and culture in their works. Coming from a different cultural background and context, their arts, too, are provocative statements about acculturation in the contact zone. Their works also revise the misconstructions that their Euroamerican predecessors fabricated about indigenous Americans by exploring issues of Post-Colonialist theory and Romantic Primitivism through parody.

VI. Regional and Pan-Indian Art

American Indian artists and artisans living in the vicinity of North Florida and South Georgia have contributed by lending their support and critical comments to this exhibition. We are pleased to close this exhibition with some of their works selected and displayed in accordance with the aesthetic sensibilities of Blue Sau-Pa Pahdocony and Joe Quetone.

Acknowledgements

We would like to acknowledge a number of people for generously donating their selfless support, knowledge and assistance. Dr. J. Anthony Paredes, Professor of Anthropology and a leading scholar on Native American cultures, helped constitute the Advisory Board and has participated in many facets of this exhibition including reading the finished catalogue. Patricia R. Wickman, Director, Department of Anthropology and Genealogy, Seminole Tribe of Florida, took time out of her schedule to critique the Seminole papers. Dr. Ruth Phillips, came to give a seminar and ended up offering us some advice and wisdom from her experiences in curating a number of very successful exhibitions on Native American art. Dr. Robin Rhodes, Adjunct Lecturer in the Department of Anthropology at Florida State University came to our assistance with her extensive knowledge on Plains Indians. Sandra Starr-Tanner was a key figure in introducing us to some of the finest private collections of Native American art found in Florida. She also came to our aid by sharing her knowledge and collection of American Indian art as well as her expertise in the field of design by helping plan the installation. Sara W. Reeves and Keith Reeves, well-known collectors of American Indian art, even fed us while we were allowed to select pieces from their collection. Mr. Reeves also volunteered his time and the assistance of his firm, Architects Design Group, Inc., of Winter Park, where Director of Graphic Design Anna McCambridge designed the striking cover of this catalogue; Mr. Reeves also made insightful comments and corrections on the Seminole patchwork paper. Elise LeCompte, of the Florida Museum of Natural History wins our admiration for her kindness in allowing myself and students to go to the museum storages to select pieces—only to later change our minds and ask for others. Marian Rodee, Curator of Southwest Ethnology at the Maxwell Museum, and Christie Sturm, Director of Collections at the School of American Research (both in New Mexico), patiently let a few of us visit the museum storages and then responded to all our many inquires with informative documenta-

tion and photographs. Sandra Greene of Glenn Greene Galleries came to our rescue in finding certain works that we needed. We are clearly indebted to Joe Quetone and we wish to thank the high school students from his Florida Indian Youth Program who have given us permission to quote from prose and poetry what they feel about being a Native American living in Florida. People across the country have also given invaluable assistance—James C. Faris, Hulleah Tsinhnahjinnie, Colleen Cutschall, Rosalind M. Plank, Elaine Reichek, and Mark Tansey: we thank you. So many people have helped us in so many ways that I hope I / we have not slighted anyone. Furthermore, these acknowledgements do not in any way bind the persons mentioned to my or the students' interpretations of the acculturated arts found in the contact zone, for it is only that, an interpretation and, ultimately, if it is incorrect, the error rests with me.

[1] Nelson H. H. Graburn, ed. *Ethnic and Tourist Arts, Cultural Expressions from the Fourth World* (Berkeley and Los Angeles: U of California P, 1976). This book is a landmark in analyzing acculturated art forms from the Fourth World. For more on the interpretation of acculturation in the arts see: Nelson H.H. Graburn, "The Evolution of Tourist Arts," *Annals of Tourism Research* 11.3(1984): 393-419; Erik Cohen, "Introduction: Investigating Tourist Arts," *Annals of Tourism Research* 20.2 (1993): 128-161.

[2] Mary Louise Pratt, *Imperial Eyes: Travel Writing and Transculturation* (London and New York: Routledge, 1993).

[3] Mary Louise Pratt 6.

[4] Mary Louise Pratt 6.

[5] Lucy R. Lippard, *Mixed Blessings: New Art in a Multicultural America* (New York: Pantheon Books, 1990) 9.

[6] Mary Louise Pratt 7.

[7] See Michael M. Ames, *Cannibal Tours and Glass Boxes, The Anthropology of Museums* (Vancouver: U of British Columbia P, 1992); Janet C. Berlow and Ruth B. Phillips, "Vitalizing the things of the past: museum representations of Native North American art in the 1990's Museum Anthropology 16.1(1992): 29-43; Annie E. Coombes, "The recalcitrant object: culture contact and the question of hybridity, " in Francis Barker, Peter Hulme and Margaret Iversen, eds. *Colonial Discourse Theory* (Manchester: Manchester UP, 1994) 89-114; James Clifford, *The Predicament of Culture* (Cambridge: Harvard UP, 1988); Anna Laura Jones, "Exploding Canons: The Anthropology of Museums" *Annual Review of Anthropology* 22 (1993):201-220; Ivan Karp and Steven D. Lavine, eds. *Exhibiting Culture: The Poetics and Politics of Museum Display* (Washington, D.C.: Smithsonian Institution, 1991); Ruth Phillips, "Indian Art: Where Do You Put It?" *Muse, Journal of the Canadian Museums Association*, 6.3 (1988): 64-71.

[8] James Clifford, *Routes, Travel and Translation in the Late Twentieth Century* (Cambridge and London: Harvard UP, 1997).

[9] See Elizabeth Edwards, ed. *Anthropology and Photography 1860-1920* (New Haven and London: Yale UP in association with the Royal Anthropological Institute, London, 1992), including Brian W. Dippie, "Representing the other: the North American Indian," 132-151.

Hopi wickerwork plaque with whirlwind design. Florida State University Department of Anthropology, Mary D. Lewis Collection, accession #2459. (Photo: Mark Fletcher)

I.   THE ARTIFICATION OF THE INDIGENOUS ARTIFACT

Pueblo Women, Colonial Settlement, and Creative Endeavors: Power and Appropriation in Native American Ceramics

Hilary L. Scothorn

The ancient trade networks which supplied Native American artists with new ideas and innovative technology were extensive. As with earlier interaction, contact with Euroamericans is manifested in the ceramic arts through the incorporation of patterns and forms inspired by trade items and household goods.[1] The process of colonization, and its subsequent effects on individuals, emerges in the pottery art forms made by Puebloan artists in response to both external and internal demand. The meeting of cultures manifests itself in ceramics made in New Mexico during the late eighteenth, nineteenth and twentieth centuries. By investigating how aesthetic and cultural changes are reflected in the reinterpretation of symbols, one can gain insight into the complex process of art making in Native American societies. By acknowledging several combination forms, consisting of both ancient and Spanish influenced motifs, a reevaluation of artistic interaction is possible. What have previously been seen as blind adaptations of Spanish motifs should now be regarded as selectively integrated forms, thereby demonstrating the flexibility of artistic traditions and the assertion of Puebloan ethnicity during the colonial era.

Pottery arrived in the Four Corners region from Meso America c. AD 500 and was developed by ancestors of the Pueblo people into the art forms we know today.[2] By the time of Spanish "discovery" in 1540, most Puebloan peoples had settled in small communities near the Rio Grande Valley. Ceramics from this period are commonly known as biscuit wares. Having left traditional clay and temper sources behind in canyon areas, Puebloan artists had difficulty with clays available in the valleys. New materials contributed to the fragility and instability of these wares, which have a tendency to flake or chip easily. Bowls tended to be larger and shallower than previous examples and were used for the storage of grain and other household items. A new jar form with a rounded bottom, flat shoulder, wide mouth and short neck evolved, and painting on these vessels was often on the design fields made by the angle of the shoulder. Serpent or winged forms

Figure 1. Side view of black-on-tan olla from Puyé, New Mexico, c. 1475-1600. Photo by Wesley Bradfield. Courtesy Museum of New Mexico, negative 90129.

often occupy these fields, painted in a few strokes of black (Figure 1).[3] This suggests some of the movement of ideas and material technology in the years before the Spanish arrived. These early Puebloan peoples were receptive to new forms when in contact with each other, and wide-scale adaptation visible to archaeologists suggests further experimentation. Jonathan Batkin notes that changes in forms such as the low shouldered jar point to the gradual expansion of new shapes among all the Pueblos. It is important to remember that "ideas moved freely between populations and geographical regions without European influence," and innovations were occurring in the arts due to cultural change before the Spanish arrived.[4]

When Francisco Vásquez de Coronado explored the Southwest for the Spanish Crown in 1540-41, he visited the Pueblos of Zuni and Hopi looking for the Seven Cities of Cibola. The Spanish realized that while the new territory was not full of precious metals and jewels, it had an enormous labor pool and mining possibilities. The missonaries settled in Native communities while government officials established large haciendas. The Spanish were ruthless in the early seventeenth century, demanding goods and labor from native peoples on a routine basis. This system, the *encomienda*, directly influenced the form of Puebloan pottery.[5] For the collection of tribute, potters created vessels which held about a bushel, half of the Spanish unit of measurement called a *fanega*.[6] Seed jars, bowls and storage vessels were set aside for the formation of these larger, round-shouldered vessels called ollas (oy-ahs). In addition to the changes in form and capacity seen with the imposition of a measurement system, painted designs changed in density, patterning and subject. The new size also had an impact on the decorative scheme by creating a larger area for design and an exploration of positive and negative space.

The period between the arrival of Don Juan de Oñate (1598) and the Pueblo revolt (1680) was the harshest for the indigenous peoples in the Southwest. Those Indians who could not pay trib-

Figure 2. Koyiti Glaze-polychrome (Glaze F) olla, 1600-1700. SAR/MNM Artifact number 8551/11. Courtesy of School of American Research Collections in the Museum of New Mexico, Santa Fe. (Photo: Mary Peck)

ute were forced into service. According to Bernard Fontana, assignments ranged from "cooks, maids, carpenters, herders, gardeners, commercial weavers, gleaners of piñon nuts, salt bearors, [to] laborers of other kinds."[7] Perhaps they were also forced to make ceramics for the household. In any case, their presence in households put them in close contact with Spanish material goods. Designs became concentrated on the shoulders of vessels, often incorporating undulating lines (Figure 2). Examples from this period are rare since little remains from the seventeenth century because of the destruction of settlements, missions and churches during the twelve-year period when the Pueblos united to oust the Spanish in 1680.

Until the Spanish returned in 1692-93, the Pueblos attempted to erase foreign influences on their culture. But one survived: the size and shape of storage jars. This probably represented a convenience in commercial exchanges. One author notes, "Governor Pedro Fermin de Mendinueta wrote in 1773 that 'the pueblos are the storehouses of all kinds of grain, especially corn. Thither come the Spanish citizens to make purchases, as well as the governor, when grain is needed...for the troops.'"[8] David Snow demonstrated the importance of the *fanega* as a unit of measurement (each *fanega* being about 2.6 bushels) in territorial terms; a man would describe crops in *fanegas*, suggesting the amount of seed necessary to sow them.[9] It is logical that the uniform measurement innovation would have been retained since it was beneficial to both Native and Spaniard. Storage jars in the collection of the Taylor Museum in Colorado and the Museum of New Mexico reflect the importance of a uniform trade measurement. The jars each have a capacity of between ten and eleven gallons (Figure 3).[10] These vessels have three horizontal design fields on the shoulders and lips as well as having bottom sections with the original red clay left visible. The artists have used undulating lines around the upper design fields and various star motifs in the center areas, which also point to Spanish influence.

Figure 3. Two Storage Jars, c. 1800-1850, with capacities between ten and eleven gallons, or approximately one half *fanega*. L: San Ildefonso or Tesuque Pueblo. R: Santo Domingo or Cochiti Pueblo. Taylor Museum of the Colorado Springs Fine Arts Center. Gifts of Alice Bemis Taylor.

By the beginning of eighteenth century, settlers outnumbered Natives, and instead of the large ranches of the earlier century, they worked small farms without the need for forced labor.[11] The Indians are thought to have been treated less harshly than in the years prior to 1680, though the pressure for religious conversions increased.[12] Missions were reestablished in the Pueblos and succeeded in gaining some converts. The increase of religious persecution manifests itself in the art forms made in this period with an increase of decoration on the shoulders of vessels. Brody notes that:

> Religious persecutions in the Rio Grande valley during the seventeenth-century forced the Eastern Pueblos to shield their rituals and related art forms from outsiders. It became common thereafter for pottery painters to isolate emblems suggestive of ritual symbolism on their utilitarian vessels.[13]

For this purpose, Puebloan artists incorporated new motifs inspired by items of everyday colonial life at a fairly rapid pace. To demonstrate a veneer of accepting Catholicism, designs inspired by Christian religious materials could have been placed on utilitarian vessels, rather than those vessels which continued to have religious functions. These new motifs would have been integrated with design schemes from the existing Puebloan vocabulary. Perhaps artists subverted the imposition of Spanish colonization by addressing this to goods with a secular purpose. This is in contrast to the pottery with aboriginal religious functions which remained hidden from outsiders and remains so today.

Figure 4. Pictograph of Masked Diety Excavated by A.V. Kidder at Pecos Ruins, Pecos, New Mexico, n.d. Courtesy Museum of New Mexico, negative 31097.

Previously, admirers of Pueblo pottery assumed that the new designs were an incorporation of motifs from trade goods introduced by outsiders.[14] In contrast, this examination of indigenous motifs suggests that some of the revolutionary changes in pottery designs were actually reinvigorated elements originating in ancient times. In the centuries of Native American domination by the Spanish and Anglo-Americans, ceramic arts became a means of asserting ethnic identity while incorporating new traditions into the indigenous aesthetic. While it is true that new items, such as silks, ceramics, jewelry and metalwork, were seen by Native Americans, the designs on these goods were reevaluated in terms of their own cultural vision. Design changes must be considered in terms of the aesthetic which existed before the Spanish arrived in New Mexico and also in terms of why some were used more often than others.

A frequent design on ceramics from the nineteenth century is an arc; often several are placed end to end to produce an undulating band. Rick Dillingham suggests that this is based upon Hispanic colcha embroidery; however, it is strikingly similar to

Figure 5. Pictograph from Pictograph Cave, Cañon de Chelly, northeastern Arizona, c. 800-1000 AD. From *Anasazi and Pueblo Painting* by J.J. Brody, © 1991, The School of American Research, Santa Fe. Published by the University of New Mexico Press, Albuquerque. (Photo: © David Grant Noble)

motifs found on rock art and kiva murals in archaeological contexts (Figure 4).[15] Native artists would surely have regarded the motifs through their own experiences and surely noted the similarity of form to their own rainbow and cloud motifs. Historical photographs and excavated areas provide examples which depict cloud, rain and stepped forms present in sacred contexts. Their presence in a religious context suggests that these motifs are a restatement of Puebloan beliefs, not merely decoration.

In *Anasazi and Pueblo Painting*, J.J. Brody notes that a multi-colored arcing form in a pictograph from Canyon de Chelly, Arizona, shares a resemblance to a rainbow (Figure 5). Brody links several other ancient sites with this motif, including Kuaua, Pottery Mound, as well as nineteenth-century locations at the Pueblos of Jemez, Isleta and Zuni. The importance of rain and accompanying weather patterns would not be lost to Puebloan women; this form could have associations with prayer and fertility. The tripartite cloud formations seen in many ritual and secular contexts seem to be comprised of several of these arcing forms which are connected to rain and associations of progeneration. By the late nineteenth century, rows of linked arcs could be found on

Figure 6. Mission Interior, Laguna Pueblo, Laguna, New Mexico, c. 1935. Courtesy Museum of New Mexico, negative 4870. (Photo: T. Harmon Parkhurst)

kiva murals from Jemez Pueblo, Awatovi at Hopi, and the devices decorate the church at Laguna Pueblo (Figure 6). The section from Jemez shows a series of linked arcs making a border on one side of the mural. Had this design been purely a Spanish decorative motif, as suggested by Dillingham, it would not likely be placed in the kiva. For an artist to innovate upon the arc and make it undulate around the shoulder of an olla would not only be aesthetically pleasing, but it might attest to veiled meaning in the object (particularly in a time of religious intolerance). To transcribe the arcing motif to pottery would transfer some of its associative properties of rain and fertility to objects used for collecting water and food. It is not unlikely that the arcs do have larger meaning since they can be linked to sacred situations, yet for the Spanish viewer, the undulating band had other associations.

For a Spaniard familiar with embroidery and cloth, the arcing band seen on pottery would seem to make reference to a familiar pattern from his / her own culture. Besides being similar to Native American designs, it is also a referent to imported majolica ware, which had dense design areas defined by wide paths of color (see Figure 7).[16] Perhaps the arcing band should be viewed as an integrated shape: the form of ancient rainbow designs linked together via inspiration by colcha embroidery and other majolica ware in order to please both Native American and Spaniard. This is possibly a visual pun, a play upon optical equivalents.

Figure 7. Puebla Blue-on-white vase (talavera ware), state of Puebla, Mexico, eighteenth century. Height 17 1/4" (42.9 x 31.1 cm). Courtesy Art Institute of Chicago. Gift of Mrs. Eva Lewis in memory of her husband, Herbet Pickering Lewis. Catalog number 1923.1448. Chinese influences in painting and form are seen in this vessel, types of which were imported to New Mexico. (Photo: © 1997, The Art Institute of Chicago. All Rights Reserved.)

By placing such adaptive patterns on secular pottery, Indians seemed to adapt to Spanish religion and culture while asserting their ethnic independence (as seen in the painting of the Laguna Pueblo Church with a mixture of Native and Spanish designs). The veil of acquiescence served to maintain a status quo which enabled underground rites to continue while placating Spanish colonizers. The appropriation of similar motifs was in fact an act of power and assertion which served a dual purpose: it maintained Native religious practices while the cultures also accepted introduced systems of belief.

The incorporation of new designs would have appealed to colonial Spaniards, who created a market for pottery made in the Pueblos. Artists adapted forms for the introduced agricultural crops which changed Puebloan diets. Puebloan women appropriated new forms which came directly for use with imported goods as well as for new cooking and dietary requirements. The expectations of colonial settlers included plates, soup bowls, pitchers

Figure 8. Polychrome dough bowl, Santo Domingo Pueblo, New Mexico, n.d. Courtesy of Museum of New Mexico, negative 88296. (Photo: Wesley Bradfield)

Santa Fe "with glazed earthenware to sell."[17] By the early nineteenth century, a vigorous market had developed for utlitarian pottery in northern New Mexico.[18] W.W.H. Davis notes that the Pueblos

> devote the greater part of their time to the manufacture of earthenware, which they sell in quantities to the Mexicans. It exhibits some skill, and is often adorned with various devices painted upon it before it is burned. This ware is universal in use in the territory, and there is considerable demand for it in the market.[19]

Examples of the pottery made during this time period suggest large, boldly painted designs which conform to Hispanic expectations. Bread bowls became popular, and those remaining from this time period show wear patterns from baking (Figure 8). Pitchers for serving were also made (Figure 9). Water jars, similar to an

and other pottery shapes allowing for dough and bread baking. Native women responded to new demands by expanding their repertoire of form; bread bowls are perhaps the most exemplary of the new forms used inside and outside the Pueblos.

Before relocating to Jemez Pueblo, inhabitants of Pecos made pottery for outside consumption. Observers of the time record that in 1694, Native Americans from Pecos Pueblo arrived in

Figure 10. Polychrome jar, Zuni Pueblo, New Mexico, n.d. Courtesy Museum of New Mexico, negative 25730.

olla in size but heart-shaped, were used within the Pueblos for gathering water at cisterns and were also popular in territorial households (Figure 10). Designs on the vessels range from strictly horizontal motifs on the rims of the bread bowls to dynamic figurative designs on water jars.

One design seen frequently on several jars from the early nineteenth century is called the "Vallero star." It is originally an eight-pointed figure, though variations continue for many years. Batkin identifies this motif as Spanish in origin which can be traced back to Moorish decorative arts.[20] This star form has a wide geographical location: it is seen on a Ranchitos polychrome from Santa Ana (Keresan) and an Opapoge polychrome from Gobernador Canyon (a Tewa area); variations are found in Acoma polychromes as well (Figure 3 right, and Figures 10 and 11). This star may well have a connection to the decorative motifs on Spanish stirrups or spurs.[21] Saddles and bridles also carried similar decorative elements with Moorish origins, made of cast metal.

Figure 9. Polychrome pitcher, Tesuque Pueblo, New Mexico, n.d. Courtesy Museum of New Mexico, negative 44084.

Figure 11. Polychrome jar, Acoma Pueblo, New Mexico, n.d. MNM artifact number 7912/12. Courtesy Museum of New Mexico, negative 86154. (Photo: Arthur Taylor)

The Vallero star has a striking similarity to a floral, or *hepakinne,* motif popular on Puebloan ceramics (Figure 12). Scholars have noted the connection to European Baroque decorative elements, but perhaps the shared design should be examined in light of its existence before Spanish arrival. Ruth Bunzel (and Ruth Benedict) identify the *hepakinne* as "sunflower," found on Salimopiya masks from Zuni Pueblo.[22] As an organic floral form, the sunflower probably had connotations of fertility and calendrical cycles. When Natives saw the parallel image also used as a decorative element, new forms of presenting the flower became possible.

Figure 12. Polychrome jar, Zuni Pueblo, New Mexico, c. 1880-1900, 23.5 cm. h x 28.7 cm. w, MNM artifact number 16185/12. Courtesy of Museum of New Mexico, negative 85704. (Photo: Arthur Taylor)

While the origins of motifs remain theoretical, it is important to evaluate the economic and social upheavals during the nineteenth century. Ceramics and their designs reflect not only the individuals who made them but the ideas which inspired the artists' innovations. As new material goods entered the territory, designs became more diverse and reflective of a changing aesthetic. A cultural preference for large, dense patterning with figurative elements almost replaced the fine hatching seen in Anasazi wares (Figure 13). In spite of the fact that most of these changes in New Mexico were due to colonization, the changes in aesthetic preferences should be viewed in a positive manner. They symbolize the ingenuity, adaptability and strength of Native people in the face of cultural peril. The evidence of politically motivated interaction in art forms testifies to the importance of the arts as a means of self-expression.

Figure 13. Anasazi Socorro black-on- white olla, 1000-1400AD. SAR/MNM Artifact number 8440/11. Courtesy of School of American Research Collections in the Museum of New Mexico, negative 70362.

The origins of particular motifs inspire the imagination with problematic assignations hundreds of years after their creation. While the true inspiration vanished with the artist, it is important to recognize more than one potential source for design inspiration as well as to speculate upon how the chosen design elements would meld with those already present in the Puebloan vocabulary. Recognition of the vast potential pool from which American Indian artists drew their sources leads to changing perspectives between colonized and colonizer. The art forms made during colonization suggest the vitality and importance of cultural memory; pottery made in the Pueblos are testaments to the survival of Native American traditions. Viewed as a response to colonization, ceramics are traditional no matter where innovations came from; they reflect the inevitable cross-cultural communication involved with existence. According to Stewart Peckham, traditions are flexible enough to be altered by individuals, and whether a tradition is introduced from outside or developed within makes no difference in the inherent value of an art form. Peckham asserts that

> whether followed from time immemorial or of relatively contemporary vintage, and regardless of whether the tradition reflects historical concerns of modern-day commercialism, such observances ultimately gain acceptance and respect by the collective.[23]

To suppose that large-scale changes would be initiated on pottery without homage to indigenous aesthetic cultural patterns disregards the value of practices and belief systems. Tradition should be regarded as a fusion of old with new directed from within to satisfy the pressures from outside. The assumption that innovation in ceramics from the Pueblos of New Mexico stems solely from a naïve fascination with materials brought to the area by outsiders underestimates the power of tradition and cultural continuity. From their introduction over a thousand years ago to the present-day art forms seen in galleries around the nation, ceramics are important expressions of identity and ethnicity which lend insight into the human experience.

[1] "Foreign" rule in the area of present-day New Mexico began with Spain (1540-1821), followed by Mexico (1821-46), and ends with the United States (1846-present).

[2] This is a simplified date; see Stewart Peckham, *From This Earth: The Ancient Art of Pueblo Pottery* (Santa Fe: Museum of New Mexico, 1990) for a concise review of the archaeology.

[3] Archaeologists have also documented the movement of the Southern Tewa, or Tano, from the Galisteo Basin to the base of La Fajada Butte. When they arrived, they were employing an Anasazi vegetal paint tradition, but by the 1300s, they adapted a mineral paint tradition and a creamy yellow slip. Some of these Tano people moved into the Puyé area and eventually to the area of present-day Santa Clara Pueblo. To Santa Clara they brought a red slip which was incorporated into the local tradition, the first of Tewa polychromes to be created. Peckham 87.

[4] Jonathan Batkin, *Pottery of the Pueblos of New Mexico 1700-1940* (Colorado Springs: Taylor Museum of the Colorado Springs Fine Arts Center, 1987) 25.

[5] Batkin 24.

[6] See David H. Snow, "A Note on Encomienda Economics in Seventeenth-Century New Mexico" in Marta Weigle, Claudia Larcombe and Samuel Larcombe, eds., *Hispanic Arts and Ethnohistory* (Santa Fe: Ancient City Press, 1983).

[7] Bernard L Fontana, *Entrada: The Legacy of Spain and Mexico on the United States* (Tucson: Southwest Parks and Monuments Association, 1994) 81. See also Marc Simmons, "History of Pueblo-Spanish Relations to 1821" in Alfonso Ortiz, ed., *Handbook of North American Indians* 9 (Washington DC: Smithsonian Institution Press, 1979) 183.

[8] Simmons 190.

[9] Snow 350. (A bushel is eight gallons).

[10] Batkin 24.

[11] Simmons 187.

[12] Simmons 187.

[13] Larry Frank and Francis Harlow, *Historic Pottery of the Pueblo Indians 1600-1880* (West Chester: Schiffer Publishers, 1974) 14 in J.J. Brody. "Pueblo Fine Arts" in Ortiz (1979) 603-608.

[14] Rick Dillingham, *Acoma and Laguna Pottery* (Santa Fe: The School of American Research Press, 1992) 140-142.

[15] Dillingham 143.

[16] Majolica ware is tin-enameled, soft-paste earthenware, also known as faience or delftware. It was brought to the colonies by Spaniards, and a large industry with a pottery guild was established at Puebla, Mexico by 1653. For more information, see Gabrielle Palmer and Donna Pierce, *Cambios: The Spirit of Transformation in Spanish Colonial Art* (Albuquerque: U of New Mexico P, 1992).

[17] Jose Manuel Espinosa, *Crusaders of the Rio Grande: The Story of Don Diego de Vargas and the Reconquest and Refounding of New Mexico* (Chicago: Institute of Jesuit History, 1942) 198, quoted in Batkin 25.

[18] In 1881, an American noted that "a Pueblo Indian and squaw knocked at the door; they wanted to sell pottery, of which I bought half a dozen pieces …" and "During my present visit, the Indians were very busy making pottery, not for household use alone, but for sale in Santa Fe as well." Lansing Bloome, "Bourke on the Southwest," *New Mexico Historical Review* 10.4 (1935): 271-322, quoted in Batkin 25.

[19] W.W.H. Davis, *El Gringo or New Mexico and Her People* (Santa Fe: The Rydal Press, 1938), quoted in Batkin 25.

[20] Batkin 134.

[21] The significance of the addition of horses to Puebloan lifestyle should not be overlooked; horses enabled the Spanish to complete their conquests and increased productivity in agricultural situations.

[22] Ruth Bunzel, *The Pueblo Potter: A Study of the Creative Imagination in Primitive Art* (New York: Dover Publications reprint 1972) 92. Ruth Benedict supplied some additional information to the chart located on page 92 and following pages. See Klarr, this volume, for further discussion of the *Hepakinne* motif.

[23] Peckham 4.

Reproduction, Revival and Tradition in Native Art—Southeastern Pottery

Diana Roman

Historical Framework

The idea of reproducing and reviving the techniques, shapes and designs of pre-contact indigenous American art probably began when archaeologists and artists combined their interests and expertise. At the turn of the century, archaeologists, such as Jesse Walter Fewkes, Kenneth Chapman and Edgar Lee Hewett, working among the Pueblos of the southwestern United States encouraged the potters there to return to the ancient styles found during their digs.[1] Indigenous artists such as the famous potter Nampeyo (Hopi-Tewa) began recreating Sikyatki (*c.* 1450 AD) shapes and designs. Her collaborative work, done in conjunction with her husband, Lesou (who was a field worker at the site) and at the suggestion of Fewkes, set the pace for the fine art market trend of reviving old techniques along with designs.[2] At San Ildefonso in the 1920s, María Martínez and her husband Julián reinvented oxygen-reduced fired black on black ware through trial and error. Later, Lucy Lewis painted Mimbres motifs on her Acoma pots. This re-production of ancient artifacts by twentieth- century people was happening all over the Americas: wood and soap stone carvers of North West Coast, beaders and featherworkers of the Plains, and basket makers and potters in the South. In the Southwest their products were marketed by the many trading posts: Fred Harvey, Hubbell's and Keams Canyon catered to the growing tourist trade that was spawned by the coming of the railroad in the 1880s.[3] Further, the museum / art community was also in the business of collecting and trading in fine revivalist pieces through agents sent into the field. These practices raise questions regarding the way contemporary artists (and art historians) define cultural property of vanished or victimized peoples and challenges the notion of "traditional" style being exclusive to a particular time or place.

Critical Language

Reproductions and reinterpretations of Native American "traditional" forms are still being created by many contemporary artisans and artists of both Native and non-Native descent. In analyzing these issues of replicating ancient works of art Eric Hobsbawm and Hillel Schwartz distinguish between the act of reproducing and reviving forms. Museums sell reproductions, their audiences (consumers) want nearly exact duplicates of the pieces they have seen to handle and carry home with them. Reproduction implies the intent to copy something, as closely as possible to the original. The copy should evoke not only the sense of the original, but be visually identical in every way.[4] Once we pick up the copy, or examine it more closely, we may find subtle differences between it and the original piece. It probably weighs less, may be of smaller or larger dimensions, or the decoration may be arranged in a slightly different way. This is because, according to Bruce Baugh, "all. . .art is created for its time."[5] In other words, what is important to contemporary tourists is a visual replica that evokes past (or foreign) aesthetics, not necessarily a pot that will function in a practical way. The reproduction is not a forgery unless it falsely claims to be the original, and not just a visual stand-in.[6]

The revival of certain forms or creative processes, such as Nampeyo's, carries with it the notion of continuity in an ancient tradition, while still being a unique form. Depending upon the artist, what begins as replicating older works can be transformed into new styles that utilize designs or patterns from ancient sources, but re-combine them to create distinctly modern products. Revival implies that its predecessors, the original customs, have passed into disuse or that the people who practiced them perished.[7] Schwartz comments on the revivalism of "living museum" demonstrations as tending to "choose that which authenticates over that which is authentic. . .that we should be able to renew as we reenact."[8] Therefore, aspects of the past that are deemed valuable to contemporary audiences are incorporated, such as Nampeyo's feather motifs, while others are discarded in favor of efficiency or profit, such as minimizing pot sizes. Certain designs or shapes inspire nostalgia, which fits our romantic vision of an "authentic" past, one unspoiled by modern technology or foreign contact. Roger Keesing, examining reinvented pasts in Pacific cultures, compares Western "mythologizing" with Native "quests for identity," and notes that the "symbolic power" and force of revival can lack accuracy from either sphere.[9] Revival must be recognized as fragmentary at best, because there are always temporal issues and contextual changes that arise both through contact with other traditions and independent adaptations.

This brings us to the complex concept of tradition and its role in culture. Tradition is "the contrast between the constant change and innovation of the modern world and the attempt to structure at least some parts of social life within it as unchanging and invariant."[10] It is therefore repetitive, historical, and formalized. Hobsbawm recognizes that the building blocks of tradition are customs, they are intertwined and must be flexible because "life is. . .so."[11] Rapid changes in societies cause new traditions and / or customs to be invented and utilized, "not because old ways are no longer available or viable, but because they are deliberately not used or adapted."[12] These may be peaceful or violent changes, adaptations in technologies or belief systems. Robert Hobbs points out that, "After five hundred years of living together, our traditions are intertwined. . .[both Native and Euroamericans have] selected aspects of [one another's] culture based on their sense of themselves and their needs."[13] Culture is idea swapping and tradition grows from the repetition of those idea-based practices. Ralph T. Coe interviewed Native artists, students and activists concluding finally that tradition has different meanings for every individual: it includes "the old ways," "connections with my people," handed-down customs, and adaptations performed to promote harmony.[14] Tradition is definitely larger than style or technique; although it may include knowledge of both, it is something that changes while still providing a sense of continuity.

The Role of Museums

Museums and the educational mission espoused by them rely on the assumption that visitors and students will gain some understanding and respect for the creators of the objects through exposure to imitated techniques and re-created environments.[15] It has been recognized as an industry:

> The commoditization of the past in the context of tourist arts can be seen in heritage industry souvenirs: in the sale of real and "fake" antiquities, in the reproduction industry, and in the incorporation of ancient symbols into modern tourist arts—all of which can be loosely placed under the heading of antiques and antique-style arts.[16]

Therefore, reproductions, revival and tradition are at work today in the space of the museum to inform our multicultural masses about where "we" all have come from. In this portion of the exhibition the ceramic work of two artists can be examined, along with some of the indigenous pieces that inspired them.

J. Martin Haythorn and Michael Stuckey have created copies of the pieces in Southeastern museums as well as their own unique vessels. They strive through many comparisons and experiments to emulate the motifs and techniques that the ancients once used. They manufacture and sell their wares in museum gift shops and at American Indian heritage festivals and powwows. These two non-Indian artists have been selected because they create contemporary versions of the pre-contact styles of pottery originally produced by the people native to our Southeastern region, especially present-day Alabama, Georgia, and north Florida. (Some Southeastern American Indian people themselves continue to make pottery, notably among the Choctaw of Mississippi and Tennessee, the North Carolina Cherokee, and, most especially, the Catawba of South Carolina.) Their goals are to teach others to

Figure 1. Ceramic double-headed bird effigy, perforated design. Washington County, Florida, c. 900 AD. 8.5 inches high. (Photo: Museum of the American Indian, cat.# 17/4875)

Figure 2. Ceramic bird effigy, incised design. Franklin County, Florida, c. 900 AD. 8 inches high. (Photo: Museum of the American Indian, cat.# 17/4088)

appreciate the indigenous process of creation through demonstration firings and pottery classes. By examining what these artists do, why they do it, and how it reflects the standards of the pre-Columbian Southeast we will see cultural reproduction at work. Perhaps through Stuckey and Haythorn's art work we can attempt to re-capture some of the cultural significance the pottery held for its original users while gaining new insights on modern issues of representation and identity.

Ancient Potters of the South

The cultures represented can be identified as Southeastern Woodland groups, distinguished by ceramics, mound building and agriculture.[17] The excavation of mounds, both burial and midden types, in the Southeastern United States has yielded evidence for the existence of flourishing pre-contact communities in the region. Included are several distinctive regional groups who occupied parts of Southeastern Alabama and Southwestern Georgia all the way down to Gulf-coastal South Florida; dating from approximately 400 to 1200 AD.[18] Of particular importance is the Weeden Island culture, which showed a new degree of complexity for pre-contact Florida. This has been concluded from the archeological record, which demonstrated new diversity of resource procurement, stratification manifested through burial forms, artistic excellence in carving and pottery, and signs of population expansion.[19] Both David Brose and Jerald Milanich have noted a certain amount of continuity in pottery decoration from the earlier Swift Creek people of the Southeast (c. 1-500 AD). The settlements uncovered range in size from one or two small midden (refuse) mounds to large sites consisting of multiple platform mounds with evidence of perishable structures built atop them and purposefully arranged burials inside. They apparently practiced elaborate mortuary ceremonies that included burying the deceased accompanied by both plain and decorated pottery, carved mica gorgets, sacrificed animals, and burned substances, like incense.[20] The ceremonial ceramic vessels were often adorned with sculptures of animal faces and bodies, incised with geometric or wave patterns, and some were ritually "killed" (holes cut into them or broken) for burial purposes. Population increases and diversification of subsistence patterns are possible reasons for the rise in ceremonial vessel use and production.[21] Because many material remains were destroyed due to environmental conditions such as humidity or modern human impact such as construction, the more enduring materials of ceramics have been used to piece together the lives of the mound-builders.

Animals were important to native peoples for many reasons. Therefore, birds and other animals play a prominent role in this art. An examination of the visual motifs reveals many bird and mammal shapes and designs (Figures 1 and 2). Some of these were seasonal food sources, while others were probably not eaten at all. The functions of their forms as utilitarian wares or transactional sculptured vessels have determined their classification as "high art," "artifact," or "folk art." The integrated role of ceramic vessels within ceremonial and mortuary contexts brings into question these classifications. "Utilitarian" plain wares take on new meaning when buried with an elite member of the community. Exotic vessels, those with special incisions or adornments, have "functions" that range from sacred purposes to everyday cultural reinforcement. Each participating member of the community (as well as surrounding populations) may attribute different significance to the ceramics based on his or her position within (or outside) the society. Mallory McCane-O'Connor elaborates on the differences in quality and content of ceramic vessel design as a "sacred / secular dichotomy."[22]

The original vessels seen here could be considered as "exotic" wares, differing from their daily-use, utilitarian counterparts in iconography, function, and ultimate disposal.[23] (Figures 3 and 4) The zoomorphic features are emphasized by the vessels' cut out and incised sections. Their beaks, wings, and other details have either been sculpted and added to the coiled pots or carved into the surface of the clay before firing. The predominance of bird images in the context of these sacred or ceremonial wares has been noted by various authors.[24] "Birds in a variety of motifs. . .appear with such frequency that the avian theme must be regarded as central to an understanding of Mississippian religion."[25] Jerald Milanich refers to them as possibly "spirit guardians of the dead," due to their placement within burial mounds.[26] Charles Hudson views them as part of the three-tiered world paradigm; birds occupy the upper world, frogs and serpents the under world, while humans exist between with the deer and the panther.[27]

The stylized animals and prolific punctations set these vessels apart in function as well. Cut-outs precluded use as containers and the effigies are more complex in workmanship and detail than the Deptford Culture stamped (using a cord wrapped paddle) utilitarian wares. Milanich speculates that they "were probably used in rituals requiring preparation of sacred medicines, as well

as in other ceremonial contexts."[28] Further, the vessels were found broken and scattered within burials, not discarded with the trash in the midden mounds situated near the village complexes. This fact adds a dimension of artistic imagination to any reconstruction of the original pieces or the culture of their creators.

Contemporary Potters of the South

While J. Martin Haythorn was an art student, he met and worked with Ivan Gundrum, an expatriate-Yugoslavian artist who made reproductions of Southeastern pottery with molds and house paint.[29] Haythorn admired Gundrum's sources himself and began to experiment with more traditional techniques. Now he teaches classes in pottery through the community center in Thomasville, Georgia. There he puts to use the same hand-building and pit-firing methods that ancient residents once utilized. Haythorn comments, "my intention is. . .to honor the art work that the Mound Builders did. . .because when you appreciate someone's art work, you understand them better."[30] His work relates to his own dual heritage; his mother is of Sioux Indian descent and she is now an honorary member of the Creek tribe as well as a practicing medicine woman.[31] He cites the "extremely brutal and dis-

Figure 4. Ceramic turkey-vulture effigy vase, by Michael Stuckey, 1996, 9 inches high. (Photo: courtesy of the Artist)

ruptive" invasions of the Spanish who destroyed "not only. . .their physical beings but. . .their culture too," which he sees as extremely connected to nature and the spirit world.[32] Haythorn therefore emphasizes the complex nature of the Southeastern Natives' religious beliefs and practices, as evidenced by their burials and the animal and curvilinear motifs on their artifacts.

Michael Stuckey enjoys relating the arrowheads and pot shards found around the bays and inlets near his home on the Northwest Florida coast to the people he knows once lived in the region. Raised in Florida, Stuckey lives in the Panhandle, not far from a Weeden Island culture archaeological site, Buck Mound (c. 500-800 AD).[33] He has spent a great deal of his professional artistic development learning the techniques used to create the coiled ceramic vessels of the first Floridians. Stuckey explains,

> I just gradually started learning how to do it
> on my own, through experimentation. . .and
> then I realized that there was a philosophy
> going along with it, that I was working from a
> two or three thousand year old local tradition
> that's just as valid as any other."[34]

His expertise was gained by observing and working on archaeological survey and data-recovery crews for some construction and dig sites in the area. By reading the work of scholars who have reconstructed the lifeways of pre-contact indigenous people, he grew to admire their systems of agriculture and their efficient use

Figure 3. Marriage Bowl, Southeast Ceremonial Complex, Pickens-Pencak Ceremonial Site, Walton County, Florida, c. 1350-1500, ceramic, 4 x 8 inches. Indian Temple Mound Museum, Ft. Walton Beach, Florida (#1253).

Figure 5. Ceramic bat effigy rattle bowl, by Michael Stuckey, 1996, 3.5 inches high. (Photo: Diana Roman)

that the head had once served as a rattle.[38] His version is not an exact reproduction, it is an original composition based on the ideas gathered from the several examples that were on display. The wings, which are incised on some of the originals, are modeled in three dimensions on Stuckey's vessel. He did construct it as a rattle, so the bowl makes a soft clatter when shaken. It was fired during a demonstration of pit-firing at the local Indian Heritage Week event. The form and firing method serve one another: the air pocket of the rattle would have caused it to explode in kiln conditions (Figure 5). This is labor intensive, but exemplifies the work of the Mound Builders.

Martin Haythorn creates owl-effigy jars which he feels conjure up the fascination the birds must have held for indigenous hunters trying to achieve their stealth and accuracy and ancient priests requesting the assistance of their power to cross the bounds of earth, sky and water. He digs his own clay, just as Stuckey does, and pit fires at area sites or events. Pit firing heats the pots slowly and gives them distinctive colorings or smudges according to how near or far they are from direct heat and each other. Haythorn incises his vessels with an assortment of tools similar to the variety the Mound Builders must have used (Figure 6). Both artists reproduce pedestaled bird-effigy vases based on ancient prototypes, with punctations or cut-outs and the beaked head adornos (Figure 7).

Figure 7. Ceramic double-headed bird effigy vase, by Martin Haythorn, 1997, 10 inches high. (Photo: Diana Roman)

of the surrounding environment. When asked how he would interpret the iconography of the ancient artifacts, he responded, "everything had a practical side, and a mystical interpretation."[35] For example, the burning of cedar or some type of incense in a ceramic pot could be said to "cleanse the lodge of spirits. . .but also the smoke keeps out mosquitoes." He cites the ideas of animals as signs of prosperity or warnings and carriers of beneficial traits as well as Native people's dependence on them as food and skin resources. "As they traveled. . .on the war path or hunting. . .if they came across an animal that carried a bad omen, they would just turn around."[36] Stuckey emphasizes that his work is "inspired by pre-[contact] art. . ." and ". . .you know when you get into that flow, you're. . .learning as you go with it."[37] Although practical and interesting, Stuckey's views are intuitive rather than reflective of the archeological tradition.

Process and Purpose

The influences of ancient southeastern native pottery can be seen in the techniques, style, and design of the contemporary works of these two artists. Michael Stuckey saw a bat effigy bowl during an exhibition at the museum in Moundville, Alabama. He liked the image and shape and was intrigued by the possibility

Stuckey and Haythorn attempt to understand the people and traditions they admire by emulating the process of the art work as much as the objects themselves. They have reproduced the production methods as closely as possible to the older traditions. The technique used to produce the pottery presented (both pre-contact and contemporary) is pit-firing of limestone and shell-tempered local clays (Figure 8). Some of the pots are burnished or have a mica temper that causes shine, but most are not slipped or painted. They have color variations based on oxidation that takes place during firing. Both artists have researched the evidence left by their ceramic-making predecessors. Martin Haythorn has expedited the process by making molds of his most common vessel shapes, which he then decorates by hand. Each piece becomes a unique creation with the addition of the incised designs. Whereas the Weeden Island people commonly made vessels for daily use and more rarely for ritual purposes or exchange, Stuckey and Haythorn make vessels as commodities for exchange and sale. Martin Haythorn has even branched out into ceramic reproductions of wood carvings and original beads.

Remembering through Revival

These artists and others working in the same genre treat their subjects with reverence as well as realism. They have chosen the

Figure 6. Ceramic owl effigy vases—pre- and post-firing (post-firing on the left)—by Martin Haythorn, 1997, 6 inches high each. (Photo: Diana Roman)

Figure 8. Demonstration of pit-firing method, Martin Haythorn's installation at the Tallahassee Museum of History and Natural Science, 1997. Pit 5-6 feet across. (Photo: Diana Roman)

most technically demanding pieces to reproduce and have invited the public to witness the ancient processes. Reconstruction of pre-contact people's lifeways in this manner encourages the repatriation of real artifacts and provides the insight necessary to support or challenge scholarly research. Vital religious items such as Iroquois False Face masks, Zuni war-god images or Plains vision-painted shields are not meant to be publicly displayed. Therefore, "the most important thing about an object may be the way in which it restricts the gaze."[39] In this case we may have burial objects that should remain buried or honored. Reproductions can serve as mundane replacements for sacred artifacts. Some will become commodities when they hit the art market, depending upon their workmanship and reflective qualities. "Authentic antiquities are looked upon as non-renewable resources worthy of investment and their relative commodity value is informed by the politics of connoisseurship."[40] Part of what makes copies of antiquities valuable to the consumer is the nostalgia mentioned earlier. Kevin Walsh also refers to this as "the idea of empathy, a promotion of the idea that we can travel back to the past."[41] We get this sensation from viewing a demonstration firing at the Tallahassee Museum of History and Natural Science or from taking a miniature turkey-vulture effigy vase home from a Native festival. By reviving the "old ways" we question the purity of any cultural commodity.

The past must be kept in perspective, for there are many things that are forgotten or misrepresented. "Antiquities act as ancestral precedents for later artistic creations—but more through the process of artistic revivals than through the process of artistic continuities."[42] Both of these artists have claimed that they want to revive the ancient pottery tradition that they simulate. Haythorn states, "to see if other people can start doing original work based on this tradition of pit firing, incise work and effigies."[43] Stuckey and Haythorn also hope that exposing tourists, students and art consumers will promote renewed respect for original inhabitants of this country. Again, Haythorn elaborates, "some of the attitudes toward life and the meaning of life and nature that Native Americans had is a valuable perspective for all people."[44] How-

ever, "It is debatable as to whether tourists' imaginative re-creation of the distant past when they come into contact with ancient objects and texts can be called equally authentic. The discovered past is inevitably interpreted by the present and hence filtered through a distorting time-lens."[45] Deborah Root succinctly notes that to the spectator or consumer "authenticity is the currency at play in the market place of cultural difference."[46] While addressing authenticity in African tourist arts, Sidney Kasfir reminds us that for many cultures

> imitating a well-known model is considered neither deceptive nor demeaning; rather, it is viewed as both economically pragmatic and a way of legitimating the skill of a predecessor… or paying homage to a fellow artist. . . ."[47]

Keeping all of these perspectives in mind, we can conclude that from the Pueblos at the turn of the century to the contemporary potters of the Southeast, revival of ancient forms and techniques can be both deceptively romantic appropriation and pragmatically honorable. Consumers choose how they will participate in the ongoing debate, yet the realm of their choices can be conscientiously provided by a critically-aware museum / education community. This may be the only true way to involve the twentieth-century public in remembering our collective and individual past.[48]

1   For general reference, see Schroeder and Simmons' sections in the *Handbook of North American Indians, Southwest*, ed. Alfonso Ortiz, vol. 9 (Washington: Smithsonian, 1979) 5-14, 219. Ruth Bunzel also worked closely with Pueblo potters; their techniques and aesthetics are dealt with in intimate detail in *The Pueblo Potter: A Study of Creative Imagination in Primitive Art* [1929] (New York: Dover, 1972) 57.

2   For more on this trend see J. J. Brody's work in the *Handbook*, vol. 9, "Pueblo Fine Arts," 605.

3   Brody, "Pueblo Fine Arts," 604.

4   Hillel Schwartz, *The Culture of the Copy: Striking Likenesses, Unreasonable Facsimiles* (New York: Zone Books, 1996) 278. This author uses a multi-disciplinary approach to examine the role of replication in modern society.

5   See Baugh's article, "Authenticity Revisited," in *The Journal of Aesthetics and Art Criticism* (1988): 477-487, where he discusses how authenticity is linked to context.

6   For a concise, informative presentation of legal issues in art, see Leonard D. DuBoff, *Art Law in a Nutshell*, 2nd edition (St. Paul: West Publishing, 1993) 67.

7   See Eric Hobsbawm's introduction, "Inventing Traditions" in Hobsbawm and Ranger, eds., *The Invention of Tradition* (New York: Cambridge UP, 1983) 4. He deals with both the need for and the construction of cultural homeostasis through "traditional" practices, whether they are weeks or centuries old.

8   Schwartz 279.

9   Although studies of non-Western societies have not been used for general sociological comparisons, we see in Keesing's article evidence of the post-modern reclamation of fourth-world cultural productivity that accentuates historical Western appropriation and how the same process is being reversed. See Roger Keesing, "Creating the Past: Custom and Identity in the Contemporary Pacific," *Contemporary Pacific*, 1 (1989): 19-42.

10 Hobsbawm 2.

11 Hobsbawm 3.

12 Hobsbawm 8.

13 See Robert Hobbs, "Recent Considerations in the Study of Native American Art," *Northeast Indian Quarterly* 7 (1990) : 67-70.

14 See Ralph T. Coe *Lost and Found Traditions: Native American Art 1965-1985* (New York: American Federation of Arts, 1986) 48. This is a catalog of an important exhibition demonstrating continuity within change and upheaval in Native cultures. For further Native American opinion on authenticity and tradition see Joseph Marshall III, *On Behalf of the Wolf and the First Peoples* (Santa Fe: Red Crane, 1995).

15 With the public audience in mind, these are very important and yet tenuously understood issues. For a sampling of the current discourse, see Peter Stone and Brian Molyneaux, eds., *The Presented Past: Heritage Museums and Education* (New York: Routledge, 1994) 14.

16 From Deirdre Evans-Pritchard, "Ancient Art in Modern Context," *Annals of Tourism Research* 20 (1993): 9-31, wherein she discusses Costa Rican reproduction arts as well as appropriation of ancient motifs for national symbolism.

17 There are categories and chronologies that overlap here, as in any cultural discussion. These Native Americans will be referred to as Woodland groups, Moundbuilders, and members of the Southeastern Ceremonial Complex. For Woodland reference, see David Brose, et.al., *Ancient Art of the American Woodland Indians* (New York: Harry N. Abrams Inc., 1985) 68.

18 See Jerald T. Milanich and Charles H. Fairbanks, *Florida Archaeology* (New York: Academic Press, 1980) 20. For more on Native Floridians and contact, see Milanich's *Florida Indians and the Invasion from Europe* (Gainesville: UP, 1995).

19 See Charles M. Hudson, *Four Centuries of Southern Indians* (Athens, Georgia: UP, 1975).

20 See Vincas P. Steponaitis, *Ceramics, Chronology, and Community Patterns* (New York: Academic Press, 1983) 83-90.

21 Milanich and Fairbanks 78-79.

22 See Mallory McCane-O'Connor, "Prehistoric Ceramics: the Weeden Island Tradition," *American Indian Art Magazine* 5 (1980) : 48-53, and Roy C. Craven, Jr., "Pre-Columbian Artist Craftsmen of the Southeast," in *Of Sky and Earth: Art of the Early Southeastern Indians*, ed. Dickens, Georgia Department of Archives and History (Dalton, Georgia: Lee Printing Company, 1982).

23 See Milanich and Fairbanks, and Steponaitis, as well as Barbara Purdy's two volumes, *Indian Art of Ancient Florida* (Tallahassee: UP, 1996) [catalog] and *The Art and Archaeology of Florida's Wetlands* (Boca Raton: CRC Press, 1991).

24 See previously cited material, McCane-O'Connor, Brose et. al., and Milanich.

25 See Strong's chapter on the "Bird-Man Motif," in *The Southeastern Ceremonial Complex: Artifacts and Analysis*, edited by Patricia Galloway (Lincoln: Nebraska UP, 1989) 211.

26 Milanich and Fairbanks 141.

27 Charles M. Hudson, *The Southeastern Indians* (Knoxville: Tennessee UP, 1976) 123-124.

28 Milanich and Fairbanks 141.

29 For biographical sketch and primary source artistic interpretations, see Ken J. Uyemura, "The Artistic Works of Ivan Gundrum with Particular Reference to his Reproductions of Clay Artifacts of the Florida Gulf Coast Indians," (unpublished Master's Thesis, Tallahassee: Florida State University, 1967) 30.

30 First in a series of interviews with the artist, March 12, 1997.

31 Second interview, conducted over telephone, June 1997.

32 Personal communication, March 1997.

33 See Yulee W. Lazarus, *The Buck Burial Mound: A Mound of the Weeden Island Culture* (Fort Walton Beach: Temple Mound Museum, City of FWB 1979).

34 First in a series of interviews with the artist, March 7, 1997.

35 Personal communication, March 1997.

36 Personal communication, March 1997.

37 Second interview, conducted over telephone, June 1997.

38 Personal communication, March 1997.

39 See Janet C. Berlo and Ruth B Phillips, "The Problematics of Collecting and Display, Part 1," in *Art Bulletin* 77 (1995) : 6-10.

40 Evans-Pritchard 10.

41 See Kevin Walsh, *The Representation of the Past: Museums and Heritage in the Post-Modern World* (New York: Routledge, 1992) 101.

42 Hobsbawm 11.

43 Personal communication, March 1997.

44 Personal communication, March 1997.

45 Evans-Pritchard 10.

46 See Deborah Root, *Cannibal Culture: Art, Appropriation, and the Commodification of Difference* (Boulder: Westview Press, 1996) 78.

47 See Kasfir's well-debated article, "African Art and Authenticity: A Text with a Shadow," in *African Arts* (1992) : 41-53.

48 For a brief introduction to the contemporary importance of a surviving pottery tradition for maintaining tribal identity within a specific southeastern American Indian community, see Wesley DuRant Taukchiray and Alice Bee Kasakoff, with photographs by Gene Joseph Crediford, "Contemporary Native Americans in South Carolina" in *Indians of the Southeastern United States in the Late 20th Century*, edited by J. Anthony Paredes (Tuscaloosa: U of Alabama P, 1992).

The Artification of the Hopi Kachina *Tihu*

Noah Young

Amidst the stark and arid landscape of the plateau area of northeastern Arizona, the Hopi Indians have been residing on three mesa tops for as long as anyone can remember. Their strong culture and a system of intensive agricultural practice have allowed them to survive in a land which averages only ten to thirteen inches of rainfall a year.[1] These sedentary people have developed an elaborate seasonal cycle of ceremonial observances in order to maintain a balanced and harmonious relationship with the spirits of the natural world.

The relationship between the Hopis and the forces of nature is codified in the existence of the Kachina Cult and its ritual manifestations. The word *Kachina* means "spirit father," or one who sits with the people, and refers to the spirit intermediaries who visit the Hopi villages for six months out of the year. Kachinas are supernaturals embodying the spirits of living things and spirits of deceased ancestors who spend half the year with the Hopis[2] and the other half in their mythic domain of the San Francisco Mountains, located in central Arizona. They are spirit beings who cross the boundary of the natural and supernatural worlds acting as intermediaries between man and the spirit world. The Hopi (an ancient people who speak a language which is part of the Uto-Aztecan language family) feel that interaction with supernaturals is a symbiotic relationship.[3] The Hopis provide what the spirits desire (prayer feathers, corn pollen, and rituals) while the Kachinas act on the Hopis' behalf by bringing rain to the arid land in rituals which are mutual gift-giving ceremonies.[4] The Hopi literally *become* the spirits in masked dances during the great winter festivals in order to materialize and celebrate their spirit helpers. They also carve symbolic representations of Kachinas, and Kachina dancers, which are given to members of Hopi society during the masked dances.

This article addresses the artification of the indigenous artifact as it relates to the art of Kachina carvings called *tihu*, practiced by the Hopi Indians.[5] It will also explore the cultural context in which this art is produced, and the unique ability of the Hopi *tihu* to retain its sacred applications, while at the same time adapting to the demands of a non-Native market.

The "Kachina Doll"[6] (or called by its Hopi name *Tihu*—meaning child[7]) is primarily used to introduce young women and infants to the presence of the Kachinas (Figure 1). It is regarded as a prayer for supernatural association and assistance, and is given by the female's masked relatives (the Kachinas). The carving is considered a Kachina and *tihu* at the same time, because the term *tihu* also refers to the masked personator.[8] Thus the dancer and the carving are both vehicles for the manifestation of the Kachina spirits.

The *tihu*'s role in Hopi society can be viewed as a representation of the greater efficacy of the Kachina Cult. The socio-religious use of the *tihu* serves to ameliorate the separation of the sexes in regards to religious practice. Therefore it fosters integration of knowledge by both sexes and creates a balance of experience for the whole society. Just as the Kachina Cult serves to redistribute food and integrate its members, so too the giving of *tihu* to females points to the redistribution of spiritual association and affiliation from the male-dominated religious sphere to

Figure 1. A *tihu* such as this example, would be given to a young female by the Kachinas at one of the ceremonies, thus associating that female with the powerful spirit beings, *c.* 1940s, height 8 1/8 inches. Collection of Sara W. Reeves and I.S.K. Reeves V. (Photo: Beverly Brosius)

the female sphere of Hopi society.[9] The symbolic use of the Hopi *tihu* also serves as a material codification of Kachina ideology for the culture which originally had no written language. Thus the *tihu* can be viewed as an essential part of Hopi culture, which serves to maintain and reinforce the Hopi world view. It is essential to note that there are problems with making blanket statements regarding the *tihu*'s use in Hopi society. This dilemma is made clear through the words of Alph Secakuku (himself a carver, painter and sculptor from Second Mesa):

> ...Because the Hopi religion is so complex, and has no written tribal language, the philosophical responses to the underlying concepts of the katsina dolls surely vary among the Hopi people themselves.[10]

The historical context within which this art form developed dates back to the introduction of the Kachina Cult itself.[11] The earliest evidence of what may be a *tihu* was found in Double Butte cave near Phoenix, Arizona, dated around the twelfth or thirteenth century.[12] Its head is carved in the shape of a mask, painted, and the body is rigid and frontal,[13] much like the early examples which ethnographers found in the late nineteenth century.[14] Frederick Dockstader[15] feels that the elaboration of the art form of *tihu* carving was affected due to importation by the early Spanish[16] priests of carved figures of the Catholic saints. It is interesting to note that the formal affinity of early *tihu* with *pahos*

Figure 2. An example of a "Kachinoid" made by a Navajo carver, c. 1915-16, height 6 inches. Collection of Sara W. Reeves and I.S.K. Reeves V.

(prayer sticks decorated with feathers offered as messages to the gods) may point to an independent origination of the carved representations of the Kachinas.

The *tihu*, in order to be considered acceptable in the eyes of a Hopi, must fulfill two conditions: first, it must be carved from the water-seeking root of the cottonwood tree, and, second, it must be painted in order to reproduce the design of the mask and costume of the particular Kachina represented. Originally, the *tihu* was anonymously carved by men, in the seclusion of the kiva,[17] prior to the ceremonial use of the carving, and was (and is) given to a female by the Kachina. The child would then take the

tihu home and hang it by a string from rafters within the house.[18]

The contemporary *tihu* has gone through a process of aestheticization[19] moving from being valued as a cultural artifact (by early ethnographers), to being a tourist curio / commodity, and finally into the aesthetic valuation as a work of art. This process has changed the formal qualities of the Hopi *tihu* and has opened the way for the contextual appropriation by non-Puebloan peoples and the subsequent secularization of the art form.

For the past one hundred and fifty years the Hopi *tihu* has been collected by non-Pueblo peoples.[20] The early ethnographers were the first to collect large numbers of dolls, and this scientific query had a great impact on the subsequent valuations of the *tihu*.[21] These early collections spawned interest in the *tihu*, and found their way into many natural history museums throughout the country, signaling the institutional reinforcement of the *tihu* as an ethnographic artifact.[22] These early carvings were acquired for what they represented (in context of the culture in which they were produced) as opposed to their formal stylistic characteristics.[23] The early missions of these ethnographers provoked great interest in the Hopi *tihu* and soon private collectors started buying the carvings from the Hopi[24] whose taboos on selling their ritual art were superseded by increasing economic pressures. As the market opened up for the Hopi *tihu*, within the non-Indian culture, the art of carving *tihu* was met by market demands which would transfigure the technique, context, and stylistic appearance of the *tihu*. In this case a formalist approach combined with an analysis of the various contexts is applied in hopes of providing a key to unlock the *tihu*'s morphological history.

The stylistic transformation of the carvings is concurrent with the evolution of the contexts in which the carvings are valued. In this light the *tihu*'s style unfolds from the roughly hewn, frontal, static, iconic images of antiquity, (and so valued by the early ethnographers) to the highly refined, exquisite naturalism of today's carvings so highly valued by the "high" art market and connoisseurs.

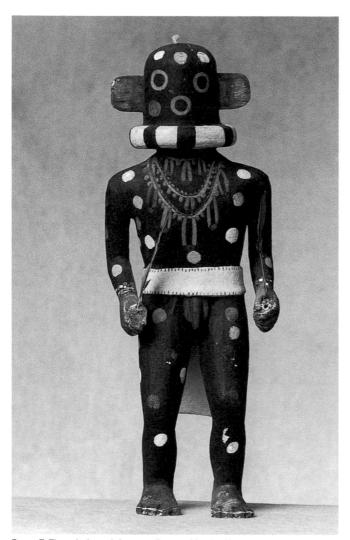

Figure 3. The split-legged design is illustrated by this Hopi Kachina Kohosorhoya which is c. 1945-1950, height 10 inches. Collection of Sara W. Reeves and I.S.K. Reeves V. (Photo: Beverly Brosius)

Arts and Crafts Act) all produce numerous Kachina doll carvings for sale, and these are not considered *tihu*, but are referred to as "Kachinoids," or fakes which are primarily bought by tourists. An example of an exceptional "Kachinoid" (Figure 2) is identified by its jumbled iconography (a trick of early Hopi carvers[27]) and was made by Navajo carvers. Few of the carvings produced by these groups are accurate representations of Kachinas, and it is estimated "that well over one-half of Kachina dolls in the typical Indian curio store are not made by Hopis."[28]

Once the *tihu* transcended the status of tourist curio, the context in which it was valued changed, and it was deemed "authentic" by the institution of non-Native ethnography.[29]

The stylistic continuum of the Hopi *tihu* evolved along with its changing contexts and displays the influence of Western esthetics. The early carvings showed none of the highly realized three-dimensional naturalism seen today, and the sculpturally in-

Figure 5. The widespread use of a base for the *tihu* can be seen in this exquisite example of a Butterfly Maiden (not technically a Kachina) which was carved in 1978 by Ronald Honyouti. The elaborate tablita headpiece this carving 'wears,' reveals many motifs which are central to the Hopi artistic vocabulary. Height 16 inches. Private Collection. (Photo © 1998 Manley Gallery, Tucson, Arizona)

Within the context of the tourist market the Hopi *tihu* became a commodity which could adapt to the acculturated tastes and needs of early collectors. Such is the case with mass-produced, lathe-turned dolls, which were sometimes painted by "Indians" in order to fool buyers into thinking they had purchased an "authentic" carving.[25] Hopi artists also had a hard time supplying the demand of the tourist market, and many non-Hopi carvers have taken up the slack.[26] Native Americans from other tribes and non-Indians (against the 1990s Indian

Figure 4. The 'action' pose is illustrated by the upraised arms and foot of this Eagle Dancer (Kwahu) Kachina, carved by Alvin James, c. 1972, height 12 inches. Private Collection. (Photo © 1998 Manley Gallery, Tucson, Arizona)

dependent limbs of contemporary carvings were not observed in early types. The bodies of the early *puchtihu*[30] gave way to the split-legged design (Figure 3),[31] and the dolls adapted the convention of the flared skirt.[32] Tihu also acquired their "action" poses, a convention which would last into the 1990s (Figure 4). This phenomenon is thought to have been caused by the encouragement given to the carvers to represent the dancers[33] whose sculptural interplay appealed to the Western world's adherence to the tenets of naturalism and contrapposto pose, thus removing some of the iconic quality of the early carvings and signaling a shift in Native aesthetics.[34]

The emphasis on the naturalistic depiction of the Kachina dancers presented a problem for the producers. Since the "action" poses were often represented with bent legs, a structural base had to be employed. Many carvers enlarged the feet of their *tihu* in order for them to stand on their own, while others joined a base to the legs of their carvings. Often carvers will anchor their creations to a thin piece of the cottonwood root, thereby integrating the media of sculpture and base (Figure 5). Thus the doll was transformed (by market demand) from a ritual object (made to be hung or handled) to a free-standing sculpture with a base (as in the European tradition).

Along with sculptural developments, the Kachina carving became more and more elaborately clothed, often displaying the paraphernalia used by the dancers in ritual ceremonies (Figure 6). Buckskin, feathers, yarn, and even seaweed have all been employed in order to give the dolls a more ornate (hence more marketable) appearance.[35]

A fascinating example of the stylistic changes which took place was the new reliance on commercial pigments for the decoration of the carving. Some carvers experimented with stains and oil paints, but the vitality of acrylic paints is generally favored.[36] This is especially intriguing due to the fact that the rigid symbology of color is an essential element in Kachina iconography.

An important step in the process of the artification of the *tihu* was made in the early 1930s, when Harold Colton (of the Museum of Northern Arizona) persuaded Jimmie Kewanwytewa

Figure 6. This Black Bear (Hon) Kachina carved by Neil David exemplifies the trend towards decorating the *tihu*, with the carver employing fur, shells, and buckskin to give the carving a robust appearance, c. 1974, height 19 inches. Private Collection. (Photo © 1998 Manley Gallery, Tucson, Arizona)

to sign one of his carvings,[37] thereby fulfilling the fine art market's emphasis on individual attribution.[38]

After 1945 the Kachina *tihu* had been established as a valued (and valuable) art object. This was prompted in part by the advent of modernist esthetics earlier in the century (which by the end of WWII had been formally accepted and embraced by the art institution) and the credibility attributed to an artifact which had been placed in the context of fine-art institutions. The ideological blending of ethnographic contextualism and artistic formalism was the non-Native basis for the valuation of the Hopi *tihu* as a universal masterpiece of human culture.[39]

The first major shift to an

Figure 7. The elongated body of this Zuni Shalako Kachina represents the contemporary carver's interest in manipulating the form of the *tihu*, and in representing the tall form of the Shalako, c. 1945, height 14-1/2 inches. Collection of Sara W. Reeves and I.S.K. Reeves V. (Photo: Beverly Brosius)

aesthetic contextualization was the "Exposition of Indian Tribal Arts" in 1931 at New York's Grand Central galleries, where 650 ancient and historic artifacts were shown in the context of a major art exhibition, in which many of the pieces were available for purchase.[40]

The 1941 Museum of Modern Art show "Indian Art of The United States" is extremely important in the elevation of the *tihu* in particular, and Native American art in general, to the status of fine art. This show put Native American art in the same context in which leading American fine art was shown, thus lending "institutional credibility" to the objects in the show.[41] The appropriation of "Indian" culture was seen as a vital national prototype of "American" culture, which could give American art the solidarity of historicity.

Further inroads have been made by the Hopi *tihu* into the world of the international art market and have established its place among the finest art in the world. In the mid-sixties Hopi carvings were cast in bronze (a medium exclusive to fine art) in attempts to further expand the market for Kachina related art.[42] Other non-essential changes have explored the manipulation of

Figure 8. Further modulations in the *tihu* can be seen in the enlarged head of this Kokopelli Kachina, carved by Clark Tenakhongua of First Mesa, c. late 20th century, height 5 3/4 inches. Collection of Sara W. Reeves and I.S.K. Reeves V. (Photo: Beverly Brosius)

Figure 9. Carvings such as this "non-traditional" example of a "Skunk" Kachina, by Clark Tenakhongua, as well as the Koyemsi, or mud-head clown, and the Koshare, or sacred clowns, are popular with the contemporary Kachina market, c. late 20th century, height 12 1/2 inches. Collection of Sara W. Reeves and I.S.K. Reeves V. (Photo: Beverly Brosius)

scale (Figure 7), proportional shifts (Figure 8), the production of genre "scenes," and the figuration of non-kachina figures. Carvings such as this example of a "skunk" kachina (Figure 9), as well as the *Koyemsi* or mud-head clown, and the *Koshari*, or sacred clowns, are popular with the contemporary Kachina market.

The Hopi *tihu* bridges the worlds of its original ceremonial art context and the context of the high art market and can be considered a "metamorphosed" object, one which has been appropriated and valued by the non-Native culture, yet which is not produced by the non-Native culture.[43] Through the valuation of a sacred, ceremonial art by early ethnographers, to the demands of a tourist market (and the economic pressures of wage-labor and reservation economics), and by the fulfillment of certain aesthetic and historic criteria, the Hopi *tihu* has risen to the status of high art. This phenomenon has had an impact on the Hopi use of the *tihu*, but strangely has not entirely stripped the *tihu* of its sacred / social function, and this art form has in many ways resisted the Orpheus-like glance of the non-Native culture. Perhaps this is due to the inherent adaptability of Hopi culture (a culture which has weathered the vicissitudes of time) which extends its survival

techniques to its rich art form of *tihu* carving. In this light the Hopi *tihu* can be viewed as a symbol of cultural solidarity, achieved through the methods of adaptation, flexibility, and the belief in and respect of the spiritual exigencies which serve to shape existence.

1   Frederick Dockstader, The Kachina and the White Man (Albuquerque: U of New Mexico P, 1985) 2.

2   The ceremonial season of the Kachinas lasts from Soyal (the winter solstice) to Niman in mid July. Barton Wright, Hopi Kachinas (Flagstaff: Northland Press, 1977) 7.

3   Robert Boissiere, *Meditations with the Hopi* (Santa Fe: Berr. and Co., 1986) 18.

4   Wright, *Hopi Kachinas* 4.

5   The Hopi have developed this craft to a greater degree than the other western Pueblo Indians (except perhaps than the Zuni, who also have a rich kachina complex) and have allowed the most outside contact with their Kachina iconography.

6   Tihu are commonly referred to as Kachina Dolls; however, this term is not applicable to the carvings used ceremonially by the Hopi, but rather designates the secular context of a carving produced for sale.

7   "The term *tihu* is applied to all figures carved more or less as effigies, but the word means a small person: a child." Barton Wright, *Hopi Material Culture* (Flagstaff: Northland Press, 1979) 107.

8   Dockstader 96.

9   This is alluded to in John T. Erickson, *Kachinas—an Evolving Hopi Art Form* (Phoenix: Heard Museum, 1977) 9.

10 Alph Secakuku, Introduction, *Following Sun and Moon—Hopi Kachina Tradition* (Flagstaff: Northland / Heard Museum, 1995) x.

11 A major drought in the last quarter of the thirteenth century, along with the pressures of the Navajo, Ute, and Apache tribes, saw the Hopi mesas populated with refugees from the north. Helga Teiwes, *Kachina Dolls: The Art of Hopi Carvers* (Tucson: U of Arizona P, 1991) 24. This increase in population signaled a greater need for integration of the divergent elements of the society (a function fulfilled by the Cult's universal membership). Charles E. Adams, *The Origin and Development of the Peublo Katsina Cult* (Tucson: U of Arizona P, 1991)160. Evidence points to the development of the Cult out of a diffusion of culture from the advanced southern Mesoamerican states, upwards through Casas Grandes in Chihuahua, which was then a trading center important for the dissemination of ideas and culture. Teiwes 23.

12 Clara Lee Tanner and John F. Tanner, "Kachinas" in *Hopi Kachina: Spirit of Life*, ed. Dorothy K. Washburn (California Academy of Sciences, 1980) 81.

13 Clara Lee Tanner, *Southwest Indian Crafts* (Tucson: U of Arizona P, 1968) 152.

14 The existence of the Cult at this time is further corroborated by twelfth-century petroglyphs of masked beings and the Kachina-like forms in kiva murals at Awatovi. Polly Schaafsma, *Indian Rock Art of the Southwest* (Albuquerque: School of American Research, Santa Fe, and U of New Mexico P, 1980) and Dockstader 35.

15 Dockstader 128.

[16] When the Spanish first saw the *tihu* they were denounced as idols of a "primitive" religion, along with the ritual Kachina dances, and many attempts were made at eradicating the native religion. John G. Bourke, *The Snake Dance of the Moquis of Arizona* (London: Sampson, Low, Marston, Searle, and Rivington, 1884) 43. Despite limited contact with the Spanish in the ensuing years, the Hopi mesas were left in relative isolation until 1821, when the Santa Fe trail opened and brought the Hopi in contact with non-Pueblo people and their manufactured goods. William Walker and Lydia L. Wycoff, *Hopis, Tewas, and the American Road* (Albuquerque: U of New Mexico P, 1983) 63.

[17] A ceremonial room found in the Southwest with the following features: sipapu—a ritual opening to the spirit world below, benches, ventilation, deflectors, and a fire pit. Fred Plog, "Prehistory: Western Anasazi," *Southwest.* 9. *Handbook of North American Indians,* ed. Alphonso Ortiz (Washington: Smithsonian Institution, 1979) 120.

[18] Dockstader 95.

[19] "The authoritative validation of the objects as intrinsically fine works of American art worthy of modern consideration." James Clifford, *The Predicament of Culture* (Cambridge: Harvard UP, 1988) 117.

[20] The first *tihu* to be collected was in 1851 or 1852 when a certain Dr. Palmer, a U.S. Army surgeon managed to purchase some dolls associated with the Zuni Shalako ceremony. Walker and Wyckoff 98.

[21] Formal collection of *tihu* began in Hopiland in 1879 with James Stevenson's Bureau of Ethnology expedition. By the turn of the century ethnographers like John Wesley Powell, Stewart Culin, and Jesse Walter Fewkes had collected over 1000 examples of *tihu*. J. J. Brody, "Kachina Images in American Art: The Way of the Doll," *Kachinas in Pueblo World*, ed. Polly Schaafsma (Albuqerque: U of New Mexico P, 1994) 149.

[22] Clifford 199.

[23] Brody 154.

[24] "Thomas Keam, a trader, and Alexander Stephen, an ethnologist, would initiate the commercial market for Hopi material culture." Richard O. Clemer, *Roads in the Sky: The Hopi Indians in a Century of Change* (Boulder: Westview Press, 1995) 50.

[25] Dockstader 105.

[26] Dockstader 157.

[27] Such as Chief Tawaquotewa, of Old Oraibi, whose sense of cultural taboo (selling kachinas) was side-stepped by mixing iconographic elements, so as to render the sculpture "meaningless" to him and his people, and allow it to be sold to outsiders. Wright, *Hopi Kachinas* 17.

[28] Quoted from Dockstader 157.

[29] Clifford 225.

[30] Flat dolls with little in the way of bodily description, which are given to infants. Teiwes, *Kachina Dolls: The Art of Hopi Carvers* 40.

[31] Erickson 27.

[32] A convention which may have been a suggestion from the non-Natives: prudish social attitude was uneasy with the Hopi's representations of male genitalia on the early carvings. Erickson 24.

[33] Sculptural interplay appealed to the Western world's adherence to the tenets of naturalism and contrapposto pose.

[34] Brody, "Kachina Images in American Art" 153.

[35] Dockstader 105.

[36] Erickson 55.

[37] He was castigated by other Hopi who felt that he had transgressed the boundaries of tradition, which dictated that the production of a *tihu* was done anonymously, and in seclusion. Helga Teiwes, "Contemporary Development in Hopi Kachina Doll Carving," *American Indian Art Magazine* 14.4 (1989) : 41.

[38] Tanner and Tanner, "Kachinas" 83.

[39] Clifford 200.

[40] Jackson W. Rushing, *Native American Art and the New York Avant Garde* (Austin: U of Texas P, 1995) 99.

[41] Rushing 193.

[42] Barton Wright, "Kachina Carvings," in American *Indian Art Magazine* 9.2 (1984): 38-45.

[43] J. J. Brody, *Anasazi and Pueblo Painting* (Albuquerque, U of New Mexico P, 1991) 15.

Cultural Weavings in Sweet Grass, Swamp Cane and Yucca: Basketry of the Choctaw, Seminole and Hopi

Diane Clark

Basket weaving is considered the oldest portable art form made by Native Americans. The basket has served significant functional, social and ceremonial purposes in various cultural contexts over the centuries and still survives as a contemporary art form. This essay will focus on the basketry produced by modern Choctaw basket weavers who live in Bogue Homa, Mississippi.[1] In addition, comparisons will be made in this exhibition with tourist baskets made by the Florida Seminoles and with Hopi basketry plaques.

The Choctaws formerly inhabited large parts of Louisiana, Mississippi, Alabama and Florida. As one of what was known as the Five Civilized Tribes of the southeastern United States, the Choctaws were forced to migrate to Indian reservation territories in Oklahoma during the 1830s. However, a few Choctaws refused to leave Mississippi and remained behind to live as squatters on former tribal lands. After the Civil War, these people worked as sharecroppers and tenant farmers in isolated areas, but the Mississippi Choctaw tribe was not officially recognized as a group until 1918, when it was given reservation lands.[2] Slowly, over the course of the twentieth century, the Choctaws of Mississippi have improved their economic status while retaining their native language and many of their customs.[3]

In the field of southeastern American Indian basket weaving, questions of foreign influences and cultural diffusion are problematic. Across this large geographic region, baskets were plaited out of river or swamp cane by several tribes including the Choctaw and the Cherokee.[4] The similarity of techniques and designs among these groups suggests that information and skills were widely traded. Since the earliest period of contact in the southeast, baskets were made as trade items. By the nineteenth century, baskets were also produced as commodities for sale with deference to the aesthetic preferences of non-Indian consumers. New items created for this market included baskets with handles such as purses, wastebaskets, and lidded storage baskets.[5] Traditional items such as the burden basket continued to be made for use within the community, but utilitarian baskets were eventually replaced by commercially mass-produced metal and ceramic wares during the 1800s. Today, Choctaw baskets are created almost exclusively as aesthetic objects for the non-Native art market which includes dealers, collectors and tourists. Phillip Martin, the chief of the Choctaw tribe in Philadelphia, Mississippi, still presents baskets as gifts to visiting dignitaries.[6] In this context, exceptional baskets function as markers of tribal identity and pride in the continuity of traditional art forms which are recognized as items of artistic

merit by the non-Indian art world. In response to the recent development of commercial markets on the Internet, the Choctaw Museum of the Mississippi Band of Choctaws now sells fine baskets by means of a website.[7]

The functional origin of basketry is fundamental to an understanding of its form and meaning. One typical shape, the large burden basket, would be suspended from a strap across the forehead onto a person's back to carry a wide variety of goods. The utilitarian burden basket was created to fulfill a specific function and has a recognizable shape common to other Native American groups. The burden basket in this exhibit was created by Ms. Jeffrey Denson Solomon, a Choctaw basket weaver from the Philadelphia, Mississippi area. Ms. Solomon also made the double-woven wastebasket in the exhibition. According to a study by Timmy Bookout, the double-woven technique of Choctaw basket weaving was revived as a direct result of encouragement by the Bureau of Indian Affairs and the Indian Arts and Crafts Board in the 1960s.[8]

The practical utility of the basket also gave it an important economic value. According to oral history reports, baskets were exchanged in a barter system for items such as coffee, sugar, flour, and meat.[9] Today in Bogue Homa, baskets continue to be an important source of cash for gasoline and are often made as needed to raise funds for emergency expenditures.

Women have traditionally been the primary basket makers, and the production of baskets was an important economic contribution to the family. During the winter months, women wove baskets for trade or cash, and the non-Native appreciation and purchase of basketry gave women a level of economic power and status in the tribe. However, the assimilation of mass-produced containers transformed the basket from a utilitarian object in the Choctaw culture into a marker of ethnic identity created for the outside market. Today, the Choctaw basket has a symbolic function as a tribal art form which is created solely as a commodity and is rarely used within the Native population. Baskets serve utilitarian or decorative functions in the homes of non-Native buyers.

The fieldwork which I began in October, 1996, took place in the small Choctaw settlement of Bogue Homa near Sandersville in southeastern Mississippi.[10] This village of less than 300 people is isolated from the main Choctaw reservation in Philadelphia, Mississippi, as well as surrounding communities. The basket makers of Bogue Homa have not been mentioned in most studies of Choctaw basketry which dealt with the more well-known artists around the main reservation.[11] The recent inception of the Pine Hills Culture Program in 1996 at the University of Southern Mississippi included the artists of Bogue Homa for the first time in a traveling exhibition of Native American art and an oral history project.[12]

My research at Bogue Homa produced results which challenge assumptions about the transmission of art in tribal communities. According to a commonly-held view, tribal art is practiced by "tradition bearers" within the culture who learn the process in childhood from older artists.[13] By this criterion, the last traditional basket maker in Bogue Homa would have been Lonie Wallace, who died in 1984. Mrs. Wallace learned the art of basket weaving in her childhood, including the techniques for harvesting the swamp cane and dyeing it with natural colors obtained from organic products such as plant roots, tree bark, and clay. Mrs. Wallace's daughter Louise Wallace remembers that her mother camped out in the woods for several days in the fall to harvest the cane needed for basket making over the winter.[14] Lonie Wallace was a role model for the present day basket makers of Bogue Homa, but none of them learned the art from her as children—which would have been the context of a traditional art transmission. The characteristically Choctaw "elbow" shaped basket in the exhibition was made by Lonie Wallace in 1976.[15]

At least five women in the community of Bogue Homa still make cane baskets. The four basket makers I interviewed were Louise Wallace, Martha Jim and Dorothy Nickey, daughters of Lonie Wallace, and Berdie Steve, their neighbor.[16] All of these women consciously chose to learn the art of basket making as adults, and the weaving process has been

Figure 1. Martha Jim splits long green cane with a butcher knife. (Photo: Diane Clark)

modernized. Instead of gathering the cane, which is now difficult to find, they usually purchase it in bundles from a tribal harvester. Rather than using natural materials for dyeing the split cane, they prefer the convenience of using commercial Rit dye.[17] The use of Rit dye is viewed by the basket makers as an improvement over earlier methods because it saves a great deal of time and allows a broader range of color such as pale blue, purple and orange, in addition to the traditional colors of red and green. However, these modern basket makers continue to produce many of the traditional shapes and designs of Choctaw basketry while also creating individual innovations in shapes, colors and sizes.

Choctaw baskets are characterized by the use of reversed cane for the colored design areas. In a typical Bogue Homa basket of today, the smooth, shiny surface of the natural cane contrasts with the rough texture of the back of the colored cane. This practice is unique to these baskets and distinguishes them from other southeastern cane baskets such as those made by the Chero-

kee, who use the smooth side of the cane on the exterior for both natural and colored areas.

Choctaw baskets are made using the technique of plaiting, with either a diagonal or perpendicular weave. The top rims are wrapped rather loosely with cane and the handles are often roughly wrapped. As early as 1902, Otis Mason commented on the lack of finish characteristic of Choctaw basket handles, but more experienced Choctaw basket makers do carefully wrap the rim and handles with uniform turns of cane when they produce a fine basket.[18]

Martha Jim, the oldest basket maker living in Bogue Homa, does not speak very much English. Despite the language barrier, she was enthusiastic about demonstrating the techniques of basket making. Ms. Jim showed me how she split the cane into four sections using a butcher knife and then separated the outer layers of cane off the core with a smaller knife (Figure 1). She then wound the coils of split cane into round bundles to be dyed in pots on the kitchen stove.

Color symbolism in Choctaw basketry has not been previously documented, but according to Louise Wallace, the Choctaws used the colors red and green to symbolize the playing of stick ball games. She said that the color red stood for the "red man" while green represented the grass upon which the stick ball game was played. Older Choctaw baskets, such as those made by Lonie Wallace, often have alternating horizontal design bands of red and green cane. The assignment of symbolic meaning to these colors transforms the apparently abstract geometric design into a stylized landscape field with culturally significant meaning for the informed tribal viewer.

Several design motifs used in Choctaw basket weaving reflect the importance of animals in this tribe. According to Louise Wallace, the diamond-shaped motif represents the rattlesnake, a creature which was viewed as a protector of the Choctaw tribe. Hunters performed a ceremonial dance around a rattlesnake, and if someone was bitten, the "medicine man" was ready with an antidote. This diamond pattern appears often on Choctaw baskets, in whole or half motif form.

Wallace also creates colorful baskets which she calls "Mother Earth" baskets using her own personal color symbolism (Figure 2). She interprets the colors red and green traditionally as Native people and the grass, with conventional descriptions of the brown for the earth, blue for the sky, and yellow for the sun, combined with the use of black to symbolize the "black man." She conceives of the basket wall as a field for the representation of an abstracted landscape, in addition to the repetition of geometric motifs one sees. Wallace produces her Mother Earth baskets in the egg basket shape and said that she often dreams about her designs and colors before making them. Her work is represented in this exhibition by a characteristically Choctaw heart-shaped basket.

Of interest is the fact that the modern basket makers interviewed at Bogue Homa do not keep models to refer to when they create a new basket. Apparently all of the baskets made today are sold as soon as they are completed. However, the weavers are able to see examples of earlier works when someone brings in a basket to be repaired. Wallace showed me two older baskets made by her mother which were awaiting repair—a flat, round basket with a broken handle and a large, natural colored hamper. Wallace and her sisters told me that they can recognize their mother's baskets and identify works made by others they know. The basket makers also regularly visit the homes of collectors to study and count out previously produced designs.

Berdie Steve learned the art of basket making as an adult by watching Lonie Wallace work, and now she makes the most elaborate baskets in Bogue Homa, often using the difficult double-woven technique. These baskets have strong double walls and now command high prices.[19] Steve told me that she perfected her basketry techniques after the ghost of Lonie Wallace visited her in a dream on the night of her death. She dreamt that Wallace came to her door with strips of cane, and after this dream, the difficult process of double-woven basketry became easy for her although she said that it still took three years to perfect her technique. Steve is now recognized as one of the most highly-skilled Choctaw basket weavers; she shuns publicity and did not want her photograph included in this publication.

Figure 2. Louise Wallace at work on one of her "Mother Earth" baskets. (Photo: Diane Clark)

The shapes of Choctaw baskets, like the Cherokee baskets, have been adapted for the non-Native market since before the nineteenth century.[20] In Otis Mason's catalog of 1902, he describes the characteristic heart-shaped gift basket of the Choctaw which was extremely popular with collectors in the Victorian era. Choctaw basket makers were also known for their "elbow" shaped baskets that have two openings connected by a single handle (which can be hung on a wall like the heart-shaped baskets). Wastebasket shapes were developed for use by Euroamerican buyers, as were the two-handled vase-shaped baskets and handled purse baskets. More traditional egg and gathering baskets were sometimes modified and or miniaturized to appeal to the non-Indian buyer.

The use of certain colors is often specified by non-Native collectors or buyers who want either a specific color combination for interior decoration purposes, or else a more "authentic" revival style using the traditional color scheme of red and green, or red and blue-black.[21] But even when certain basket types or color

combinations are requested, it is practically impossible for the Bogue Homa basket makers to reproduce previous examples exactly.

Research into the current status of Choctaw basket making in Bogue Homa revealed that the baskets are not kept as keepsakes or decorative items within the Choctaw community, presumably because of their economic value. Ironically, while the women who make these baskets view them as symbols of their ethnic heritage, those who actually enjoy them as visual art forms in their homes are the non-Native collectors.

Florida Seminole Basketry

Until the twentieth century, Seminole baskets were made from the traditional southeastern medium of swamp or river cane, as illustrated by the sifter in the exhibition.[22] However, in the early 1930s, Deaconess Harriet M. Bedell introduced the method of making coiled sweet grass baskets to the Seminoles as a way to raise money through sales to tourists.[23] This introduced form of basketry became recognized as the typical Seminole basket. Today, modern Seminole basket makers like Mary Frances Johns have perfected the sweet grass technique, originally created for the tourist market, as an aesthetic art form.[24] In this new role as a sign of ethnic identity, outstanding examples of Seminole coiled baskets are now given as gifts by the tribe to important visitors.[25]

Hopi Basketry Plaques

Basket weaving in other Native American cultures has developed along similar lines as a result of acculturation. The mid-twentieth-century Hopi basketry plaques included in this exhibition from the Mary D. Lewis Collection at Florida State University reflect the two characteristic styles of Hopi basket making utilizing the techniques of coiling and wickerwork.[26]

The Hopi live on three mesas in northeastern Arizona, and distinctive basketry continues to be produced both for use by the culture and for sale to the art market.[27] Coiled baskets are made almost exclusively on the second mesa while wicker baskets are typically produced only on the third mesa. The first mesa, which is known for its pottery, no longer produces baskets but purchases them from the second mesa for ceremonial use.

Plaques—flat, round basketry trays—are made for use in Hopi society to fulfill a variety of purposes, including as gifts for newborns and young children, at basket dances when young women are initiated into clan groups, as ritual wedding paybacks, and for carrying cornmeal in religious ceremonies to the kiva. Plaques are also used in the home for serving food and for wall decoration. As demonstrated by archaeological evidence, the plaque shape has a long history in the Hopi culture. Despite the fact that plaque baskets are still part of the living culture of Hopi societies, almost all Hopi baskets are eventually offered for sale in the ethnic art market.[28] The exception to this is the groom's wedding basket, which is never supposed to be sold. This special basket is kept by the man until his death and buried with him to speed his journey to the underworld.[29]

The basketry plaques in this exhibit illustrate the characteristic designs and techniques of Hopi basket weaving. The coiled plaque is decorated with abstract, stepped-cloud motifs typical of mid-twentieth-century Hopi basket making.[30] The design represents clouds, which are believed to be the spirits of the *kachinas*, in geometric, stepped patterns. Bright aniline dyes were used to color the yucca strips sewn around the foundation coils of galleta grass. The coils are rather fat, unlike the thinner coils of more recently produced Hopi plaques.[31]

The wickerwork plaque in the exhibition was certainly created by a Hopi artist on the third mesa and is an excellent example of this style. The sophisticated whirlwind design of the plaque is created using natural earth colors (Figure 3).

In conclusion, it is possible to recognize in Native American basketry a transformation from its previous status as a utilitarian craft object into a symbol of ethnic identity, examples of which have been recognized by the fine art world. This exhibition of modern Choctaw baskets made by virtually unknown basket makers in Bogue Homa, Mississippi, also demonstrates that the direction of Native American basketry can be influenced by a small number of locally significant contemporary artists who are interested in continuing a tribal art form. A hopeful sign for the future of Choctaw basketry occurred in the Spring of 1997, when both Louise Wallace and Berdie Steve received grants from the Mississippi Arts Commission to teach the "folk art" of basket weaving to others in their tribe.

Figure 3. Hopi wickerwork plaque with whirlwind design. Florida State University Department of Anthropology, Mary D. Lewis Collection, accession #2459. (Photo: Mark Fletcher)

making, see the following sources: Patti Car Black, *Persistence of Pattern in Mississippi Choctaw Culture* (Jackson: Mississippi Department of Archives and History, 1987); Timmy Joe Bookout, "Traditional Basketmakers in the Southeastern and South Central United States," Diss. Florida State University, 1987; Carol Norton, "Choctaw Cane Baskets," *Shuttle, Spindle & Dyepot* 21 (Summer 1990): 56-58; Kenneth York, "Choctaw Arts and Crafts," in *Made by Hand: Mississippi Folk Art* (Jackson: Mississippi Department of Archives and History, 1980); Stephen Flinn Young, "An Introduction to Mississippi Choctaw Crafts," in *Mississippi Choctaw Crafts* (Jackson: Craftsmen Guild of Mississippi, Inc., 1983) and "The Evolution of Mississippi Crafts," in *Mississippi Crafts* (Jackson: Craftsmen Guild of Mississippi, Inc., 1983).

2 For the history of the Choctaw peoples in Mississippi, see Samuel J. Wells and Roseanna Tubby, eds., *After Removal: The Choctaw in Mississippi* (Jackson: UP of Mississippi, 1986); Clara Sue Kidwell, *Choctaws and Missionaries in Mississippi 1818-1918* (Norman: U of Oklahoma P, 1995); Jesse O. McKee, *The Choctaws: Cultural Evolution of a Native American Tribe* (Jackson: U of Mississippi P, 1980); Carolyn Keller Reeves, ed., *The Choctaw Before Removal* (Jackson: U of Mississippi P, 1985).

3 For an overview of these recent economic developments, see Bert Gildart, "The Mississippi Band of Choctaw: In the Shadow of Nanih Waiya," *Native Peoples* 9 (Summer 1996): 44-50.

4 Diane Dixon, "Native North American Cane Basketry," *Shuttle, Spindle & Dyepot* 23 (Fall 1992): 40-41; Frank W. Porter, ed., *The Art of Native American Basketry: A Living Legacy* (New York: Greenwood Press, 1990) 86-87.

5 These adaptations had occurred by the end of the nineteenth century and are reflected in the collections formed during this period as illustrated in Otis T. Mason, "Aboriginal American Basketry: Studies in a Textile Art without Machinery," in *Report of the U.S. National Museum* (1902).

6 This information was obtained during an interview with basket maker Berdie Steve in Bogue Homa, Mississippi, on October 6, 1996.

7 This site can be found at http://allcatalogs.com/choctaw/baskets.html.

8 Bookout 133. According to Bookout 138, Jeffrie Denson Solomon was born in 1919, learned basket making from her mother, and specializes in double-woven containers. Both Jeffrie and Lela Solomon (born 1921) had exhibition catalogs prepared by the U.S. Department of the Interior.

9 Bookout 134.

10 The Bogue Homa basket makers often travel to Laurel, Mississippi, where I was first introduced to them at the Lauren Rogers Museum of Art in the early 1980s. This museum has an extensive collection of Native American baskets on display. The basket makers sold their work door-to-door in Laurel and included the museum on their rounds. Today their baskets are sold in the museum gift shop.

11 See Bookout and Young at note 1. The Bogue Homa basket makers were probably neglected due to their isolation from the main reservation in Phila-

1 This project was undertaken for a Tribal Arts methodology seminar taught by Dr. Jehanne Teilhet-Fisk at Florida State University in the Fall of 1996. These observations and interviews were the result of three visits to the Native American settlement of Bogue Homa, Mississippi, 1996-97. The basket makers from this area were previously undocumented in the literature concerning Choctaw basketry. For information about Choctaw basket

delphia and the fact that their work is relatively recent.

12 As part of an oral history project for the Pine Hills Culture Center, the Bogue Homa basket makers Louise Wallace and Berdie Steve were interviewed by Martha Garrott, the manager of the Mississippi Crafts Center on the Natchez Trace Parkway near Jackson, Mississippi. Mrs. Garrott provided valuable information about locating and talking to these artists in two telephone interviews. I also listened to her taped interviews with Berdie Steve and Louise Wallace.

13 This definition was used by the oral history project of the Pine Hills Culture Center and was found in John W. Suter, ed., *Working with Folk Materials in New York State: A Manual for Folklorists and Archivists* (New York: Folklore Society, 1994) 22.

14 In interviews, Louise described how her mother carefully cut the cane plants low to the ground and buried the ends to encourage new growth. Unfortunately, the supply of wild cane has declined in recent years as natural wetlands have decreased due to development.

15 This basket, on loan from the Lauren Rogers Museum, is the only basket I found in the museum's collection made by one of the local Bogue Homa basket makers. Other examples of local basketry have been borrowed from private collectors.

16 Another basket maker in Bogue Homa whom I did not interview is Mary Chapman. I was told by the collector Mary Lyon that Ms. Chapman only occasionally makes small, rather quickly formed baskets when she needs money.

17 It is easy to recognize the home of a basket maker in Bogue Homa in the fall by looking for the pile of green cane stalks lying beside the carport.

18 Mason (1902).

19 Double woven baskets by Berdie Steve are now sold in the range of $400-$900.

20 Dixon 40.

21 Interview with Mary Lyon, August 1997, Laurel, Mississippi.

22 David M. Blackard, "Patchwork and Palmettos: Seminole / Miccosukee Folk Art Since 1820," *American Indian Art Magazine* 15 (Spring 1990): 66-83.

23 Patricia West, "Glade Cross Mission: An Influence on Florida Seminole Arts and Crafts," *American Indian Art Magazine* 9 (Autumn 1984): 58-67.

24 Dorothy Downs, "Contemporary Florida Indian Patchwork and Baskets," *American Indian Art Magazine* 15 (Autumn 1990): 63.

25 Downs 62.

26 For more information about the Mary D. Lewis Collection, see Theresa Harris, "Contextual Curation of the North American Indian Baskets from the Florida State University Department of Anthropology Ethnographic Collection," undergraduate Honors Thesis, Florida State University, 1993.

27 Helga Teiwes, *Hopi Basket Weaving: Artistry in Natural Fibers* (Tucson: U of Arizona P, 1996).

28 Sheryl F. Miller, "Hopi Basketry: Traditional Social Currency and Contemporary Source of Cash," *American Indian Art Magazine* 15 (Winter 1989): 62-71.

29 Teiwes 56. For this reason, few Hopi wedding plaques appear in museum collections. Today, since the value of the plaque has increased so tremendously, wedding plaques are not buried with the deceased, but kept by a

sister as a memorial.

30 Clara Lee Tanner, *Indian Baskets of the Southwest* (Tucson: U of Arizona P, 1983) 53.

31 Tanner 55.

Pictorial Tapestry, 1960, length 153 cm. Courtesy of the School of American Research, Santa Fe, New Mexico. (Photo © School of American Research)

History Reconfigured: Haida Argillite Carving

Teri Robin Yoo

The many tribes living along the Northwest Coast of North America, stretching from Yakutat Bay in Alaska to what is now southern Oregon, are known for their sumptuous artistic traditions. One of these tribes, the Haida, inhabits the Queen Charlotte Islands (Haida Gwaii) which are separated from British Columbia by the Hecate Strait and the southern part of the Prince of Wales Islands in Alaska.[1] The Queen Charlotte Islands are the exclusive source of an unusual and atypical Northwest Coast medium, argillite. This medium was rarely quarried until after the seaborne fur trade had been firmly established within the Northwest Coast area. But, with the dwindling of the sea otter population around the early nineteenth century, the resourceful Haida soon turned to providing other trade goods, which now included carving argillite souvenirs, as a means of continuing their trade with the Euroamericans (Russians, British and Americans).[2]

With the establishment of permanent trading posts such as those of the Hudson Bay Company around the 1820s, the carvers increased their production of argillite carvings, initially producing fanciful argillite pipes, many of which could not be smoked. It is possible, however, that argillite was carved before 1820 in the forms of amulets, labrets and even smokeable pipes.[3] Robin K. Wright makes a strong case against the notion that the Haida argillite pipes were solely invented as a response to the tourist trade as originally suggested by Leslie Drew and Douglas Wilson.[4] Drawing on the research of Knut Fladmark, Alexander MacKenzie and J.R. Swanton, Wright makes a convincing argument that the Haida smoked common pipes of argillite fashioned after simple clay trade pipes. These were used for casual smoking; other argillite pipes were smoked during the "tobacco feasts" that were held within funerary ceremonies.[5] External trade with Euroamericans, however, clearly changed the types of argillite carvings that were made. In response to the demand for curios, the Haida began to produce, over a one hundred year span, non-functional "panel pipes," miniature replicas of "totem" poles (Figures 1 and 2), "shaman" figures (Figures 3 and 4), circular dishes, platters (Figure 5) and group carvings.[6]

What sets these "contact zone"[7] carvings apart from other acculturated souvenir arts made by Native Americans is their early

Figure 1. (frontal view) Miniature "totem pole" with figures bottom to top—bear, human, eagle, bear, c. 1865-1910. Argillite. 18 3/4 inches h x 2 1/2 inches w. Collections of the Anthroplogy Department of the Florida Museum of Natural History, FLMNH Cat. No. P1006.

entrance and longevity in a foreign market, relatively high standards of artistic quality, unique choice of medium and varied subject matter. After the 1820s, argillite became the dominant medium associated with carvings because it appealed to the Euroamerican market as well as to the Haida. The shiny black of argillite resembled the jet carvings that were so popular in the Victorian era.[8] Like jet, a subbituminous coal, argillite contains just enough coal to color it black. There are other colors of argillite but black is the Haida color of choice. Not only is black argillite in more abundance than the other colors, but, in the Northwest Coast, black has symbolic connotations. Black is often used for primary form-lines in painted and woven works.[9] Black is also the color of Raven, who in giving the gift of the burning hot sun to the Haida, scorched his beautiful white feathers black.[10] Even the sea otter, whose glistening fur once clothed the Haida and served as the main trade item with the Hudson Bay Co., was black. According to John Jewitt, prominent chiefs would paint on their faces and then dust a fine, black shining powder over them. The powder was highly valued, and while the substance in Jewitt's account was probably mica, it indicates the esteem in which the shiny black substance was held.[11]

The main source of fine quality argillite is found on a moun-tainside at Slatechuck Mountain ("slate and water" literally) near the village of Skidegate. The quarry was probably discovered by the Haida around the beginning of the nineteenth century.[12] Since the Skidegate family clan owned that particular area of land, the majority of carvers purchased the argillite from them or used an inferior grade. The stone is kept moist before and during carving because it tends to split into slabs if it is allowed to dry too rapidly. As Wright points out, argillite does not harden measurably after it is quarried and can be carved just as easily centuries later.[13] Today the argillite is initially quarried with hand tools and cut into blocks that are able to be carried for several miles. The blocks are fashioned with wood-working tools and the medium is treated as if it was hard wood. The rough shape is formed with an adze and blocked out using a hand saw.[14] The sculpting is done with files that have had the tips reshaped by the carvers. The surfaces are smoothed with sandpaper and then fine steel wool. The desired glossy finish comes from the sweat and natural oils of the carver's hands. However, there are different degrees of polishing that the carver deems appropriate for each individual piece.[15]

According to Kaufmann, by the mid-nineteenth century one way of assessing Haida social achievement was through economic gain and the refined production of these argillite items as commodities became an important part of their new economy.[16] But, to paraphrase Wright, even though these argillite carvings had their own origin as commodities for the tourist market, that should not preclude their recognition as "a respectable art form."[17] Furthermore, as Kaufmann points out, the images and style helped the Haida culture by providing them with a new miniaturized means to continue their established art of form-line carving since many of the Haida's monumental "totem" poles were being cut down for fire wood by 1892.[18] What can be deemed inauthentic is their impractical size and intentional lack of a truly functional use within the Haida clans.

Changes in the style and content of argillite carvings also correspond with different events in Haida history.[19] A heuristic model has been adopted here only as a means to place the exhibition pieces within a relative time frame and to give the reader a better understanding of their content. Initially the Haida drew on their own crest imagery as subject matter for the argillite pipes made for sale or trade to Euroamericans.

> These images, called crests by anthropologists, were symbols of the beings from whom a clan traced its origin and the origin of its possessions. Any object which had been decorated with a crest was imbued with the vital forces of the spirit world and was considered to be alive.[20]

The images of Haida crests (animals, birds, sea monsters and mythic beings) used in the period from 1800-1835 are rendered in their "traditional" style and iconography, but reconfigured in a meaningless manner devoid of cultural context to escape the possibility that these crests could ever be misused.[21] These nonsensical images appealed to the uninformed tourist as manifestations of Haida culture, while not jeopardizing the inherent meaning of these crest images. Sheehan and others borrow Duff's nomenclature and label this style "Haida Non-Sense."[22]

The second period of argillite carving (1830-1865) overlaps with the first and is referred to as the "White Man's Non-Sense"[23] or the "Western" period.[24] Crest images were replaced, as Wright explains, with subject matter taken from eighteenth- and nineteenth-century sailing ships, paddle wheel steamers, ornate figureheads, decorative billetheads and complex floral motifs.[25] Building on Wright's research, Dr. Jehanne Teilhet-Fisk proposes the idea that by incorporating the imagery found on these vessels that came into their harbors, the Haida may have been appropriating Euroamerican ships' names or prow "crests" as a way of tapping into the vessels' lineage and

Figure 2. (side view) Miniature "totem pole" with figures bottom to top—bear, human, eagle, bear, c. 1865-1910. Argillite. 18 3/4 inches h x 2 1/2 inches w. Collections of the Anthropology Department of the Florida Museum of Natural History, FLMNH Cat. No. P1006.

power. At the same time, the images that the Haida artists carefully selected would also convey meaning to the Euroamerican people who traveled on the vessels, making carvings more desirable as purchased mementoes of the trip. Furthermore, the imagery of Euroamericans is often humorous, anecdotal representation of dress and customs that probably did appear non-sensical to the Haida peoples. In some ways these images may also be seen as Haida constructions of the Euroamerican (colonizer's) world in order to engage the sailors, colonizers and officials, on their terms. They are a kind of "autoethnographic expression" to borrow Mary Louise Pratt's term.[26] If Teilhet-Fisk's assumption is correct, then the Haida choice of European imagery makes sense.[27]

Most of the exhibition pieces can be placed in the third period (1865-1910). This phase is marked by a resurgence of culturally-relevant themes in response to the massive depopulation of the Haida after the smallpox epidemic of 1862 and the advent of missionary activity, colonial government and slow demise of their potlatch ceremonies. This period is called "Haida-Sense." The images returned to more faithful representations of Haida crests.[28] The Haida wanted to perpetuate, in these argillite carvings, visual depictions of their myths that validated the ancient covenants between man, spirit-beings and their animal benefactors.[29] The carving of these myths helped keep Haida narratives vital, for themselves and future generations as well as for the outside world. This period is marked by the increased popularity of fully sculpted miniaturized "totem poles."[30] The Haida were noted for their large—up to 60 feet—crests, erroneously referred to as totem poles.

The last period (1910-present) is somewhat arbitrarily divided into two different trends and also overlaps with the third stylistic period. One trend has artist or artisan continuing to use Haida themes, but often lacking the artistic skills and aesthetic integrity of the previous argillite carvers.[31] In the other trend, artists strive to recreate the sculptural use of complex form-lines that swell and wane to form elaborate images in a high standard of technical and creative excellence. Many of these early Masset and Skidwell argillite carvers were building reputations as fine artists: Charles Edenshaw, George Gunya, Charles Gwaytihl, Tom Price, John Robson, Jim Macay, John Cross and Henry White to name a few working in the late nineteenth and during the twentieth century. Their works, once labeled tourist art, are eagerly sought by collectors, dealers and museums as pieces of fine art. According to MacDonald, "argillite carving went into decline after the First World War until the 1950ties."[32] But, artists, such as Reg Davidson, Robert Davidson and Pat Dixon have revived and further transformed the medium into a contemporary art form that is appreciated by and made for the American Indian and non-Indian world.

This exhibition highlights a few of the many hundreds of

early twentieth-century argillite sculptures originally owned by Col. Leigh Morgan Pearsall. Col. Pearsall had been collecting argillite pieces even before he contacted Thomas Deasy in 1922.[33] Deasy, the federal government Indian agent at Masset, was known to have owned the largest collection of argillite carvings in British Columbia and that explains why he became Col. Pearsall's main supplier until 1925.[34] The pieces in this exhibition date from the third and fourth period and are good examples of late nineteenth and early twentieth-century argillite carvings.

The miniaturized "totem pole" (Figures 1 and 2)[35] belongs in the "Haida-Sense" period, which suggests that the crest imagery of bear, human, and eagle illustrates one or more Haida myths. However, since the Haida have some seventy crest figures that identify the owner's moiety and lineage it is difficult to "read" a totem or crest pole without a thorough knowledge of the thousands of recorded myths.[36] We do know that throughout the Northwest Coast, the bear seems to "encapsulate ideas of predatory ferocity, competition, and indiscriminate, immoral, voraciousness as an all-pervasive process."[37] Bear is also the most "human like" animal with its ability to walk on his hind feet leaving prints that imitate those of man; front legs can be used as arms and hands that dig, crush, pull apart and carry. Eagle is an important clan that is one of the moieties (socio-ceremonial division into halves) of the Haida, the other being Raven. Eagle is often perched on top watching the world below. As masterful predators of flight they can use their keen vision and talons to carry their prey away. Human, bear and eagle form "an important triumvirate of creatures, all united in their mutual dependence on salmon, and they form an important set of conjoined representations,"[38] and alternative transformations that go beyond boundaries between the mythic and modern world. Through the display of totem pole crests, humans are linked to each other and outside forces.[39]

The Shaman figure (Figures 3 and 4) is attributed to the third (or fourth) period because it is not until this time that Christianity firmly made its presence known in Gwaii (Queen Charlotte Islands), and with Christianity came certain restrictions.[40] As Wright explains, souvenir carvings of argillite shamans would have been improbable during a time when shamanism was active because that type of imagery was sacred and for use only in their domain.[41] Before Christianity objects made for and used by shamans were never traded and usually buried with them.[42] In general shamanism "consisted of a belief in spirits which interfere with the lives of the people and whose power can only be broken through the knowledge of a few, the shamans."[43] The Haida shaman could be male or female and had in possession all kinds of paraphernalia, such as carved bone spikes, soul catchers, charms,

Figure 3. (frontal view)   Figure 4. (side view)
Shaman wearing bear headdress, c. 1865-1910. Argillite. 12 inches h x 3 3/8 inches w. Collections of the Anthropology Department of the Florida Museum of Natural History, FLMNH Cat. No. P752.

rattles and drums, that were used to cure the sick, bring on good weather, bring about large fish runs and other similar acts.[44] The argillite shaman shown here wears a finely carved headdress in the shape of a bear that appears to be sitting on the shaman's shoulders and holding firmly to his head. The shaman is dressed in an apron decorated with a crest image that is carved in a distributive style which obfuscates meaning. He wears a necklace with powerful charms that look like bear claws or teeth, and in his hand he carries a globular rattle that makes a particular sound needed for use in certain ceremonies.

The argillite platter is attributed to Tom Price (Chief Ninstints, Haida), a well-known artist working at the turn of the century. It features a large shark or "dog fish" elegantly carved in bas-relief to fit the shape of the platter. According to Walens, the spiney dogfish can be both equivalent to and an enemy of the salmon.[45] They are more common than salmon, eat the same food as salmon and are often caught on hooks that have been baited for salmon. As a symbol, they indicate how uncontrollable hunger can bring about one's downfall. In their frenzy to take bait they are killed by fishermen. Compared to other sharks found in Northwest Coast waters, they are the smallest and stand in relation to larger sharks as common people stand to chiefs.[46]

In summary the Haida people were the sole proprietors of argillite, a somewhat impractical medium that was rarely, if ever, used before the nineteenth century. Capitalizing on its uniqueness the Haida began making functional and non-functional pipes for sale or trade among themselves, other tribes and outsiders, but the brittle nature of the medium led to its being admired more for its abstract aesthetic qualities (such as its shiny, smooth black finish) and its rarity thus making it a highly competitive product in the tourist market. As changes in the social structure were brought about by outside forces, the Haida began channeling their distinctive carving techniques and crest imagery into these miniaturized argillite sculptures that retained their "tourist art" label. This essay sides with recent literature that takes umbrage at the indiscriminate use of the term "tourist art," especially as applied to the argillite carvings, because such a term undercuts the role these argillite forms played as meaningful carriers of the formline style.[47] By manipulating this "tourist" venue, the Haida were able to produce a range of argillite sculptures that are sold to non-Indian and Indian communities—each perhaps buying for very different reasons.

1 Philip Drucker, *Indians of the Northwest Coast* (Garden City: The Natural History Press, 1963) 12. George F. MacDonald, *Haida Art* (Seattle: Washington Press, 1996) 3-4.

2 Aldona Jonaitis, *From the Land of the Totem Poles* (New York: American Museum of Natural History and Seattle: U of Washington P, 1991) 42.

3 Carole N. Kaufmann, "Functional Aspects of Haida Argillite Carvings," *Ethnic and Tourist Arts,* ed. Nelson H.H. Graburn (Berkeley: U of California P, 1976) 59.

4 Leslie Drew and Douglas Wilson, *Argillite Art of the Haida* (British Columbia: Hancock House Publishers Ltd., 1980) 60-61. Robin K. Wright, "Haida Argillite Carved For Sale," *American Indian Art* 8.1 (Winter 1982): 48-49.

5 Wright, "Carved For Sale" 49.

6 Drew and Wilson, verbal communication from William Newcombe to Canadian ethnologist Marius Barbeau, 1928, 61.

7 Mary Louise Pratt, *Imperial Eyes Travel Writing and Transculturation* (London and New York: Routledge, 1992) 6-7.

8 MacDonald 97.

9 Bill Holm, *Northwest Coast Indian Art: An Analysis of Form* (Seattle: U of Washington P, 1971) 29.

10 Stanley Walens, "The Weight of My Name Is a Mountain of Blankets: Potlatch Ceremonies," *Arts of African, Oceania and the Americas,* eds. Janet Catherine Berlo and Lee Anne Wilson (Englewood Cliffs: Prentice-Hall, 1993) 179-180.

11 Drew and Wilson 44.

12 Sheehan, *Pipes That Won't Smoke: Coal That Won't Burn* (Glenbow: Glenbow Museum, 1981) 59.

13 Robin K. Wright, "Haida Argillite Pipes—The Influence of Clay Pipes," *American Indian Art* 5.4 (Autumn 1980): 43.

14 Peter L. MacNair and Alan L. Hoover, *The Magic Leaves—A History of Haida Argillite Carving* (British Columbia: British Columbia Provincial Museum, 1984) 17.

15 Drew and Wilson 54-55.

16 Kaufmann 58.

17 Wright, "Carved For Sale" 48.

18 Kaufmann 58.

19 Sheehan 18-27.

20 Walens, "Potlatch Ceremonies" 189.

21 Sheehan 22.

22 Sheehan uses the thematic periods coined by William Duff and elaborated on by Carol N. Kaufmann 67-80.

23 Sheehan 22-23.

24 Kaufmann 67.

25 Robin K. Wright, "Influence of Clay Pipes" 43. While she only investigated pipe imaging, her findings support Duff's theory. She identifies three types of pipes that were carved, Haida motif, ship pipes, and clay type pipes. The pipes were functional initially, but as the carvings became more intricate, the holes that were nearly always fully drilled became too small to be used. Wright feels that there is evidence that all three types of Haida argillite pipes were produced at the start of the argillite carving tradition, and uses Fladmark's findings as proof.

26 Pratt 7.

27 Personal communication November 20, 1997.

28 Sheehan 25.

29 For more on the importance of myth see Stanley Walens "The Weight of My Name Is a Mountain of Blankets" 184-195.

30 MacDonald 97.

31 Sheehan 27.

32 MacDonald 98.

33 Drew and Wilson 271.

34 Drew and Wilson 271.

35 The argillite "model totem poles" are not replicas of totems but of crests.

36 MacDonald 8.

37 Stanley Walens, *Smoke and Mirrors, New Perspectives on the Critical Discourse of Northwest Coast Indian History and Art* (unpublished manuscript, n.d.) 662.

38 Walens, unpublished manuscript, 664.

39 Walens 184.

40 E. Michael Whittington, "The Bear-Mother Theme: Exploring the Narrative in Haida Argillite," *Athanor* VIII (Tallahassee: Museum of Fine Arts of Florida State University 1990) 23-24. The missionaries prohibited the carving of crest imagery on wood poles and *potlatching.*

41 Wright, "Carved For Sale" 50. Implied in this is the possibility that power of the shaman could be turned against the profane.

42 MacDonald 67. Shamanism is a religious phenomenon that defies a perfunctory definition. For more information on shamanism see Mircea Eliade, *Shamanism* (Princeton: UP, 1964).

43 Drew and Wilson 69.

44 Drew and Wilson 69.

45 Salmon are the mainstay of the Haida diet.

46 Stanley Walens, *Feasting With Cannibals* (Boston: Little, Brown and Company, 1969) 121.

47 Aldona Jaunts, "Traders of Tradition, The History of Haida Art," *Robert Davidson, Eagle of the Dawn,* ed. Ian M. Thom (Seattle: U of Washington P, 1993) 3-23.

Figure 5. Platter possibly by Tom Price, Skidegate carver, c. 1910-1925. Argillite, abalone inlay, 20 1/6 inches x 2 1/4 inches x 10 inches w. Collections of the Anthropology Department of the Florida Museum of Natural History, FLMNH Cat. No. P1203.

Picturing St. Augustine: Images of a Florida City through Native Eyes

Heather Waldroup

In her book *Sending My Heart Back Across the Years,* narrative historian Hertha Dawn Wong writes, "Self-narration is part of the process of self-construction and self-representation. When our stories change, when silences are spoken or narrative vacancies become inhabited, we are transformed."[1] This thought is especially applicable to the second half of the nineteenth century, when time sped up and cultures collided.

In the twenty years after the Civil War, the small Atlantic coast town of St. Augustine was explored and represented artistically by people from vastly different cultures. Easily reached by the new steam-powered ships, St. Augustine became a popular winter vacation destination, especially for former Union soldiers who had fought in the South during the war. Lured by photographs, especially widely-circulated stereoscopic views with captions such as "Florida: The land of flowers and tropical scenery," Northerners arrived in search of unusual scenery and warm weather in the slightly decrepit, but quaint seaside town. In May 1875, an entirely different sort of people arrived in St. Augustine. A group of around 70 American Indians from the Great Plains, including Cheyenne, Kiowa, Comanche, Arapaho, and Caddo, were held prisoner for three years in the sixteenth-century Spanish fort Castillo de San Marco, known at that time as Fort Marion. Since this exhibition is taking place in Florida, only a few hours' drive from St. Augustine, this discussion concentrates on drawings of the town and surrounding landscape produced by the prisoners during their interment.

The first known drawings from the Fort Marion period appeared in August 1875,[2] some three months after the prisoners' arrival, and they continued to be created until 1878, when the prisoners were released. During their interment at the Fort, the prisoners produced drawings of various subjects, including hunting, courting and wildlife scenes, their month-long journey to Florida, and the new surroundings into which they had been forced. Scholars have approached the drawings from numerous perspectives. Karen Daniels Petersen's 1971 monograph, *Plains Indian Art from Fort Marion,* focuses on the Florida drawings as part of a long tradition of Plains pictorial imagery produced under remarkably different circumstances. Joyce M. Szabo's publications have explored several issues concerning the drawings. Her 1994 monograph *Howling Wolf and the History of Ledger Art*[3] discusses the work of the artist Howling Wolf and his contributions to the history of ledger art. She has also written on the aesthetics of ledger art as a combination of both the Native artist and non-Native audience[4] and the function of the drawings as a means for the artists to explore and understand their new surroundings.[5]

There remains further room for interpretation of the drawings, however. This paper will focus on the Fort Marion captives' portrayal of their surroundings as an art of the "contact zone." This term is borrowed from Mary Louise Pratt, who defines the "contact zone" as areas where vastly different cultures find themselves colliding, intertwining, and trading ideas, but ultimately continuing, though sometimes taking on new forms or added dimensions.[6] In some senses the prisoners' representations of St. Augustine are like photographs made of the town for the Euroamerican tourist market. Both artforms were intent on portraying the State of Florida as an exotic geographic locale. Further, the captives often did sell their drawings to tourists or visiting officials. However, the way the Native Americans chose to portray their Florida experience can be seen to articulate the needs and desires of a captive people who once roamed free on land which was quickly being transformed, both physically and spiritually, by the encroaching Euroamerican world and its concepts of land ownership and control. Created in the zone of contact between the worlds of the Euroamericans and of the Native Americans from the Great Plains, the often autobiographical images created by these prisoners speak

Figure 1. Native American prisoners at Ft. Marion, St. Augustine, Florida. c. 1870s. Florida State Archives.

of the representation of this contact and the way both worlds were irrevocably changed.

At the time of the prisoners' arrival in St. Augustine on May 21, 1875, American Indians from many nations had been subjected to decades of brutal warfare among themselves as well as directly with Euroamericans as a result of the pressure from the continuous expansion of the white frontier. Additionally, Euroamerican culture had been brought closer by new technologies, such as the expanding railway system, and postwar philosophies of manifest destiny. The winter of 1874 had been especially harsh, and with the dwindling buffalo population many Plains people were near starvation. In desperation they surrendered to the U.S. Army, and the Plains reservation system was put into full swing. In April 1875 the army hand-picked about 70 "notorious hostiles"[7] for even further restriction—in the form of imprisonment in Florida—than that enforced by the reservation system, in hopes of forcing the remaining Native Americans on the reservation into submission. Imprisonment was a form of humiliation. The families of the prisoners assumed that their loved ones were on their way to execution, and indeed the prisoners themselves believed that they would be killed.[8] Instead, they were sent to Florida by train and steamship under the control of Lieutenant Richard H. Pratt, finally arriving after a month of travel.

The creation of so many drawings from the Fort Marion period was directly through the encouragement of Pratt. Pratt's assimilationist theories—his desire to "civilize the savage"—may seem degrading and racist from a postcolonial perspective.[9] His chief goal was to absorb the Indian warriors into Euroamerican society through the implementation of militaristic discipline.[10] As illustrated in a photograph from the

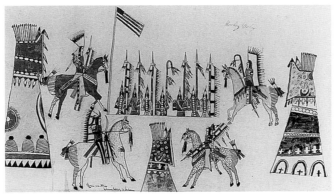

Figure 2. Howling Wolf (Cheyenne), ledger drawing, possibly of Bowstring Society ceremony. c. 1875-1877, 24 1/2 x 22 3/8 inches. Collection Sara W. Reeves and I.S.K. Reeves V. (Photo: Beverly Brosius)

Florida Archives, Pratt dressed the prisoners in Army uniforms and led them in practice drills (Figure 1). However, it must be recognized that Pratt's philosophies, and his treatment of the captives, were radical for his time. Pratt did respect the intelligence and resourcefulness of his captives. Although it took the deaths of several prisoners from the dampness in the Fort and other illnesses to spur him to action, Pratt took initiatives to change his prisoners' situation of confinement. He removed their shackles and educated them in English and other typical school subjects with the assistance of female volunteer teachers. He allowed the warriors to work in the town, harvesting oranges and performing manual labor, providing them with pocket money for themselves and to send home to their families. Most importantly for this discussion, Pratt encouraged his prisoners to draw. He requisitioned the needed materials: pens, colored pencils, inks, and paper. There was certainly an eager audience in St. Augustine for the easily portable, colorful and fairly inexpensive artwork pro-

duced by the captives at the Fort, and Pratt used the drawings as "goodwill propaganda" to demonstrate the industriousness of his charges to his superiors.[11] For the artists themselves, the drawings served as an outlet for their creativity, as a way for them to explore their new surroundings and captive situation in a way in keeping with their cultural traditions. Contemporary Cree-Chipewyan artist Jane Ash Poitras has said, "For the survival of the soul, the mind is always free through art,"[12] and the drawings became a way for the captives to make sense out of the senseless changing of their lives. Disoriented, stripped of their honor and status, the prisoners were able to retain their dignity and honor as warriors and as artists; as Berlo writes, "to draw the past is to remember it."[13]

The drawings were in keeping with a rich pictorial tradition in Plains arts. Produced only by men, figurative imagery derived from symbolic sign painting used to convey messages to both insiders and outsiders in a clear, concise form of visual shorthand. Calendric records used by the Kiowa and Cheyenne were a public record of historic events. As a public display of an individual owner's deeds, painted robes and lodge covers made of buffalo hides depicted autobiographical deeds of war and bravery. These hides were then used as a dwelling or were worn wrapped around the body, and the process of rendering the images themselves was considered a powerful act.[14] With increasing warfare, both with Euroamericans and other Native American groups, and the dwindling buffalo population, the portability of books became more appealing over hides, and paper became a frequent drawing medium.[15] As Mary Louise Pratt has noted, peoples of the Third and Fourth Worlds may not be able to control what items are introduced to them by Westerners, but they do choose which ones they assimilate and transform into something uniquely theirs.[16] The artists recognized the power of books as a result of contact with Euroamerican culture, but also respected the intrinsic power of images and the importance of the past for pre-contact Native American art.[17] Ledger books and drawing materials were acquired through trade with soldiers stationed at military outposts, in times of peace, or as post-battle spoils during less peaceful times. These soldiers formed a new market also, as they began to commission books from Native Americans for themselves or to send home to their families.[18]

Szabo has written on the nature of the Fort Marion drawings as an art of transition, bridging traditional and contemporary Native American representational imagery, and combining the desires and fulfilling the needs of Pratt, the public and of the prisoners themselves.[19] Much pre-reservation ledger art focused on deeds of glory, such as battles and horse raids, and was a form of self-

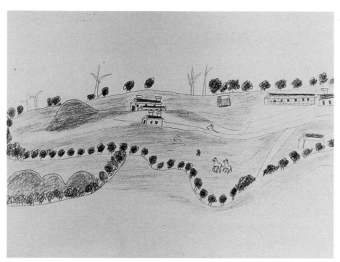

Figure 3. Wo-Haw, *Camping Out in Florida* (also known as *Ft. Sill*), pencil and crayon on paper, c. 1875. Missouri Historical Society, St. Louis, accession # 1882 018 0013.

aggrandizement.[20] There was little focus on landscape. In the Fort Marion drawings, these glorified, self-centered subjects were transformed from didactic, culturally-based genre images of personal narrative for an audience of insiders into a medium for articulating the values and aesthetics of the entire culture to outsiders.[21] Since they were intent on being released as soon as possible, the Indians wished to appear peaceful.[22] A drawing by Cheyenne artist Howling Wolf, 1875-1877, represents a ceremonial rather than a battle scene (Figure 2). Keith Reeves has suggested that this image may illustrate a ceremony for the Bowstring Society, of which Howling Wolf was a member. Although the name of ledger artist Roman Nose appears in the bottom left of the drawing, Reeves feels that, rather than being a collaborative effort, the piece is the work of a single artist, and that Howling Wolf included the name of the other warrior as a tribute to Roman Nose's membership in the Bowstring Society.[23] Images such as courting scenes and wildlife illustrations, which would have been considered more suitable subject matter by a white audience, replaced battle images. Hunting scenes were popular also, allowing the prisoners to relive the achievements of their past without alienating their captors.

The American Indian prisoners themselves were entwined in a web of tourism, both as creators of tourist art and as tourist attractions themselves. John Urry has described the "tourist gaze" as the tourist's desire to depart from his or her everyday, mundane existence by seeking out the exotic or different.[24] Sold for two dollars[25] to an audience who knew nothing about Plains art, Szabo has suggested that the Fort Marion books offered "a way of coming into contact with these potentially dangerous events and men while simultaneously keeping safe and removed from them."[26] The appeal of the cultural "other" and the suggestion of danger was extended to the prisoners, who performed reenactments for a tourist audience. Buffalo hunts (with a steer as a stand-in animal), dances and singing were performed at Pratt's suggestion, and the admission charged was used to raise money to send the prisoners to schools in the northeast after their release. A drawing done

by Kiowa artist Etahdleuh Doanmoe, 1876-1877,[27] illustrates one of these performances in the central courtyard of the Fort. The caption, added by a typewriter, reads, "An Omaha dance given by the prisoners on the solicitation and to please their new friends in St. Augustine as well as to amuse themselves." Wade and Rand have stressed that with captions such as these, "Anglo is speaking directly to Anglo."[28] However, the image can serve both communities. To an outside audience, captors become sincere "friends;" a dance performance is a form of "amusement." From another perspective, Berlo has suggested: "To make a picture can be a revolutionary act, an autobiographical act, an act of covert resistance."[29] To the artists themselves, both the creation of the image and the act of performance itself are imperative as ways to maintain cultural traditions while imprisoned by a Euroamerican culture which wanted them ultimately to disappear peacefully through absorption.

In contrast with Western ideas of ownership, control and domination, Plains philosophy did not allow for concepts of the land as a commodity.[30] Contemporary Cheyenne artist Edgar Heap of Birds has described the Plains as a land of round shapes: the sky, the horizon, the dwellings of the people, working in a circular

Figure 4. Buffalo Meat, *Buffalo Meat in His Sunday Clothes*, before March 12, 1878. Collection Sara W. Reeves and I.S.K. Reeves V. (Photo: Beverly Brosius)

Figure 5. Wo-Haw, *Woman, Birds, and Indians,* pencil and crayon on paper, c. 1875. Missouri Historical Society, St. Louis, accession #1882 018 0009.

cycle of life.[31] For the prisoners, the Western world into which they had been thrust was one of linear conquest, harsh and inorganic. While Szabo has noted that maps and postcards were readily available for examination by the prisoners and may have provided them with some inspiration in their own works,[32] for these artists the land was not a commodity to be controlled. A drawing by Kiowa artist Wo-Haw of a camping trip to Anastasia Island demonstrates a new purpose of ledger art: rather than as a recorder of a person's own deeds, drawing becomes a way of observing this new world (Figure 3).[33] As the prisoners were allowed to roam free around St. Augustine and were taken camping on Anastasia Island, landscape became a strong element in their drawings. In this image the natural bushy vegetation and sand dunes of the island are portrayed, as well as dead trees in the background. Wild ponies perhaps reminded Wo-Haw of those at home.

Many ledger drawings articulate the exchange of Euroamerican and Native American traditions through iconography and the use of Western modes of visual representation. A drawing by Buffalo Meat (Figure 4) depicts the appropriation of Western goods, including an umbrella and a top hat. The horse's head is represented from the front view, a Western technique, while the body is in profile, the more conventional pictographic convention.[34] Another of Wo-Haw's images articulates the isolation of the prisoners and the collision of cultures while at the same time serving as an outlet to draw the new forms of wildlife surrounding them (Figure 5). The woman to the left of this image is interpreted by Moira Harris as being one of the prisoner's white teachers.[35] Wo-Haw's curiosity with the woman lies not in her sexuality—as an object of the male gaze—but in her dress, in which Wo-Haw has fused elements of Native and non-Native attire. The woman is wearing typical Euroamerican dress, but has her hair long and loose, decorated with feathers, and wears large, dangling earrings. The Native American woman on the right of the image, wrapped in a blanket, is wearing similar earrings. Wo-Haw himself seems to grow out of a stubby bush on which two birds sit. The shape of his body, the color of his clothing and his lack of arms echo the bird above him. This confusing image hints at the loneliness of

the prisoners, and their grief at being separated from their families. In contrast with Wo-Haw's enigmatic long-haired women, the artist Making Medicine in 1876-1877 depicted Euroamerican women as stiff and hairless.[36] In this image, two prisoners are instructing a group of women in archery practice, while another two women look on. The women are static and stiffly dressed, and seem to be guarded by a large, collared dog.

An image by Wo-Haw from the Fort Marion period demonstrates the state of transition, both culturally and personally, for almost all American Indians at the end of the nineteenth century. This image contains Sundance iconography in the form of specific celestial bodies in their position in the summer sky, as well as a Sundance lodge, and could be interpreted to be a representation of the dance and its importance in Plains culture (Figure 6).[37] While serving as an outlet for the preservation of traditional iconography and concepts, this image could simultaneously be seen as providing an outlet for yet another form of exploration. Both Petersen[38] and Harris[39] have interpreted this image as Wo-Haw's vision of the future. In the drawing, the artist, in traditional dress and with long hair, stands in the center, facing a bull, which is breathing its power at him. A Western frame building sits by his foot. On Wo-Haw's other side, representing the past, are a tipi and a buffalo. Directly above Wo-Haw is the sun. On the left side of the image are the moon and Venus, but the sky on the right side of the drawing has been left empty. Altogether, the image suggests to this author the position of American Indians in the late nineteenth century: while the white culture converges upon them, they have retained their traditional beliefs through acculturated materials.

In depicting the world of their captors, prisoner artists combined aspects of personal narration along with an exploration of a landscape dominated and controlled by man. Instead of being a world of excitement and romantic mystery, St. Augustine and its surroundings appears stark and forbidding in the images, created from artificial materials. A drawing by Wo-Haw (Figure 7) illustrates the lighthouse on Anastasia Island as existing on an island

Figure 6. Wo-Haw, *Indian Between Two Cultures,* pencil and crayon on paper, c. 1875. Missouri Historical Society, St. Louis, accession #1882 018 0030.

Figure 7. Wo-Haw, *St. Augustine Lighthouses on Anastasia Island*, pencil and crayon on paper, c. 1875. Missouri Historical Society, St. Louis, accession # 1882 018 0027.

devoid of vegetation and cut off from the rest of humanity. A Euroamerican man highlighted in the lighthouse looks out at the world with a gaze of power and control. Like the ships watched over by the lighthouse, the prisoners are surrounded by, and cannot escape from, the world of their captors.

To look at the Fort Marion drawings through postmodern eyes is a haunting experience for the viewer today. In these images, created over a century ago, we are presented with the results of a cultural "other" transplanted into the world of their most opposing enemy. The images functioned as a way for them to continue their cultural traditions using appropriated materials while isolated from their homes and families. Through the Fort Marion drawings, Native American prisoners were able to keep alive a strong and powerful cultural tradition in spite of the threat of assimilation and destruction.

1   Hertha Dawn Wong, *Sending My Heart Back Across the Years* (New York: Oxford UP, 1992) vi.

2   Karen Daniels Petersen, *Plains Indian Art from Ft. Marion* (Norman, OK: U of Oklahoma P, 1971) 21.

3   Joyce M. Szabo, *Howling Wolf and the History of Ledger Art* (Albuquerque: U of New Mexico P, 1994).

4   Joyce M. Szabo, "Howling Wolf: Autobiography of a Plains Warrior-Artist" (Oberlin, OH: Bulletin of the Allen Memorial Art Museum XLVI, 1992) 10.

5   Joyce M. Szabo, "Chief Killer and a New Reality" (*American Indian Art Magazine,* Spring 1994) 56.

6   Mary Louise Pratt, *Imperial Eyes: Travel Writing and Transculturation* (London and New York: Routledge, 1992) 6-7.

7   Petersen 15.

8   Petersen 15.

9   After his tenure at Fort Marion, in the 1880s Pratt opened the Carlisle Indian Training School in Pennsylvania, which had as its chief goals the erasure of Native American culture. This was accomplished by dressing the Native Americans in Euroamerican clothes and schooling them in the Western tradition in order to remove all aspects of their culture.

10   Szabo, *Howling Wolf and the History of Plains Ledger Art* 66.

11   Joyce M. Szabo, "Shields and Lodges, Warriors and Chiefs: Kiowa Drawings as Historical Records," *Ethnohistory* 41.1 (Winter 1994): 6.

12   Jane Ash Poitras, "Paradigms for Hope and Posterity: Wohaw's Sun Dance Drawings," in *Plains Indian Drawings 1865-1935: Pages From a Visual History,* ed. Janet Catherine Berlo (New York: Abrams, 1996) 68.

13   Janet Catherine Berlo, "Drawing and Being Drawn In: The Late Nineteenth-Century Graphic Artist and the Intercultural Encounter," in *Plains Indian Drawings 1865-1935: Pages From a Visual History,* ed. Janet Catherine Berlo (New York: Abrams, 1996) 14.

14   Szabo, *Howling Wolf and the History of Plains Ledger Art* 10.

15   Gloria Young, "Aesthetic Archives: The Visual Language of Plains Ledger Art," in *The Arts of the North American Indian: New Traditions in Evolution* (New York: Hudson Hills Press, 1986) 59.

16   Pratt 6.

17   Berlo 16.

18   Young 59.

19   Szabo, "Howling Wolf: Autobiography of a Plains Warrior-Artist" 10.

20   Joyce M. Szabo, "Howling Wolf: A Plains Artist in Transition," *Art Journal* (Winter 1984) 368.

21   Wong 58.

22   Wong 71.

23   Keith Reeves, personal communication, November 14, 1997.

24   John Urry, *The Tourist Gaze* (London: Sage, 1990) 2.

25   While relatively expensive for the time, the popularity of the books indicates that this amount was not out of the price range for at least upper-class tourists.

26   Szabo, "Chief Killer and a New Reality" 55-56.

27   Permission to reproduce this image was not granted. For an illustration see *Plains Indian Drawings 1865-1935: Pages From a Visual History,* ed. Janet Catherine Berlo (New York: Abrams, 1996), catalogue no. 88.

28   Edwin L. Wade and Jacki Thompson Rand, "The Subtle Art of Resistance: Encounter and Accommodation in the Art of Fort Marion," in *Plains Indian Drawings 1865-1935: Pages From a Visual History,* ed. Janet Catherine Berlo (New York: Abrams, 1996) 48.

29   Berlo 18.

30   J. J. Brody, *Indian Painters and White Patrons* (Albuquerque: U of New Mexico P, n.d.) 51.

31   Edgar Heap of Birds, "Of Circularity and Linearity in the Work of Bear's Heart," in *Plains Indian Drawings 1865-1935: Pages From a Visual History,* ed. Janet Catherine Berlo (New York: Abrams, 1996) 66.

32   Szabo, "Chief Killer and a New Reality" 55.

33   This image has alternatively been captioned by the Missouri Historical Society's archives as "Fort Sill," the fort in Oklahoma where the prisoners were interred before being transported to Florida. The attribution to Anastasia Island is found in Moira Harris, *Between Two Cultures: Kiowa Art From Fort Marion* (N.p.: Pogo Press, 1989) 122. The location is not easily identified; certainly the dunes / rolling hills, sparse vegetation, wild ponies and small clusters of buildings are typical of both central Oklahoma and coastal Florida. The drawing was created *c.* 1875, after Wo-Haw had visited both states. Therefore, an alternate interpretation to the one I have presented in the body of the text is that the image be considered a composite image of his experience in captivity.

34   People were generally represented in pictographs with profile heads and frontal bodies to ensure recognition (Szabo, *Howling Wolf and the History of Plains Ledger Art* 7). This tradition continued in ledger art, but horses were generally depicted entirely in profile. The dual perspective used for horses is unusual.

35   Moira Harris, *Between Two Cultures: Kiowa Art From Fort Marion* (N.p.: Pogo Press, 1989) 118.

36   Permission to reproduce this drawing was not granted. For an illustration see *Plains Indian Drawings 1865-1935: Pages From a Visual History*, ed. Janet Catherine Berlo (New York: Abrams, 1996), catalogue no. 60.

37   Jane Ash Poitras describes the Sundance ceremony as follows: "The Sun Dance is one of many powerful ceremonies carried out to initiate young warriors to the sacred. After enduring excruciating pain, a Sun Dancer is blessed by receiving visions and spirit helpers. After his ordeal, the Sun Dancer is reborn to the sacred. The more rebirth a visionary survives, the more power he has in the sacred world—power used to help, to heal, and to communicate good to the community" (Poitras 69).

38   Petersen 90.

39   Harris 129.

Blurred Boundaries: Jewelry as Visual Art and Cultural Identity

Caroline Klarr

Jewelry production can be described as multi-dimensional in the sense that it can be conceptualized in terms of form, technology, history, and culture. Jewelry, broadly defined, is a near-universal art form which has proven to be a vehicle for uniting geography, society, and community throughout time. For thousands of years native peoples of the southwestern United States have produced items for personal adornment made from shell, turquoise, and other semi-precious stones, mined locally or obtained through trade. The appropriation of silver technology in the nineteenth century revolutionized jewelry production in the Southwest until it grew into an international industry. Throughout the twentieth century turquoise silver jewelry has grown in popularity world-wide due both to its aesthetic and economic value.

While many different groups of Native Americans produce turquoise silver jewelry, particularly in the Southwest, this article will concentrate on the role of Diné and Zuni artists. The Diné, more commonly known as the Navajo, are located in northeastern Arizona, while the Zuni are located in northwestern New Mexico. These two groups were chosen to be representative of this much larger tradition because of the Diné's contribution in the early historic record in the assimilation and dissemination of the technology of silversmithing and because of the Zuni's contribution in the lapidary arts. The Diné were the first to learn silver working and allegedly to introduce it to the Zuni; consequently, early examples of jewelry from both groups are very similar.[1] During the 1930s and 1940s the Diné and the Zuni were even involved in cooperative efforts in order to meet the increasing demand for jewelry.[2] In spite of their shared history, jewelry produced by the beginning of the twentieth century exhibited distinct aesthetic preferences associated with each cultural group. The jewelry made by the Diné tended to emphasize the silver while the Zuni emphasized the stones. The increase in jewelry production was proportional to the increase in numbers of artisans. As more men and women began to make jewelry as either a source of additional income or as full time smiths, the aesthetics of jewelry, the "styles," designs, and other formal elements, became increasingly diverse. No longer restricted by access to proper tools and ample materials, artists

Figure 1. Squash blossom necklace by unknown artist, Diné Reservation, Arizona. Star / Fire Collection—Sandra Starr-Tanner.

created a wide variety of techniques and stunning forms inspired from their past and their present.

One medium common throughout the history of the Southwest is the "sacred sky stone" of turquoise. We know from archaeological evidence that the ancient ancestors of the Southwest valued, collected, and traded turquoise. For example, one site known as Chetro Ketl, at Chaco Canyon, New Mexico, dated *c.* 1100-1300 AD, yielded over 10,000 pieces of turquoise which had been worked, ground, and shaped.[3] Even so, it seems turquoise was not common among the general populace. Culturally, turquoise was valued for its beauty and its intrinsic qualities. It was used in burials, in offerings to the gods, and worn on ceremonial occasions.[4] Turquoise is referred to as the "sky stone" because it is the color of the sky and water, and thus associated with rain, growth and fertility. Rain is precious to any culture, however in desert cultures its value is the difference between life and death. It is not surprising that many of the indigenous religious beliefs and practices are related to the blessings of rain for good crops and fertility. Turquoise makes reference to these beliefs and its beauty is held in high regard in all Southwestern cultures.

Turquoise has been worn for personal adornment for hundreds, if not thousands, of years. In ancient times stones were often shaped into discs, beads, or pendants. The ancient Zuni carved turquoise into fetishes of small animal forms such as bear or mountain lions.[5] Early examples of turquoise mosaics were made by shaping individual stones to be set on a foundation of wood or shell.[6] Shell was another popular material due to its association with water and its prestige as a trade item; the enduring beauty of shell is still appreciated by artists today.

In contrast to the indigenous lapidary arts, silversmithing is an acculturated art form. It is undetermined when silversmithing first arrived in the Southwest; however, the residents there were exposed to silver items by the Spanish who first arrived in 1598; the Mexicans who governed the area from 1821-1846; and by the southern Plains tribes with whom the peoples often traded.[7] While there remain many unknowns, the history of silversmithing is best documented in *The Navajo and Pueblo Silversmiths* by

John Adair. Even today Adair's book remains the authoritative source on the history of Southwestern jewelry. According to Adair, the Navajo acquired the art of silversmithing from the Mexican *plateros* or silversmiths.[8] The first man to learn the art was Atsidi Sani, whose name means "Old Smith." Atsidi Sani first learned to work in iron during the 1850s.[9] By this time there was also an iron working shop on the Zuni reservation.[10] Atsidi Sani learned silversmithing between 1850 and 1870; some say prior to the Long Walk to Fort Sumner and some say after the Diné returned home.[11] Another Diné who learned at this time was Atsidi Chon or "Ugly Smith." Atsidi Chon is credited with not only setting the first turquoise stone in silver but also passing on the knowledge of silversmithing to a Zuni man, Lanyade, who learned in approximately 1872.[12] This began the "First Phase" of jewelry from 1868-1900.[13]

Late nineteenth-century examples of jewelry tended to emphasize the silver material. This was partially because turquoise was relatively rare at this time and it was not until the opening up of commercial mines in the 1880s that turquoise became more readily available.[14] Silver was a new material and as such came into popular fashion. Because of their isolation early smiths had to employ relatively simple technologies utilizing bellows, forges, and crucibles to produce silver jewelry. The silver material had to be annealed, or tempered, by heating and cooling rapidly in order to relieve internal stress so as not to crack.[15] In addition to fashioning silver, early Diné smiths learned to cast pieces using fine-grained sandstone. This technique is referred to as sand casting.[16] The beautiful works produced at this time exacted a high price since often the bright fires and poor conditions caused smiths to go blind.

While early examples of silver jewelry were either plain or simply decorated, various techniques were employed to decorate the silver after it had been fashioned into its final shape. The first designs were often etched or engraved with a file or an awl.[17] These techniques died out by 1875 with the invention of stamping using metal dies.[18] Dies are metal tools bearing a design which is impressed into a piece of silver jewelry by hand hammering.[19] Die technologies and designs are often correlated with those used in Mexican leather work and it seems Diné artists may have appropriated them for silversmithing.[20] Initially very popular, the use of dies has continued into the present day and remains especially popular with Diné artists. Another important development during this time was soldering. Soldering enabled silver pieces to be joined, filigree to be attached as ornament, and bezels to be fashioned for the setting of stones.[21] These

Figure 2. Cluster work by Lee Weebothee, Zuni Pueblo, New Mexico. (Photo: Caroline Klarr)

Figure 3. Late nineteenth-century example of a horse headstall, Navajo, c. 1890-1900, silver, 15 1/4 x 16 3/4 inches. Collection of Sara W. Reeves and I.S.K. Reeves V. (Photo: Beverly Brosius)

breakthroughs in technology initiated the revolution and Native jewelry would never be the same.

The earliest written record of silver jewelry production was recorded by Washington Mathews in his 1880-81 Bureau of American Ethnology report on Navajo silversmithing.[22] Among the items in his report, Mathews describes plain silver *conchas*, mounted on leather and used for belts; rings and bracelets either cast flat or wrought round; hollow silver beads; bridle ornaments; and tobacco canteens.[23] Mathew's contemporary, Lieutenant John G. Bourke, mentions additional items such as silver loop earrings, horse ornaments, silver buttons, bow guards and mother-in-law bells. With exception of mother-in-law bells, the majority of jewelry types are still produced today.[24]

Concha belts derive their name from the Spanish word *conchas* which means shells. The origin of *concha* belts is still unclear; however, a leading theory is that the style was derived from the Plains Indians who wore long strings of *conchas* in their hair.[25] Plains silver *conchas* were usually made of German silver and worn strung on a leather strap.[26] The nomadic nature of the Diné fostered contact with the Plains peoples through trade and raids.[27] This theory credits the Diné with the translation of Plains hair pieces into waist ornaments or *concha* belts. Visually the two types are distinguished by the outer edge of the oval disc; a smooth edge is characteristic of Plains *conchas*, while a scalloped edge is characteristic of Diné *conchas*.[28] The first *conchas* necessarily required a hollow center in order to thread the multiple silver discs onto straps of leather which would then be worn around the body. However, with the invention of soldering, loops could be attached to the backs of the *conchas* creating a solid background for stamping designs and, later on, for setting stones.

Before silversmithing was known, rings and bracelets were made of copper and brass metal wire bent around the finger or wrist. Metal rings and bracelets from the First Phase were generally hammered, wrought, or cast. In contrast to rings, silver bracelets were most often set, usually with stones. The first bracelets were set with turquoise about 1880 and by the 1920s most bracelets incorporated stones.[29] It has been noted that bracelets may be the most popular jewelry form, perhaps due to their size, portability and the fact they are worn by both men and women.

Besides adorning their own bodies with jewelry, the peoples of the Southwest ornamented their horses. Horses were introduced to America by the Spanish in the late sixteenth / early seventeenth century.[30] Among the Native peoples, horses were highly-prized, prestige items. Following Spanish tradition, when the Southwestern peoples adopted horses, they adopted horse gear and ornaments (Figure 3). Silver bridles were made with elaborate head stalls featuring *conchas* and a pendant ornament called a *najahe* or *naja*. *Naja* are three-quarter circle design pendants believed to derive from the Spanish who obtained the design from the Moors, the latter of which believed it a charm against the evil eye.[31] The *naja* design was appropriated for use as a pendant in necklaces referred to as "squash blossoms" (Figure 1).

Squash blossom necklaces are predominantly composed of hollow silver beads. Before soldering was invented a fully hollow bead could not be made; therefore Adair dates the appearance of squash blossom necklaces to post-1880.[32] Squash blossoms generally consist of two rows of smaller, round silver beads attached to a single row of larger, round silver beads alternating with "squash blossom" beads. The necklace is completed with a naja pendant which hangs in the center. While the exact origin of the term "squash blossom" is unknown, it has been attributed to the Spanish decorative motif of a pomegranate blossom (used to ornament clothing items) which the bead blossoms resemble.[33] The squash blossom necklace is unique to the Southwest and is one of the most widely recognized forms of Southwestern Native jewelry.

Necklaces of this First Phase tend to emphasize the silver, to consist of heavy proportions, and to be executed in simple designs.[34] During this period most jewelry was produced for internal use and there were relatively few pieces produced for outside sale. However, several factors accelerated the commercialization process. The first historic event was the arrival of the Santa Fe Railroad in 1880 and with it a steady tourist market. This market was targeted by intrepid traders who traveled west to start businesses. Traders were to have a great influence on Southwest jewelry. For example, as early as 1884 one trader, C. N. Cotton, recognized the potential market and hired a Mexican *platero* to teach silversmithing at the Ganado Trading Post on the Navajo Reservation.[35] Another trader, C. G. Wallace, who arrived in Zuni in 1918, at which time there were only five silversmiths, went on to sell the work of over 300 Zuni and Navajo silversmiths.[36] Another trader who had an enormous impact was Herman Schweizer, a buyer for the Fred Harvey Indian Department, who recognized the tourist market wanted portable and affordable souvenirs. In order to meet demand, he began to supply silversmiths with ready-made silver sheets and wire, as well as precut stones.[37] This allowed artists to produce jewelry faster and cheaper, which likewise helped to keep jewelry affordable, making it one of the most popular tourist mementos of the period. From this time on it has become a general rule that tourists prefer lighter-weight jewelry, while Native people continue to like heavier jewelry.[38] Collectors have favored this heavier style; the first two decades of the twentieth century are often referred to by collectors as the "classic phase" of Southwest Native jewelry.

By the 1920s the Zuni lapidary arts began to take on a dimension very distinct from the Diné jewelry. Instead of creating a balance between the two materials, metal and stone, the Zuni began to use the metal work as a foundation for multiple-stones settings. Stones began to be set on all types of jewelry, but it is in the bracelets where the different forms were most prominent. "Row bracelets" were decorated with stones laid out in either a single or multiple parallel rows. These row bracelets are still popular today, although now they tend to be more complex and delicate in design. For example, the contemporary Zuni artist Pam Mahooty specializes in row work. Each delicate stone is ground down in order to capture the clear sky blue color preferred by most Zuni artists. The delicate drops of silver are melted down from individual wires. Each part of the process is hand made; no ready-made materials are used.[39] All hand made jewelry, while very time consuming, results in some of the highest quality jewelry made in the world.

Another style known as cluster work developed in the 1920s. This style was made by both Diné and Zuni smiths. Cluster work refers to a group of stones, each with its own bezel, laid out in a circular fashion often around a central stone (Figure 2).[40] The final design recalls a floral pattern, thus the motif is often termed "blossom" or "sun flower." Cluster work made by Diné artists tends to use larger and fewer stones. Cluster work is typically made by Zuni who characteristically incorporate multiple circular rows of small stones. The individual stones are called "drops" by Zuni artisans, recalling the association of turquoise with rain.[41] Throughout history, cluster work has remained one of the most popular types of designs of jewelry, including manta pins, bracelets, necklaces, and *conchas*. It is also used to adorn sacred *kachina* masks.[42]

Another technique which flourished during the first part of the twentieth century was the figural design inlaid in a mosaic fashion. It was at this time that representational motifs such as the Knife Wing or Thunderbird image became popular. Although the

Figure 4. Petitpoint style bracelet by Edith Martza (Zuni), 1970, silver with turquoise, 6 x 2 1/2 cm. Courtesy of School of American Research, Santa Fe, New Mexico, SAR. 1989-7-204.

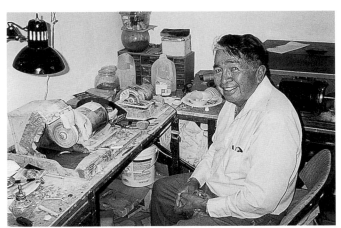

Figure 5. Lee Weebothee in his workshop, Zuni Pueblo, New Mexico. (Photo: Caroline Klarr)

Knife Wing figure is taken from religious iconography, when the image is reproduced as ornament the Zuni no longer assign it any religious meaning.[43] Other images produced at this time were Zuni maidens, Rainbow deities, and clowns. The outsiders' taste for representational designs contributed to the cooperation of Diné and Zuni artists as they combined efforts to keep up with the growing demand for inlay style jewelry. In this cooperative effort, the Diné would fashion the silver casings which would later be set with stones by Zuni artists.[44] It was during this time that the technique of channel work developed. In channel working the stones are set in mosaic fashion but each stone is encased in a silver housing. This results in thin walls of silver around and between each stone.

Other cooperative efforts took place within the family unit. Between 1925 and 1945 the jewelry industry accounted for 65% of the Zuni Pueblos' cash economy.[45] This demand for jewelry was brought about in part due to the arrival of the automobile to the Southwest and the wave of people on their way to California. Like the tourists before them, these outsiders wanted to take with them mementos of their travels in the Southwest and their encounters with Native cultures. It was during this time that women began to play a more substantial role in jewelry production by providing additional support to their husbands and fathers, or by starting up businesses of their own. Silversmithing tended to be taught within the family and if extra assistance was needed it would likewise come from a family member. In these cooperative efforts, women typically were responsible for the grinding and polishing of the stones while their male counterparts worked the silver. Through their cooperative participation women had the opportunity to learn silversmithing by watching their husbands or family members and even ventured into business on their own. Already by 1926 a Zuni woman, Della Casi, held her own account with traders. Casi is credited as the first independent woman silversmith, but soon thereafter many women were to follow her example.[46]

The influence of these women silversmiths on the aesthetics and designs of jewelry is rarely discussed, probably because in Western thought women's arts are conceived of as being produced in soft materials (cloth, clay, basketry) and remain marginalized by the designation of "craft."[47] These stereotypes are apparent in the androcentric scholarship, composed of male scholars documenting male art forms (metallurgy, sculpture, carving). Consequently, women jewelry makers have only received equal attention in the last decade or two—following on the heels of the feminist movement in the West. In reality, Zuni women have been actively involved in production since at least the 1920s. Additionally, by the 1940s women made up two-thirds of the total silversmiths in Zuni.[48] Perhaps it is not a coincidence that it was during this time that the techniques of needlepoint and petitpoint were developed at Zuni. Their names, needlepoint and petitpoint, derive from needlework which by the twentieth century was considered women's work.[49] The difference between the two styles is that needlepoint uses small stones with pointed ends while in petitpoint the stones have one end which is rounded (Figure 4). Both needlepoint and petitpoint are characterized by small, elongated stones, each set in fine toothed bezels supported by thin frames of silver.[50] Delicate patterns are created by multiple rows of stones, often in the "sunflower" design in an elaborated form of cluster work. This "sunflower" motif has always been popular with women and Della Casi is known to have produced numerous pieces of jewelry of this design.[51] A possible corollary to this floral pattern is the hepakinne or "sun flower" motif commonly found on ceramic water vessels carried by the Olla Maidens or Zuni ceremonial water bearers.[52] These women represent the female counterparts of the male kachina cults, thus they bear water in the ceramic vessels which they carry on their heads, just as the male Kachinas don masks and dance in an effort to bring rain. In Zuni culture women are held as tehya,[53] precious and valuable as vessels of growth, birth, and fertility. Women bear children and, as Olla Maidens, water, both invaluable to the perpetuation of the Zuni people and their culture. These associations are implicit in the turquoise material which metaphorically and simultaneously reference these multiple associations.

In recent years artists have continued to participate in the development of new techniques—for example, the extremely difficult raised needlepoint invented by Edith Tsabetsaye. In this technique the tiny stones are curved in a crescent shape lending a sculptural quality to the stones.[54] Another technique which utilizes raised stones is three-dimensional mosaic inlay. Lee Weebothee, a celebrated Zuni artist (Figure 5), works in this style which differs from the mosaics of the past in that unlike the older pieces where the stones were polished to create a flush surface, the three-dimensional mosaics allow each stone to protrude into space. The Zuni tendency for

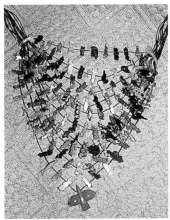

Figure 6. Fetish necklace (Zuni), c. 1960, ten strands, turquoise, abalone, jet, catlinite, and shell, 14 1/2 x 10 1/2 inches. Star / Fire Collection—Sandra Starr-Tanner.

stone carving reaches its height in the so-called fetish necklaces which consist of tiny carved stone and shell animals strung alternatively with small beads of stone or shell (Figure 6). Animal carvings may be in a variety of representational forms including frogs, birds, bears, and other mammals. Fetish necklaces are the extreme celebration of the stone material, rarely incorporating any silver at all. Sunshine Reeves, a Diné artist who won Best of Show at the 1997 Indian Market, goes to the opposite extreme with his silver miniatures which do not usually incorporate any stones (Figure 7).

By the 1940s the distinctive regional styles began to be produced by artists from diverse cultural backgrounds. The revival of turquoise silver jewelry in the 1970s resulted in an explosion of styles and designs. The theme of this era was individualism as silversmiths began stamping their names into their jewelry. This notion of a "signature" derives from a western art tradition; within the Native communities an individual would be recognized by his or her handiwork.

Figure 7. Small bowl with lid by Daniel Sunshine Reeves, Diné Reservation, 1997, silver, 2 1/4 h x 3 inches wide. Star / Fire Collection—Sandra Starr-Tanner.

Another dimension of the jewelry industry native to the Southwest is the influence it has had on contemporary artists across America. Take for example the jewelry of Denise and Samuel Wallace, a wife and husband team who have been producing jewelry in Santa Fe for twenty years. The couple moved from Seattle to Santa Fe in order for Denise to attend the Institute of American Indian Arts. They began to produce jewelry for practical reasons, although their business rapidly expanded into DW Studio in Santa Fe which regularly employs up to eight other artists. Their jewelry is unique in terms of technology, material, and design (Figure 8). Designs are most often figurative representing scenes from daily life, religion, and art which are inspired from Denise's Aleutian heritage. Materials such as fossilized walrus ivory etched with scrimshaw designs are combined with silversmithing to create elegant and dynamic imagery. Technically, the jewelry is versatile and sophisticated; the individual elements, such as pins and pendants, are linked together to create belts which have diverged a long way from their concha predecessors. Another innovation are the hinged masks which open up to reveal the person's or animal's inner spirit, particularly associated with northwest coast beliefs and art. The couple is best known for their

Figure 8. Samuel and Denise Wallace (Inuit), King Island Dancer I, 1989, pin of silver and fossil ivory, 14K with mask, 1 5/8 x 1 3/4 inches. Collection of Sara W. Reeves and I.S.K. Reeves V. (Photo: Beverly Brosius)

belts which may sell for as much as $50,000.

Today turquoise silver jewelry continues to be a multi-dimensional art form appreciated by Indians and non-Indians alike. Traders continue to operate throughout the Southwest but they are now joined by Native groups such as the Zuni Arts and Crafts Cooperative and the Navajo Arts and Crafts Guild. The Diné and the Pueblos still choose to make and wear their jewelry as sources of cultural pride and wealth. Since the 1970s more and more Native peoples outside of the Southwest have begun wearing turquoise silver jewelry as a symbol of their Native American heritage. At the close of the twentieth century, the turquoise silver jewelry industry continues to employ a large number of smiths who generate a sizable portion of the total cash income. Currently, artists are extending the legacy of the past into the twenty-first century by creating jewelry in the older styles as well as new forms; they are fashioning the future of turquoise silver jewelry.

[1] John Adair, The Navajo and Pueblo Silversmiths (Norman: University of Oklahoma, 1944) 131. Carl Rosnek and Joseph Stacey, Skystone and Silver (Englewood Cliffs: Prentice Hall, Inc., 1976) 34.

[2] Margery Bedinger, Indian Silver Navajo and Pueblo Jewelers (Albuquerque: U of New Mexico P, 1973) 197-8.

[3] Edna Mae Bennet, Turquoise and the Indian (Denver: Sage Books, 1966) 138. In 1931 Edgar L. Hewett, an archeologist and head director at the Museum of New Mexico, excavated the Anasazi site of Chetro Ketl, located in the larger complex of Chaco Canyon (1100-1300 AD). Alfonso Ortiz, ed., Handbook of North American Indians Southwest 9 (Washington D.C.: Smithsonian Institute, 1979) 139.

[4] Rosnek and Stacey 10; Bennet 112.

[5] In this essay a "fetish" is an "object, natural or manmade, in which a spirit is thought to reside and which can be used to effect either good or evil" as defined by Marian Rodee and James Ostler in The Fetish Carvers of Zuni (Albuquerque: Maxwell Museum of Anthropology, 1990) 15.

[6] Nancy Fox, "Southwestern Indian Jewelry" in I Am Here (Santa Fe: Museum of New Mexico Press, 1989) 67. While we can not be sure what these designs meant, if anything, to the ancient people, today the Hopi refer to these earrings as tu'oynaaqa, meaning "stacked up corn earrings." This is meant to symbolize blue corn stacked in its bin for storage (Heard Museum, Phoenix, Arizona, 1997).

7 Fox 77.

8 Adair 4.

9 Adair 4.

10 Adair 121-2.

11 The Diné were incarcerated during the years 1864-1868. They were forced to walk the distance from their homeland to Fort Sumner at Bosque Redondo in eastern New Mexico, thus this period is referred to as "the Long Walk." Thomas E. Sheridan and Nancy Parezo, *Paths Of Life*, (Tuscon: U of Arizona P, 1996) 12.

12 Adair 13.

13 Cirillo 79.

14 Adair 14.

15 Fox 78.

16 Fox 78.

17 Adair 21.

18 Fox 79.

19 Rosnek and Stacey 153.

20 Adair 30.

21 Rosnek and Stacey 34.

22 Rosnek and Stacey 28.

23 Rosnek and Stacey 33.

24 According to Adair, tobacco canteens were always rare and despite a revival are not made very often (Adair 52). Mother-in-law bells derive their name for the historic Diné taboo of a son-in-law casting his eyes upon his mother-in-law. In an effort to give warning of their arrival, mothers-in-law wore cast silver bells (Adair 7).

25 Dexter Cirillo, *Southwestern Indian Jewelry* (New York: Abbeville Press, 1992) 75.

26 Rosnek and Stacey 37.

27 Cirillo 75.

28 Rosnek and Stacey 37.

29 Adair 38-9.

30 Alice B. Kehoe, *North American Indians* (Englewood Cliffs: Prentice Hall, Inc., 1981) 278.

31 Rosnek and Stacey 157.

32 Adair 44.

33 Adair 44; Cirillo 72.

34 Cirillo 79.

35 Cirillo 82.

36 Cirillo 82.

37 Cirillo 82.

38 Adair 135-136; Cirillo 82-83.

39 Pam Mahooty, personal communication, Gallup, New Mexico, August 10, 1997.

40 Rosnek and Stacey 151.

41 Pam Mahooty, personal communication, Zuni Pueblo, March 23-27, 1987. Mahooty is a well known contemporary Zuni silversmith.

42 Lee Weebothee, personal communication, Zuni Pueblo, April 2, 1988. Weebothee is a well known contemporary Zuni silversmith.

43 Adair 164.

44 Bedinger 197-8.

45 "Zuni History," in Zuni Pueblo tourist information packet (Idaho: Institute of the American West, 1983), n.p.

46 Adair 164.

47 This academic position is summarized by anthropologist Nancy Parezo who writes:
> There is a world wide tendency for men to carve with metals. . .(and) for women to make pottery, weave and produce clothing. . . .Men to produce goods. . .whose raw materials are hard and rough. Women tend to produce crafts which are compatible with child care and their frequent interruptions ("Navajo Sandpainting: The Importance of Sex Roles in Craft Production" in *Small Scale Society Contemporary Readings*, Richard Anderson and Karen L. Fields, eds. [Englewood Cliffs: Prentice-Hall, 1993] 221).

48 John Adair, "Miscellaneous notes on returning war veterans," Zuni Archaeological Society, private folders.

49 M. C. Stevenson, *The Zuni Indian* (New Mexico: Rio Grande Press, 1985) 381.

50 Rosnek and Stacey 157.

51 In an auction catalog by written by C. G. Wallace on his private collection, he described many works by Casi as having the "flower head design" (C. G. Wallace, *Collection of American Indian Art* [Sotheby Parke Bernet, Inc., 1928] n.p.). This fact is supported by Anarita Homer and Mabel Leekya, living relatives of Della Casi, who both conferred that she often worked in the flower cluster design (Anarita Homer and Mabel Leekya, personal communication, April 2, 1988).

52 Ruth Bunzel, *The Pueblo Potter* (New York: Columbia UP, 1929) 94.

53 Ortiz 502.

54 James Ostler, Marian Rodee and Milford Nahohai, *Zuni, A Village of Silversmiths* (Albuquerque: Zuni A:shiwi Publishing and the University of New Mexico, 1996) 83.

American Indian Quilts: an Indigenous Product of the Contact Zone

Jehanne Teilhet-Fisk

"Cultures that do not change with the times will die."
—Jaune Quick-to-See Smith (Confederated Salish and Kootenai Nation)

Figure 1. Nancy Blackhawk (Sioux), *Tepees 'Round the Lake,* c.1970-75, Morningstar pattern quilt, 87 x 73 inches. Star / Fire Collection—Sandra Starr-

The American Indian quilts displayed in this exhibition under the rubric of art have an appeal that crosses cultural boundaries, ethnic groups and generation gaps: they lend themselves as visual metaphors for the social fabric of life. The temporal and fragile aspects of the medium are analogous to "the vulnerability of humans, whose every relationship is transient [and] subject to the degenerative processes of illness, death and decay."[1] Most quilts have a natural end to their lifetimes, but a few achieve a kind of immortality, preserved as heirlooms or collected as works of art.[2] Most who have owned a quilt will say that its aesthetic value is often secondary to what the viewer cannot see, namely the quilt's meaningful, functional life and the social history of the people who possessed it. Quilts play multifaceted roles in contemporary American Indian cultures.

There is little direct evidence to ascertain when the different American Indian tribes began to quilt for themselves. The earliest examples of Native American quilting seem to date from the nineteenth century. By the time official government policies of assimilation and removal were in place, quilting and sewing had became a part of the female curriculum at federal and parochial boarding schools for Native Americans.[3] Forms of quilting were probably introduced earlier to those American Indian women who were indentured servants in settlers' families,[4] as well as by Christian missionary women in the 1800s who came into Montana and the Dakotas with their needle and cloth.[5] A Mennonite missionary, Martha Voth, was conducting quilting and sewing bees for the Hopi women at Oraibi in 1893.[6] Quilting was considered an appropriate and practical craft to teach American Indian girls and women, especially since the art of quilting had long been within the domain of Euroamerican women—although not exclusive to women. Furthermore, since the making of malleable, ephemeral goods was more closely connected with American Indian women than men, this division of labor was in accord with their art-making practices.[7] And quilts, like robes or blankets, evoke an association with both human reproduction and the cultural reproduction of the kin group, or tribe.[8]

The American Indian quilt is considered an acculturated[9] or "contact zone"[10] post-reservation art form because commercial cloth represents an alien material that different tribes adopted since it collated well with indigenous practices. Quilting replicated various sewing methods and appliqué processes that Native women had historically utilized. So it is not surprising that American Indian women, especially those from the Plains tribes, soon adopted this alien art form for reasons of their own. They seized upon quilting as a natural and practical substitution for some of the artistic expressions that were lost to them through subjugation, political changes, confinement to reservations, the killing off of their buffalo, and the drastic changes to their whole ecological system. As an art form, quilting became an integral part of their dynamic cultural heritage. Moreover, the use of commercial fabric neither denigrated the neotraditional value of the object nor significantly altered its meaning or usage by making

Figure 2. Victoria Fortner, quillwork, 1997. (Photo: Rebecca Miller)

Figure 3. One of the earliest Alabama Poarch Creek quilts made with ancient Southeastern Indian motifs. It was made by a Poarch Creek Community group and auctioned at a Thanksgiving Powwow in 1978. (Photo: J. Anthony Parades)

it any less authentic in expression or definition.[11]

Quilting is the process of stitching together three layers of textiles; the top layer, the interlining (or batting), and the back. The series of tiny hand or machine stitches that connect and bind all three layers together is termed quilting. This process sculpts the quilt's surface into a shallow relief with the appearance of a soft, three-dimensional plane. The textured pattern is agreeable to feel and touch, as it should be. The quilting stitches produce a series of repetitive designs that may harmonize and enhance the pieced or appliqué motif, or act as a pervasive counter-rhythm. Native Americans often quilt in the shell pattern as seen in Figure 1; the stitches run counter to the geometric star, generating a vibrant interplay of texture and motif on the surface. It is rare to find the quilting stitch used in clothing. The Florida Seminoles use a technique that does not employ a quilting stitch. Their patchwork technique is labor-intensive and would be impractical for making large bed quilts.

In general, a patchwork quilt can be *pieced* or *appliquéd*. Pieced work is the process of sewing many small bits of usually straight-edged fabrics together to form an overall design sheet.[12] The piecing process has certain affinities with quillwork in that quills were folded into diamonds, triangles, or rectangles that were appliquéd, embroidered, wrapped, or woven onto leather (Figure 2). Quillwork differs from quilting, however, in that the thread or sinew never pierces through the quill. Appliqué allows the maker to use more complex, representational designs because the process of sewing small pieces of fabric onto a larger background is quicker; both techniques can be used in a single quilt.[13] Both quilting techniques are also employed and elaborated on by inventive Native American artists, although appliqué seems to be used more often. A quilt top must have a functional edge: "it is where the pattern of the quilt ends in an intersection with setting and finishing elements."[14] Borders or sashing strips can be added to the frame and enhance the main design in a pleasing manner. Borders can also guide the way the viewer sees the quilt and interacts with the pattern (i.e. on the bed and flat, on a wall and vertical, or draped over a person or object).

Plain or "household" quilts, known to the Sioux as "winter quilts," are sewn and tacked rather than quilted.[15] They were used for warmth and other practical functions. The simple patchwork quilts are cheap since they were made from recycled pieces of old clothing, flour sacks, yard goods or whatever materials were at hand. The special or "best" quilts are more costly because they are normally made from new fabrics; they are always quilted, not just tacked, and are appreciated for their aesthetic qualities and artistic virtuosity, as well as for their symbolic and transactional

functions. A best quilt is always used for special occasions. It is, however, becoming more commonplace to find American Indians making a best quilt as a commodity for art's sake. These quilts are sold to dealers, galleries, and interested buyers, even through the Internet.

Women, especially among the Plains Indians, discovered that some of the Euroamerican patterns had visual equivalents found in their indigenous designs. Both cultures used basic geometric shapes and abstract drafting units that could, for instance, be read as an abstract triangular shape or as an iconic representation, such as a tipi or mountain. A series of tipis around an abstract center field (Figure 1) could read as a symbol for the sun with radiating rays. Native American women recontextualized the geometric shapes, drawing on indigenous sources of inspiration found in their vocabulary of painted designs used on tanned skin robes, ceremonial hides, parfleche and quillwork (Figure 2).[16] In other tribal societies different art forms have also been translated into quilts: ancient pottery and incised shell motifs appear on the Poarch Band of the Creek quilts (Figure 3), basketry designs and *katsina* representations and gifts are incorporated into Hopi quilt patterns (Figure 4), and—as with the Navajo—motifs found on rugs and shoulder blankets find replication in quilts as well (Figure 5). Of interest is the fact that American Indian quilters rarely adopt the crazy-quilt design, which is asymmetrical and usually lacks any symbolic-pattern content.

Other design sources were the elaborately beaded patterns that were appliquéd with a "spot" stitch or "lazystitch" to leather or cloth. Glass trade beads pre-date quilting and were introduced through trade with Europeans. But here, too, the preferred design units and choice of colors were carried over, as in the quilts, from indigenous sources and retained for their sacred or meaningful connotations.[17] Beads, like the Euroamerican commercial fabrics, were inexpensive substitutions for indigenous materials. Contemporary quilter Mae Whiteman, a Sisseton / Wahpeton Sioux living in St. Michael, North Dakota, notes: "I made beadwork before I started the quilts."[18] Her interest in beadwork led her to quilts, which she has been fabricating ever since.

An additional reason for the widespread acceptance of quilting is the fact that the process of making quilts lends itself to the different ways American Indian women work; to begin with, quilting can be seasonal, and the process is adaptable to one's schedule. Furthermore, Plains women work cooperatively and specialize in certain skills by dividing the preparatory and decorative tasks in making their hide robes.[19] Quilts, like skins, can be made collectively, providing the makers with an opportunity to

Figure 4. Becky E. Masayesoa, Child's Quilt, 1989, 4 x 3 feet. Courtesy of the School of American Research, Santa Fe, New Mexico.

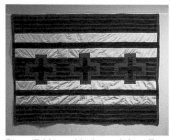

Figure 5. Navajo blanket quilt from Taos Pueblo, New Mexico, 1988 (artist preferred to remain anonymous). Private Collection, Los Alamos, New Mexico. (Photo: J. Teilhet-Fisk)

socialize, or exchange information, ideas, and stories. Quilts can also be made by a solitary individual: Navajo women can live great distances from each other, so they often weave alone and some prefer making quilts alone. Some quilters learned from their mothers, grandmothers, aunts or social organizations, like the Poarch Creek senior citizen activity center in Escambia County, Alabama. Other women, for example B.K. Courtney (Wasco / Tlingit), studied texts on quilting and attended classes.[20] Though the majority of quilters are women, men are now both quilting on their own and collaborating with women (Floyd Fox collaborates with Alice Fox and Rita Corbiere).[21] Conrad House, a Navajo / Oneida, considers his quilts as "paintings without the paint."[22] Excellent quilters are recognized for their talent in their community and beyond. Like any artist, they take great pride in their work, and some of the Plains Indian women keep "careful records, of the number and kinds of quilts they have completed. This is reminiscent of the quilling counts that Sioux women kept in former times." [23]

Quilting is labor-intensive, and the long hours required for making quilts endows them with measures of connectedness to family, tribal values and oral traditions. To paraphrase an 1850s trader, Edwin Denig, working in Plains Societies, raw bolts of cloth, just like raw buffalo hides, have little or no abstract value; it is the labor of putting raw materials into the form of a robe or skin fit for use that accords it worth.[24] And as an intimate, lengthy process, quilts are often imbued with the spirit of their maker or makers. When men make the quilts, women still maintain the larger role in the gifting of them on occasions that mark life-cycle celebrations.

Even though quilt work is often associated with the High Plains people,[25] many tribal groups have adopted this art form: Oklahoma Seminole, Florida Seminole, Potawatomi, Ottawa, Pima-Maricopa, Mohawk, Cherokee, Choctaw and the Yup'ik Eskimo,[26] among others. For some it has come to represent pan-Indianism because it can "transcend tribal and regional styles. Its elements are drawn from many tribes. . . . [and] in some cases the style serves as a unifying basis for national Indian political action."[27] Pan-Indian quilts also express a pride in the broader aspects of Native American heritage rather than articulating an identity with a particular tribe; this reflects the fact that many American Indians have descended from more than one tribal group.

Quilts from the Dakota Sioux, Hopi, Navajo and the Poarch Creek, each illustrating how the women adapted the quilt form to fit their needs and express their ethnic identity, are included in this exhibition. These acculturated products are marked by each tribal woman's preference for certain colors, designs, techniques, sizes, and by her sense of ethno-aesthetics.

In pre-reservation times, when both sexes worked in the same

medium, such as painted hides, the women's designs were geometric in distinction to the men's figurative designs.[28] Plains Indian quilters still tend to favor the abstract designs displayed on the robes worn by women and children.[29] These geometric motifs were associated with veiled, symbolic meanings about their belief system and place in it.[30] Color, shape and location in the pattern frequently indicate symbolization of the sun, day, hills, tipis, animals, and buffalo or legendary lodges. Today, contemporary Plains women make figurative motifs, but preference is still given to the bold, bright, chromatic abstractions. Primary hues of red, yellow, and blue and secondary hues of orange, green and purple tend to dominate their patterns; whites, blacks, browns and even calico and commercially-made Indian prints are employed. Mary Youngman (Sioux) acknowledged, "colors speak to me."[31] The hue and value (the interplay of dark and light) are picked by the Native quilter for symbolic values as well as for the ability to influence the visual perception of a pattern. They cause the eye to move easily from one analogous hue to another. Contrasting hues may also be abutted.[32] Although color symbolism was prominent in the American Indian art forms, the symbolic meanings were not the same for all tribes. For the Blackfoot, red "represented and clearly evoked, this energy which. . .permeated through all things essential to life."[33] Red symbolized blood, the sun as Great Power, the sunrise and sunset, and sacred red paint was used to cover the medicine woman at the Sundance.[34] To the Lakota, red is the favorite color of the spirits, though they also like blue, yellow and brownish yellow.[35] Red is the color that

Figure 6. Regina Brave Bull (Hunkpapa Sioux), *Patchwork Eagle Star*, c. 1970-75, Morningstar pattern quilt, 86 x 66 inches. Star / Fire Collection—Sandra Starr-Tanner.

Figure 7. Elaine Brave Bull (Sioux), Detail of *Morningstar Quilt, c.* 1992, Morningstar pattern quilt, 74 x 88 inches. Star / Fire Collection—Sandra Starr-Tanner.

belongs to the Sun and "represents the coming and going of the Sun."[36] Many tribes associate blue with the all-pervasive power of sky and water, while yellow connotes the powers of the earth, green represents growth and fertility and white the moon, snow or the north wind. Color is also associated with the cardinal directions for the Hopi and other tribes. Almira Buffalo Bone Jackson (Assiniboine) describes her use of color: "blue is clear sky. . .darker blue is the river waters," and "red is to show my joy and happiness."[37]

Certain named patterns have been popular in quite dissimilar cultures. From a purely formalist point of view (that does not take cultural context into consideration), it would *appear* that Native Americans assimilated into their repertoire named images commonly used by Euroamerican women, such as the eagle or the star. The eagle became a popular pattern in Euroamerican quilts after its adoption by Congress in 1782 as the emblem of the Great Seal of the United States. But the eagle and the Native personification of the mythic "thunderbird" had been sacred icons to many American Indian tribes long before the late eighteenth century. In Lakota belief, the eagle "is an *akicita* [messenger] of the sun and the *tonwan* [spiritual essence] of the sun abides in its tail quills."[38] The eagle's spirit "presided over councils, hunters, war parties and battles,"[39] and the "tying of an eagle's plume to a girl's hair was to indicate that she had matured as a woman."[40] The *eagle* is consequently a named quilt pattern adopted by two cultures, with a contextual meaning that differs according to the maker. In their interpretations of the image, Native Americans make it more meaningful to their cultural beliefs: the eagle is the "revered messenger between the earth and sky and symbol of valor and courage."[41] (Figure 6)

Gail Binney-Winslow and Edwin B. Binney assert that "Star patterns appeared on America's quilts from virtually the beginning. No other motif has been represented so profusely."[42] The star is not only considered one of the most beautiful quilt patterns, "but all told it is probably the most common motif," and Star designs can have any number of points, though eight-pointed stars are the most common.[43] The star motif has intricate, inven-

tive variations, and precision is required to prevent error. A typical central star pattern is constructed from a series of eight pieced diamond shapes, each of which contains smaller diamonds. For example, a larger diamond-shaped sub-unit is sewn from one hundred small diamond patches arranged in a grid and pieced in strips which run parallel to two opposing edges of the larger diamond; such a large number of seams and angles in the shapes of the patches magnifies the possibility of error.[44]

There are more names for the star motif than there are patterns. Each quilt name is associated with regional, local, political, biblical or historical interests, as indicated in the names "Texas or Lone Star," "LeMoyne Star," "Feather Stars," "Stars and Stripes Forever," "Patriotic Starburst" and the "Star of Bethlehem." The star pattern is also prevalent among American Indians, but the name they confer is "Morning Star." (Figure 7) This pattern is not listed in most of the Euroamerican books on quilting because this name is associated with the Northern Plains Indians, as well as having pan-Indian significance.

The morning star is a meaningful symbol that was painted, woven, quilled and beaded onto tipis, bags, hide robes, moccasins and shields long before it was quilted. This begs the question, which came first to this continent, the Morning Star, the Star of Bethlehem (through Christian contact), or the Stars and Stripes? All act as important symbols of national identity and / or religion. "For the Northern Plains Indians of Montana and the Dakotas, the sighting of the morning star still heralds a new beginning and a new dawning" cites Pulford.[45] Hammond and Quick-to-See Smith note that when Native artist Whiteman quilts, "she makes stars fly

Figure 8. Artie Crazy Bull (Oglala Sioux), *Star and Arrows,* 1970-75, Morningstar pattern quilt, 68 x 83 inches. Star / Fire Collection—Sandra Starr-Tanner.

Figure 9. Alice McGhee and her daughter Elsie Holland (Poarch Creek) working on a "Big Star" quilt in Mrs. McGhee's home, Hedpeada, Alabama, Summer, 1972. (Photo: J. Anthony Paredes)

again," a reference to the morning star which stands for renewal and hope.[46] In explanation of fabled qualities, MacDowell and Wood note that the morning star, which appears in the east in early April, represents the direction from which spirits of the dead travel to earth and thus signifies a continual link between the living and the dead."[47] The Pawnee attribute the creation of the first man to the evening and morning stars,[48] while the Morning Star, according to the Blackfoot, "was considered to be the son of the Sun and Moon and a great source of protective power," and the only child by this pair to survive, called A-pi-su'-ahts.[49] Blackfeet holy women wore robes in the Sundance ceremonies painted with symbols of the Morning Star.[50] Because of its indigenous symbolic value, the star pattern is always seen at events associated with ceremonial and ritual significance: birth, marriage, healing and death. This exhibition has one Morning Star quilt made by Elaine Brave Bull and three Plains Indian quilts that carry a variation of the Morning Star pattern (Figure7),[51] and each has the shell quilting stitch. It is possible that the arching pattern of the stitch is employed as a visual equivalent to sacred rainbows or clouds.

Regina Brave Bull, a Hunkpapa Sioux from Cannonball, North Dakota, named her quilt *Patchwork Eagle Star,* combining two powerful symbols in one pattern (Figure 6). Medicine men caution women making this pattern since a quilter has to be careful not to misuse the eagle because of its power, courage and strong medicine.[52] The eagle seen on the quilt, however, appears to be based on the thunderbird motif. The eagle and mythic thunderbird were "the principal messengers of the Creator and represented the most powerful guardian spirits one could receive through a vision."[53] Brave Bull's quilt vibrates with analogous hues, and placed on a yellow-orange ground is a blue tipped, eight-pointed star: "I use the blues of the summer sky," notes the artist.[54] In the center of the star, ablaze in both close variations as well as contrasting hues of light blue, yellow-orange, and red-orange, is an eagle with a white head, brown and white feathers and a red-orange body, floating in the center as if hovering in flight. The softly-sculpted shell quilting resembles concentric rainbows or billowing clouds. Ralph Coe writes about a similar Eagle Star quilt made by Brave Bull, only he describes the pattern as a variant of the sacred circle:

> The moment she unfolded it. . .the room was filled with radiating power and spiritual enlightenment. Light swirls from the yellow center of her quilt, carried outward on the points of color (pieced from scraps). The tips of the giant star point toward the four edges of the earth.[55]

Tepees 'Round the Lake, composed with a violet ground (Figure 1) by Nancy Blackhawk, Sioux, is a variation of the Morning

Star pattern and painted Sun motif found on tanned buffalo robes. Here the pattern is meant to be viewed as a visual pun; the form line of the eight-star motif can also be seen to represent eight tipis replete with an entrance, woods and lake. For many Plains Indians, the circle of tipis represents unity.[56] The Plains Indians have always honored the circle as sacred. Buffalo robes were painted by women with feathered circles or sunbursts; "shields were painted with sacred circles with sharp pointed symbols for sun, stars and the four winds whirling forever."[57] The Sundance lodges were round, and the tipis have a round base and cone or triangular shape that resembles the ray of the sun or the point of a star. The Oglala Sioux (Lakota) and Cheyenne all followed strict rules when they met bands of their own tribe by erecting their tipis in a great circle or Sacred Hoop with an opening facing east, the rising sun.[58] Tipis were made and owned by women, and young girls would play house with toy tipis made by their mothers; therefore, the image is fitting subject matter for women quilters. The symbolism and religious significance of many of these circular designs may never be fully understood because women members of the "Tipi Decorators" were instructed "never to disclose [its secrets]. . .in the presence of males."[59]

Artie Crazy Bull, an Oglala Sioux from Montana, created the *Star and Arrows* quilt (Figure 8). The quilt has a visually engaging motif against a bold green background. In this pattern, the star and arrow tips are visual equivalents and share the same hues. This gives the illusion that the arrows, the emblems of war and hunting societies, are shooting into space like flying stars.

The Alabama Poarch Band of the Creek Confederacy[60] make Big Star quilts that do not identify with the Morning Star or any other indigenous symbols. Nevertheless, the motif is appreciated for its complexities and beauty, and its expression of pan-Indianism. The eight-point Big Star in this exhibition is on a light blue ground. The center of the star is in red with radiating colors of white, light blue and red. This quilt has moved through its life cycle. It has a pleasant, lived-in aroma, and the used cloth is faded and worn, reflecting its rich social history.[61] Alice McGhee and her daughter Elsie Holland made a number of different types of patterned quilts as seen in Figure 9, a photograph taken in 1972 while they worked on a Big Star quilt. Even though their African-American and Euroamerican neighbors did quilt at one time, this art form has become increasingly

Figure 10. Detail of Quilt, Poarch Creek, 1980s, commercial fabric, c. 70 x 86 inches. Collection of J. Anthony Paredes. (Photo: J. Teilhet-Fisk)

indentified with the Poarch Creek community.[62] But it wasn't until the late 1970s that Poarch Creek women began searching for motifs that would link them with the ancient artistic heritage from which they had become separated. Motifs were sought from artifacts published in works on early Southern Indian pottery and shell ornaments as a way of promulgating their own tribal identity.[63] In 1994, Dr. J. Anthony Paredes was honored with a best quilt for being the guest speaker at the Poarch Creek Powwow. This quilt has no name, but it is interesting because it expresses pan-Indianism in utilizing commercial cloth with Navajo or Pueblo people sitting in front of a Navajo (?) blanket with Pueblo pottery beside them (Figure 10). The commercially symmetrical motifs form the basis of the repetitive quilt pattern.[64] The cloth's hues are printed in warm earth-tone colors.

Today we find evidence of a number of patterns that through their nomenclature reflect tribal identity and / or a pan-Indian heritage: *Arrows Shooting Into the Stars, Time to Make Dry Meat, The Story of the Assiniboine, Deer Tracks, Indian Five Star, Flying Swallows Like Indian Dancers, Sacred Medicine Pipes, Indian Dance, The Sun Dance Star, Sand Painting Quilt* and the *Basket Quilt.*

The Hopi village of Oraibi in Arizona has been quilting since the late 1800s. Their situation is uniquely different from the Plains Indians in that Hopi men were the makers of cloth.[65] (As Kate Kent Peck remarked, if weaving had been a woman's craft rather than a man's, the tradition might have continued.[66]) Missionaries introduced quilting to the Hopi women probably under the assumption that female artisans wove, thinking it would be a logical replacement for cotton robes and blankets. Nevertheless, Hopi women were culturally free to work in this medium because it did not rely on indigenous weaving techniques that were sacred to the male realm, those who worked the looms in the kiva. Unfortunately, the Anglo presence also brought about the "demise of loom weaving as a man's skill by the early 1900s and then by fostering the revival of some traditional techniques, notably belt weaving and embroidery, as women's art."[67] Contemporary Hopi women are quilting or painting traditional Hopi images on their quilts; some represent the corn symbol while others borrow from *kasina* imagery. Women are even using "traditional dyes to color the fabric for their quilts."[68] Other Hopi women quilt contemporary fabrics with children's motifs such as "Big Bird" seen in Figure 11.

A quilt of a different nature from those just discussed was purchased in the summer of 1988 from a young Navajo / Diné woman at Taos Pueblo in New Mexico (Figure 5). The quilt is interesting because it has retained the shape and size of a woman's

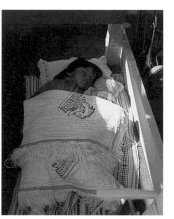

Figure 11. "Big Bird" Child's Quilt (Hopi), Fall 1993. Artist unknown. (Photo: J. Teilhet-Fisk)

Figure 12. Plains fancy-dress costume with quilted fabric, Taos Powwow, 1990. (Photo: J. Teilhet-Fisk)

shoulder blanket rather than adopting the larger size used as bedclothing or the size of a tanned skin. The pattern is in the early Navajo blanket style with traditional Navajo colors. The quilt imitates the form, scale and colors of a Navajo blanket and therefore has no soft sculptural quilting pattern. The parallel stripes of dark red, black, dark blue and white are distributed symmetrically around a wide central stripe made up of smaller stripes and three equilateral crosses. The quilt reflects the Navajo / Diné concern with "harmony in color and balance in a design structure" as being "the most important aesthetic imperatives of textile design."[69] The crosses lack the small flags at their corners, but the maker (who wishes to be anonymous) told me it symbolized the Spider Woman cross. It is said that Spider Woman taught the Navajos to weave. The quilt is unusual because careful attention has been given to the backside which has a two-striped pattern: the quilt was intended to be used as a shoulder blanket, like the weaving that it emulates, and thus has a pattern on both sides. The young maker commented that she was homesick and missed weaving, so she decided to quilt Navajo-styled blankets instead.

As we have seen, "household" and "best" quilts were used as logical, practical and reasonably inexpensive replacements for dyed quill work, painted skins and hides, and woven blankets and robes because they assumed similar functions. The Plains Indians used painted muslin and quilts as replacements for the painted skin *dew curtain* (*ozan*) that hung inside the tipi and functioned as a moisture barrier, insulator, windbreak and a didactic artwork that evoked stories. According to Ella Deloria (Yankton Sioux) the Sioux made "pictographs" on the dew curtains and "people went visiting just to hear the stories they preserved."[70] In time, American Indian quilts absorbed many of the traditional functions of skins and textiles, serving as bedding, robes, wall-hangings, door and window covers and baby carriers. But, most importantly, Native American quilts are multivocal objects where the meanings can change as the object moves from one contextual use to another. In other words, quilts, like humans, have their own life-cycle, analogous to the degenerative processes of life. When the quilt fades or becomes frayed and worn, its interactive roles or functions (utilitarian and transactional) change over time. Quilts that are kept as heirlooms usually have a rich social history that recalls particular events and people, whereas quilts made exclusively for the art market are kept for their aesthetic virtues.

In another context, best quilts have multifaceted uses as transactional markers. They are often bestowed in "give-aways" that commemorate ceremonies which emphasize and support physi-

Figure 13. Congressman Jack Edwards was presented with a Poarch Creek quilt decorated with ancient Southeastern designs on Thanksgiving Day, 1983. (Photo: J. Anthony Paredes)

cal or social change: a birth; naming ceremonies; marriage; recovery from illness or death. Give-aways are a special way of showing appreciation and recognition by publicly bestowing objects made (or bought) to elders, leaders and members of the audience. Give-aways are often seen as labors of love, a sacrifice of time, energy and spirit to benefit others in order to gain a kind of spiritual purity and social prestige. Almira Buffalo Bone Jackson, Sioux, explained that "Nothing can make one feel better than giving, giving is our way of being thankful."[71] Deloria quotes a Dakota patriarch as saying, "Give abundantly and with glorious abandon. Better not to honor someone than dishonor him by doing it haltingly and calculatingly. . . . Property always flows back in due time to those who let it flow freely forth."[72] Best quilts are also presented and / or bestowed at "give-aways" during a pow-wow.[73] "At powwows, for instance, quilts are often given to popular singers and dancers, who have befriended a family or whose talents are simply admired by that family."[74] There are as many different types of give-aways as there are occasions for generosity, reciprocity and gratitude. Regina Brave Bull was even given the name "She Who Gives Many Things," and according to Pulford, she did give away many things and excelled in all the arts which included hide tanning, beading and porcupine quilling.[75] Some quilts are specially made in gratefulness for the return of a family member from a distant place, or from an illness, or out of respect and love for a deceased, or even to redistribute wealth and raise money for a particular event or need. Also seen at the powwows are fancy dress costumes with quiltwork (Figure 12).

Quilts have metaphorical properties that bind the recipients to their ancestors and future progeny.[76] Danyelle Means, Oglala Lakota, explains that a Morning Star quilt was laid on the ground to be stood upon as her son was given his Lakota name,[77] thus binding him to a sacred symbol that appropriately stands for renewal and hope.[78]

In Hopi and Hopi-Tewa naming ceremonies, quilts are often given to the baby.[79] When a baby is born, the infant is given a naming ceremony on the twentieth day. "The parents hold the child up to the [rising] sun and choose the best name of those given [by the husband's clanswomen]."[80]

The child is presented to the sun as a new member of the tribe, and prayers are said to ensure that the child will grow in good health. After the blessings, family and friends are invited to offer a clan name to the baby. A gift of a quilt accompanies the offered name. Some babies will be the recipients of several names, and several quilts. On any trip to Hopi a visitor will always see beautiful Hopi babies wrapped in hand made quilts."[81] Though there is no documentation accompanying the Hopi quilt made by Becky E. Masayesoa, seen in this exhibition (Figure 4), based upon its size and imagery it seems likely that it was used in such a ceremony. The quilt is adorned with images of a small flat *katsina*, probably Hahay'iwuuti, one of the *katsina* mothers. The flat *katsina* are usually the very first *katsina tihu* "received by female infants."[82] In July during the Niman ceremony, a newborn will receive her first flat *katsina tihu* from the Katsinam, who also bring other traditional gifts for young children such as the bows and arrows, gourd rasp rain makers (as a prayer for moisture), and colorful lightning sticks or dance wands visible on this Hopi quilt.[83] Since the Katsinam gifts are gender coded, the rattles and bow and arrows indicate that this may be a boy's quilt.[84]

It has been observed that quilts serve as an analogue for degenerative processes of life: they can be used in funeral ceremonies to wrap the deceased. The Hopi use quilts as burial shrouds.[85] Mae Whiteman (Sioux) said, "I give most of my quilts away either to my children or to someone who needs one put on a casket."[86] The Oklahoma Seminoles often place a quilt over the casket in the grave; this protects it and muffles the somber sounds of the returning earth as it hits the casket surface.[87] MacDowell and Wood state that the "Oglala also commonly wrap a star quilt and matching pillows around a new tombstone until it is unveiled."[88] Quilts have the ability to tie the living to the dead: just as it covers the living, the quilt also comforts the dead in eternal sleep.

Quilts can be sacrosanct objects deployed as altar cloths and placed on top of sweat or purification lodges, *inipi*. Young Plains Indian men often wrap themselves "in a quilt while awaiting a vision on some secluded high place."[89] Participants in a Yuwipi ("a modern Oglala shamanistic healing ritual"), make offerings during the "Light Phase" which may include a quilt top.[90] In the "Dark Phase" of the healing ritual, the shaman tells of his vision after which he may be tied. His helpers tie his hands behind his back, then cover him with a robe or quilt that is also securely tied. The spirits free the shaman from his bonds and the robe or quilt is now found on the lap of one of the participants.[91] The tying of the shaman in a star quilt blanket invokes the gods.[92]

Quilts are created in order to honor outstanding individuals, groups, or even the community at large. The Fort Peck Assiniboine ceremony in Montana honors each member of the basketball team by giving them quilts, whereas other quilts might honor military veterans, graduates, or persons of power in a community.[93] The presentation of quilts can serve to validate and solidify bonds between groups or governments. Congressman Jack Edwards

Figure 14. Poarch Creek Star Quilt, Artist unknown. Collection of J. Anthony Paredes. (Photo: J. Teilhet-Fisk)

was presented with a Poarch Creeks quilt decorated with ancient Southeastern designs on Thanksgiving Day, 1983 (Figure 13). The gifting of a quilt marked his formal announcement of the positive recommendation by the Bureau of Indian Affairs of the Poarch Creeks' petition for federal acknowledgment.[94] Quilts can also make political statements, such as the one made by Alice Olsen Williams (Mohawk). Her quilt was a social commentary that protested the way the Canadian government was destroying the Mohawk's sacred sites to make way for commercial development.[95]

Quilts have become markers of ethnicity and emblems of tribal pride and continuity. For the Sioux, "the Star quilt has become an important display item, functioning like a banner or flag at important family and community gatherings."[96] Star quilts are even seen draped over cars, floats and horses during Powwow parades.[97]

An equally important use of artful best quilts is as a form of wealth or as an instrumental agent in the raising of funding for an American Indian community. Women will carry an open quilt "around the edges of the dance area so spectators can toss in money," or they may raffle or auction these quilts to generate money for a good cause,[98] such as the Star quilt purchased by J. Anthony Paredes from the Poarch Creek Indians (Figure 14). The money generated is rarely commensurate to the labor invested, but the quilts bring honor and prestige to the makers. Quilt makers are receiving wider recognition by entering competitions at powwows and fairs. Elaine Brave Bull's *Morningstar* (Figure 7) was made as a best quilt and entered into a quilt competition in 1992 at the well-known and highly attended Red Earth Powwow, Oklahoma, where it took first place. In reaching the status of art, American Indian quilts are finally becoming an attractive com-

modity on the global art scene and being exhibited as art hangings in galleries, museums and even government buildings. A *Star Pattern* quilt made by Nellie Menar, Rosebud Sioux, and commissioned by the National Museum of the American Indian was installed in the House Rayburn Office Building in mid-1997.[99] Many tribes are turning to quilting as a collectable art form that can bring some sort of income to its makers. This notion of the American Indian quilt as an isolated art object or commodity is, however, different from its transactional valuation as a gift. Gifting has distinctly social importance: gifts have rank. Gifts are inalienable things whereas commodities are alienable objects.[100]

By substituting needle and thread for bone awls and sinew, and commercial cloth for tanned skins or quill work, Native American women appropriated and transformed Euroamerican quilts into visible referents that retain their cultural values, integrity and vitality. American Indian quilts as multivocal "contact zone" creations are ingenious extensions of indigenous practices used in culturally appropriate ways that maintain links with the past: only the medium has changed. Quilts communicate ideological values and help social groups to reproduce themselves.

Acknowledgments: I would like to acknowledge Erin Barcinski, a graduating senior who provided research for this paper before going to West Africa on a study trip. I am indebted to J. Anthony Paredes and Sandra Starr-Tanner for sharing their knowledge, assistance and beautiful quilts. I am grateful for Professor Paredes' insightful comments on an earlier draft of this paper. These acknowledgments do not in any way bind the persons mentioned to my interpretation, for this paper is only that, an interpretation of Native American quilting.

In the course of research, I was astonished to find that most books on "American Quilting" neglect to include anything on the Native American contribution; African-American and Hawaiian-American quilts are mentioned, though often under-represented. In 1989 Florence Pulford wrote *Morning Star Quilts*, addressing the subject in a warm, chatty, reflective style. A new volume edited by Marsha L. MacDowell and Kurt Dewhurst (still in press) tries to rectify the neglect of the important roles that Native American quilts play in our vast North American continent: *To Honor and Comfort: Native Quilting Traditions* accompanies a traveling exhibition of the same name.

1   Annette B. Weiner and Jane Schneider, *Cloth and Human Experience* (Washington and London: Smithsonian Institution Press, 1989) 2.

2   John Forrest and Deborah Blincoe, *The Natural History of the Traditional Quilt* (Austin: U of Texas P, 1995) 157. This is a groundbreaking book on quilts.

3   Marsha MacDowell and Margaret Wood, "Sewing It Together: Native American and Hawaiian Quilting Traditions," in *Native American Expressive Culture* (*Akwe:Kon Journal* 11.3-4 [Fall/Winter 1994]. 109).

4   Patsy and Myron Orlofsky, *Quilts in America* (New York: Abbeville Press, 1992) 38. Orlofsky quotes a notice in the 1728 Boston News-Letter: "Ran away, an Indian woman, indented servant. . .wore a. . .homespun quilted petticoat. . . ."

5   Florence Pulford, *Morning Star Quilts* (Los Altos: Leone Publications, 1989) 7.

6   Carolyn O'Bagy, "Hopi Quilting: Shared Traditions in an Ancient Community." Internet www.patchwords.com/ofeatures/hopi.htm.

7   There are, however, the exceptions to the rule. Among Pueblo and Hopi cultures, men were the original loom weavers. With the pressures of foreign change and acculturation, women now work in textiles.

8   Annette B. Weiner, *Inalienable Possessions: The Paradox of Keeping-While-Giving* (Berkeley: U of California P, 1992) 13.

9   Clifford quotes how William Sturtevant distinguishes acculturation from assimilation. "The former involves the adoption of cultural traits, the borrowing of customs, it is a matter of degree. The latter refers to a relation between societies, the incorporation of one society into another. Acculturation, he says, has taken place among all Indian tribes." James Clifford, *The Predicament of Culture* (Cambridge: Cambridge Press, 1988) 323.

10 Mary Louise Pratt, *Imperial Eyes: Travel Writing and Transculturation* (London and New York: Routledge, 1992) 6-7. James Clifford also discusses "Museums as Contact Zones" in *Routes. Travel and Translation in the Late Twentieth Century* (Cambridge, MA, and London: 1997) 188-219.

11 For a discussion on the concept of traditional in Native American art, see J.C.H. King, "Tradition in Native American Art," *The Arts of North American Indians: Native Traditions in Evolution* (1986): 65-104. On the issue of authenticity and who determines cultural authenticity, see the controversial but informative article by Sidney L. Kasfir, "African Art and Authenticity," *African Arts* 3.3 (April 1992): 40-53, 96-97.

12 Orlofsky 94.

13 Orlofsky 91-125.

14 Forrest and Blincoe 49-50.

15 Bea Medicine and Patricia Albers, "Star Quilts," *Native Arts/West* (July 1988): 10. The Poarch Creek of Alabama also tack their household comforters. (J. Anthony Paredes, Oral Communication, October 1997.)

16 Quill work was generally made from moose hair, vegetal fibers, and splitbird quills or porcupine quills.

17 Colin F. Taylor, *The Plains Indians* (London: Salamander Books, 1994) 139-147.

18 Harmony Hammond and Jaune Quick-to-See Smith, *Women of Cedar and Sage* (New York: The Gallery of the American Indian Community House, 1985) n. pag.

19 Medicine and Albers 11.

20 Margaret Wood, "Contemporary Native Quilt Artists," *Native Peoples* 10:4 (Summer 1997): 30.

21 Wood 31.

22 Wood 31.

23 Medicine and Albers 14.

24 Edwin Thompson Denig, "Indian Tribes of the Upper Missouri," *Extract from the Forty-Sixth Annual Report, Smithsonian Institution, Bureau of American Ethnology*, ed. J. N. B. Hewitt (Washington D. C.: Smithsonian Press, 1930) 506.

25 The High Plains tribes are: Assiniboin, Blackfeet, Sarcee, Plains Ojibwa, Gros Ventre, Crow, Sioux, Arapaho, Cheyenne, Commanche, Kiowa, Kiowa-Apache, Lipan Apache, Tonkawa. Taylor 28.

26 For more information on the Yup'ik Eskimos see: Ann Fienup-Riordan "How Yup'ik Women Spoil Their Cloth: Seal Party Quilts of the Nelson Island Eskimos" in *The Magazine of Textiles, Fiberarts* 24.3 (Nov./Dec. 1997): 29-32.

7   Edwin L. Wade, ed., *The Art of the North American Indian: Native Traditions in Evolution* (New York: Hudson Hills Press, Inc. 1986) 311.

28 For more on the division of artistic labor by sex and gender, see Jehanne Teilhet, "The Equivocal Role of Women Artists in Non-Literate Cultures," *Heresies: A Feminist Publication on Art and Politics* 4 (Winter 1978): 96-102.

29 See Marsha Clift Bol, "Lakota Women's Artistic Strategies in Support of the Social System," *American Indian Culture and Research Journal* 9.1 (1985): 33-51.

30 Taylor 121.

31 Pulford 63.

32 For an excellent understanding of the use of hues and values, see Forrest and Blincoe 126-149.

33 Taylor 197.

34 Taylor 196-197.

35 James R. Walker, edited by Raymond J. DeMallie and Elaine A. Jahner, *Lakota Belief and Ritual* (Lincoln: U of Nebraska P, 1991) 108.

36 Walker 108.

37 Pulford 75.

38 Walker 230.

39 Walker 122.

40 Walker 252.

41 Pulford 38.

42 Edwin Binney, III and Gail Binney-Winslow, *Homage to Amanda: Two Hundred Years of American Quilts* (San Francisco: R. K. Press, 1984) 51.

43 Robert Bishop, William Secord and Judith Reiter Weissman, *Quilts, Coverlets, Rugs and Samplers* (New York: Alfred A. Knopf, 1982) 30.

44 Forrest and Blincoe 230.

45 Pulford 7.

46 Hammond and Quick-to-See Smith n. pag.

47 MacDowell and Wood 110.

48 William K. Powers, *Indians of the Southern Plains* (New York: Putnam, 1971) 126.

49 Taylor 126, 62.

50 Taylor 125.

51 These quilts were collected by Florence A. Pulford and subsequently purchased by Sandra Starr in 1987. I am most grateful for the generous time, articles, books, valuable advice and assistance Ms. Starr has given me. Her energy and enthusiasm for this exhibition has sustained us all.

52 Pulford 51.

53 Peter Nabokov and Robert Easton, *Native American Architecture* (New York: Oxford UP, 1989) 165.

54 Pulford 51.

55 Ralph T. Coe, *Lost and Found Traditions: Native American Art 1965-1985* (New York: The American Federation of Arts, 1986) 35.

56 Pulford 46.

57 Coe 35.

58 Taylor 40, 42.

59 Taylor 126.

60 J. Anthony Paredes, "The Poarch Creeks, Florida's Third Tribe," *Forum, The Magazine of the Florida Humanities Council* 16.2 (Fall 1992): 24.

61 This quilt was purchased by Dr. Paredes in 1972 for fifteen dollars; quilts now sell for two to three hundred dollars, reflecting their value as art commodities.

62 With appreciation to Dr. Paredes for pointing this out to me; in his article "The Folk Culture of the Eastern Creek Indians: Synthesis and Change" in *Indians of the Lower South: Past and Present,* John K. Mahon, ed., (Pensacola: Gulf Coast History and Humanities Conference, 1975) 103, he writes: "Quilting has been continued up to the present; in recent years the art has been stimulated by the saleability of quilts as craft items. Up until twenty-five or so years ago, annual spring quilt washings at nearby springs and creeks were minor social events."

63 Paredes, personal communication, October 1997.

64 Paredes, personal communication, October 1997.

65 Kate Kent Peck, *Pueblo Indian Textiles: A Living Tradition* (Santa Fe: School of American Research Press, 1983) 27-28.

66 Peck, *Pueblo Indian* 19.

67 Peck, *Pueblo Indian* 23.

68 O'Bagy n. pag.

69 Kate Kent Peck, *Navajo Weaving: Three Centuries of Change* (Santa Fe: School of American Research Press, 1985) 114.

70 Ella C. Deloria, *Speaking of Indians* (Vermillion, SD: Dakota Books, 1992) 56-57; MacDowell and Wood 109.

71 Pulford 14.

72 Deloria 41.

73 The word Powwow comes from the Algonquin word pau pau, "which refers to a gathering of medicine men or spiritual leaders in a curing ceremony." Anita Herle, "Dancing Community: Powwow and Pan-Indianism in North America" in Anita Herle and David Phillipson, eds., *Living Traditions, Continuity and Change, Past and Present* (Cambridge: Cambridge Anthropology, 1994) 17.2: 57. The powwow is now associated with secular events, fancy dance competitions, trade, and is an occasion that promotes pan-Indianism.

74 Medicine and Albers 12.

75 Pulford 42-43.

76 Weiner and Schneider 3.

77 Tanya Thrasher, "To Honor and Comfort: Native American Quilting Traditions," *Native Peoples* 10.4 (Summer 1997): 26.

78 Hammond and Quick-To-See Smith, n. pag.

79 Thrasher 26.

80 Michael B. Stanislawski, "Hopi-Tewa," in Alfonso Ortiz, ed., *Southwest* (Washington DC: Smithsonian Institute, 1979) 599.

81 O'Bagy n. pag.

82 Alph H. Secakiku, *Following the Sun and Moon: Hopi Katsina Tradition* (Flagstaff: Northland Publishing Co. in cooperation with the Heard Museum, 1995) 53. The flat *katsina* could also represent *novantsi-tsiloaka* or *kököle.* (Barton Wright, *Hopi Kachinas* [Flagstaff: Northland Press, 1984] 74, 122.)

83 Secakiku 53.

84 Mischa Titiev, "Old Oraibi: A Study of the Hopi Indians of Third Mesa," in *Papers of the Peadbody Museum of American Archaeology and Ethnology* (Cambridge: Harvard UP, 1944) 22.1: 115, 117-118.

85 O'Bagy n. pag.

86 Hammond and Quick-To-See Smith n. pag.

87 MacDowell and Wood 109.

88 MacDowell and Wood 110.

89 Pulford 7.

90 Luis S. Kemnitzer, "Structure, content and cultural meaning of *Yuwipi* a modern Lakota healing ritual," *American Ethnologist* 3.2 (May 1976): 267

91 Kemnitser 270.

92 Jerrold E. Levy, "Indian Healing Arts," in Robert L Iacopi, ed., *Look To The Mountain Top* (San Jose: Gousha Publications, 1972) 54.

93 Thrasher 26.

94 "In 1984, the Poarch Creeks won official recognition and a 'government to government' relationship with the United States. Recognition brought the right to self-government, a land base, tribal sovereignty and the services of the Bureau of Indian Affairs and Indian Health Service." Paredes, personal communication, October 1997.

95 Wood 29.

96 Medicine and Albers 14.

97 Medicine and Albers 14.

98 MacDowell and Wood 109.

99 NMAI Runner, *Newsletter for the Smithsonian National Museum of the American Indian NMAI Runner* 97.3 (May/June 1997): 3.

100 Nicholas Thomas, *Entangled Objects* (Cambridge: Harvard UP, 1991) 14-22. Commodities are objects "which are placed in a context in which they have exchange value and can be alienated. . . ." or "dissociated from producers, former users, or prior context." Thomas 39.

Seminole Patchwork: Pride of Many Colors

Ashley E. Remer and *Nessa Page-Leiberman*

One acculturated art form that managed to survive and flourish within the confines of the Florida reservations is Seminole patchwork. Kept alive by the grandmothers and mothers, patchwork has come to represent Seminole cultural heritage as well as being a lucrative commodity. Currently, there is a division between Seminoles and academics about whether patchwork is an expression of cultural aesthetics or an artistic medium highly charged with symbolic meanings. The true value of Seminole patchwork cannot be found on the art market.

At the time of European contact, when the colonial spirit was unleashed upon the North American continent, the Seminoles as an individual tribe did not exist. This was the beginning of a chain of events that caused a massive upheaval and dispersal of the native peoples of the Southeast. The Creeks, from which most of the Seminoles came, were a multi-tribal confederacy of many cultures and many languages.[1] During a series of wars between the Spanish, French and English, land rights alternated several times, and the Creeks were scattered around the Southeast. Mostly Mikasuki-speaking Lower Creeks were driven into Florida. The towns they established began to develop their own identities. When the British gained control of the Florida territory after the French and Indian War, the name "Seminole" was given to the mixture of people who fled into Florida. "Seminole" comes from the Spanish word *Cimmarón*, meaning wild or runaway.[2]

However, the real threat to the survival of the Seminole people came when the British lost control of the Florida territory after the American Revolution. Slaves, running for their lives from the newly established republic, sought refuge in Spanish Florida. This was hazardous because the bounty hunters who came in search of runaway slaves made no distinction between them and their Seminole hosts. Also, the fledgling government of the United States felt the spirit of expansion, eager to accommodate a growing population.[3] In 1817, the first of three so-called Seminole Wars began. However, it was not until after the second Seminole War that the Seminoles were driven deep into the Everglades of South Florida. After killing countless Seminoles and committing outright acts of treachery, the U.S. government claimed victory by relocating most of the tribe to Oklahoma. Those who remained were left in the wetlands of South Florida.[4]

After the wars were over, the Seminoles were mostly isolated from settlers, although some trading did occur. They hunted, grew vegetables and traded hides and furs. In 1906, the U.S. government, in order to clear land for settlers, began to drain the Everglades. By 1920, the significant loss of wildlife was rapidly becoming a loss of resources and assurance for the future of the Seminoles. Some began to live on government reservations, where they were provided with social services and education. In 1958, when the government threatened to cut them off, the "Seminole Tribe of Florida" was established.[5] Today, there are three main reservations in South Florida; Hollywood, Big Cypress and Brighton. Many people choose not to live on the reservations for either political or economic reasons.

Since the early 1800s, Seminole artistic expression has been most strongly evident in

Figure 1. Governor and Mrs. Leroy Collins, at a holiday reception with representatives from the Seminole Tribe in 1956. The governor and Mrs. Collins are wearing Seminole patchwork ceremonial clothing gifted to them by the tribe. Florida State Archives.

articles of clothing.[6] At the time of contact, the Spanish noted that the people were wearing brightly- colored cloaks and shawls made of feathers and hides. In 1765, the British distributed ready-made shirts as offerings to the Seminoles at the Treaty of Picolata. Gifting has been a way to make friends, allies and peace in Native American tribes even before Western contact. In 1956, two years before the Seminole Tribe of Florida was established, representatives came to Governor Leroy Collins to make gifts of patchwork to him and his wife (Figure 1). Later clothing styles seem to be derived from these European prototypes. The leather hunting coat became the model for a "shirt" that was made of trade cloth, which was better suited for Florida's hot and humid climate. It generally was constructed of a patterned or stripped cotton cloth, such as calico, and muted colors. It had no pockets, rather items such as flint, powder, bullets, etc., were contained in pouches that were suspended from a belt.[7] The materials they used were cotton prints such as calico. After the Red Stick War of 1814, many Upper Creeks moved into Florida, joining the ranks of the Seminoles. The customs of the Upper Creeks became acculturated with Seminole styles.

The precise date of the beginning of patchwork is unknown. With the introduction of the sewing machine in the last decades of the nineteenth century, it can be inferred that the patchwork process soon followed. The main method of clothing decoration prior to the sewing machine was appliquéwork. The difference between the two is that patchwork is part of the structure of the garment, where appliquéwork is not integral to the structure. Around the turn of the century, men's shirts began to have integrated waistbands. These horizontal bands consisted of small vertical strips of cloth sewn together. Elaborate designs and color combinations began to appear more frequently on men's "big shirts" and women's capes in varying widths of horizontal bands (Figure 2).[8] Patchwork, as it is known today, evolved in the first quarter of this century.

In the 1930s, men had to look for work in towns and found they had to conform to a Western dress code. The bands of patchwork were made thinner, placed higher on the shirt and the skirt was shortened to make it easier to tuck into the trousers. This was called the transitional shirt. Eventually, the "true jacket" appeared, which stopped at the waist. The true jacket continues today as the most popular style of male patchwork clothing (Figure 3).[9] Women's capes were made longer to incorporate more rows of patchwork designs. The strips within the rows were set diagonally, giving a different orientation in which to experiment. By the mid 1950s, men wore mainly Western clothes, wearing patchwork only for ceremonies. Satin was used for the fancier outfits for specific occasions and cotton for everyday wear. The overall popularity of earlier designs waned because there was an interest in multi-colored designs. The number of colors in one row increased, and the new designs lent themselves to the use of more color.

During the 1960s, there were mostly variations of the popular diamond-shaped design. The bands of patchwork narrowed over time, to be taken to the extreme in the 1960s with the miniature "postage stamp work.[10] The 1970s brought a revival of interest in Native American heritage within popular culture. Seminoles took charge of the marketing of their skills and arts. Annual festivals and powwows inaugurated interactions between Native Americans and non-Native Americans, becoming especially important occasions for artists to showcase their work. Modern styles of clothing began to show patchwork designs in the 1980s. Form-fitting women's skirts and casual shirt and shorts sets also displayed patchwork.[11] The 1990s attitude of "anything goes" is exemplified in that patchwork can be found on almost anything that can be sold to the tourist market. For example, handbags, placemats, eyeglass cases, even stuffed animals are made of patchwork.

The essence of patchwork is the infinite number of combinations and recombinations of shapes and colors. Cloth, usually storebought, is cut into strips. It is sewn together into bands that are then cut into larger segments and assembled in a pattern. The larger bands are then sewn into plain fabric, which can be made into garments. The sewing machine makes the stitching easier, but it is still complex. The process of making patchwork begins with early childhood education in the basics of sewing. Diane Billie of Miami was only five years old when her mother and grandmother taught her how to sew.[12] This traditional education is important for all involved, not only for the child learning but also for the time spent with close female family members. The functional aspect of patchwork is still very important. As Betty Mae Jumper's mother and grandmother told her, "If you don't learn [how to sew], you'll have nothing to wear."[13] A Seminole girl just learning how to sew first masters the basic lines, cuts and attachments and then takes on more complex designs.[14]

Figure 2. Seminole Man's Big Shirt, c. 1925. This is a man's Big Shirt with patchwork bands. In the 1920s when patchwork began to be commonly employed, the men's clothing was covered with a series of stripes with few bands of patchwork. By the mid 1920s, designs were relatively restrained, with patchwork commonly limited to four bands, those on the sleeves being different from those on the balance of the garment. Length: 43 1/2 inches. Collection of Sara W. Reeves and I.S.K Reeves V. (Photo: Beverly Brosius)

The variety in patchwork is exponential in the different designs, and the different fabrics and types of clothing that can have patchwork. At the 16th Annual Native American Heritage Festival in Tallahassee on September 27 and 28, 1997, there were baseball caps, bonnets, aprons, vests, and children's clothing. The types of materials used varied dramatically, from rough cotton to satin to even lamé. There were several gold and silver lamé blouses, covered in sequins, with a band of patchwork cutting across the center. The children's clothing was the same style as the adult

Figure 3. True Jackets. This photo was taken at the 16th Annual Native American Heritage Festival, on September 28, 1997, in Tallahassee, Florida. (Photo: J. Teilhet-Fisk)

those colors that were desired by the Seminole. The early accounts indicate that when cotton cloth became available, around 1910, that it was in the colors of red, indigo, yellow and green.

These were colors that the Seminoles liked, respected, and had a rationale for wanting on their clothing for reasons that went beyond mere availability. Indigenous people rarely choose colors arbitrarily. Color and its significance has always been an important attribute of Southeastern culture, evolving from pre-contact society. Each color primarily had a rational basis for selection that had social, religious or other significance. For example, red signifies war in Creek culture, and the Red Creek clans produced the war chief; white being the color of peace, the White clans produced the advisors to the town chief.[18]

The issues dealing with symbolism in patchwork cause conflict. Calling a shape or design a "symbol" implies that there is mythology or folklore associated with it. And without the knowledge of this information, the design cannot be understood. More often than not, the designs are iconographic in nature. This means that they are recognizable as the objects for which they are named. However, because patchwork designs are all geometric in form,

apparel, only miniaturized (Figure 4). The range in price also varied. Jackets were the most varied in price, from one hundred fifty to two hundred and seventy five dollars for satin jackets. Even the children's clothing was priced up to seventy five dollars. For high quality in such a labor intensive process, the artist must ask for relatively adequate compensation.

Designs were named primarily for identification purposes. Women usually referred to designs by what they resembled in the physical world.[15] Patterns received names like "rain," "fire," and "storm" to identify them with powerful forces of nature. But there are more mundane references like the "telephone pole" and the "ladder" designs. Seminole women, as always, were looking at their surroundings and drawing from their environment for inspiration. Not only were designs complex in composition, but they were enlivened by the use of bright colors. The traditional colors, including bright reds, yellows and blues, create a vibrant, upbeat rhythm and energy. Bobby Henry of the Tampa Seminole Reservation referred to the sleeve of his shirt when asked about the most frequently used colors. "Black, white, red and yellow are the traditional colors most used today," Henry said. "They have been incorporated into the rainbow design, which is really popular now."[16] Henry, who is a medicine man, considers the rainbow array to be "healing colors." The colors within the patterns are harmonious, whether they are contrasting or monochromatic. With an infinite number of color combinations, designs can be manipulated to create the illusion of an area coming forward or receding from the viewer. Some parts may appear to be floating while others hide in the background.[17] The patchwork clothing in this exhibition exemplifies the Seminole ability to combine bright colors into vibrant patterns. In the Seminole Man's Big Shirt (Figure 2), the primary background color is green, with patchwork colors in red, white, purple, black, blue and orange. The cloth is used as a canvas made up of many harmonious colors. The Seminole Man's Jacket (Figure 5), has red, white, pink, black, blue and orange arranged brilliantly on a field of yellow.

The early Indian traders clearly were there to make a profit and learned, within a reasonable time period, to acquire for trade

Figure 4. Linda Storm, with her daughter, Tristan, from Tampa, Florida. This photo was taken at the 16th Annual Native American Heritage Festival on September 28, 1997, in Tallahassee, Florida. (Photo: Diana Roman)

they are more abstract than natural in appearance. For example, the "telephone pole" design is composed of a vertical line crossed by two horizontal lines, just like a telephone pole. The common explanation for the name of the "rain" and "storm" patterns is that the Seminole relied on nature to provide water for them to have a good harvest. It is unclear whether they meant for the pattern to abstractly symbolize the actual forces of rain or to just represent the shape of the lightning. The fire design, which is widely used, carries a sacred connotation as life force in the Seminole ethos. On certain coats, an intricate diamond-shaped pattern taken from the diamondback rattlesnake can be found. There are also more symbolic patterns. The cross is one of the most ancient symbols in the world. A cross with four arms of equal length possibly represents the four cardinal directions. The circle of life, an important idea to the Seminoles, is implied by the cross within a circle design. A possible explanation for "the man on horseback" design is more abstract, symbolizing power and authority, not just a man on horseback.[19]

The Seminoles have explanations for patchwork designs that academics tend to overlook. At the Tampa Powwow, displaying her book on folklore and some of her art, Betty Mae Jumper expressed her own theories about the function of patchwork patterns. When asked if her patchwork had any folklore behind it, she answered, "No, none of it means anything!"[20] She says that some patterns may have had meanings in the past, but the ones she chooses are purely for aesthetic reasons. Connie Gowen of Hollywood concurred, saying that in the old days, designs and colors had special and specific meanings, but now people just choose what colors and patterns are pleasing to them. She did mention an abstract name for the alternating "T" pattern, calling it "Disagree" (Figure 5).[21] Even though most people come up with ideas on their own, ideas and designs are still exchanged between artists at powwows and festivals.[22] No one owns or copyrights a specific pattern; the only restriction is personal ability.[23]

Opposition to the idea that each patchwork design carries with it a specific symbolic meaning and origin is prevalent among contemporary patchwork makers. Perhaps sacred knowledge is not to be given out to non-Seminoles who want to "authenticate" in their minds the designs by linking them to Seminole mythology and folklore. More likely because of forced acculturation, what

Figure 5. Seminole Man's Jacket, c. 1935. This is a man's jacket with an extended "skirt." The patchwork of this period has achieved greater complexity and illustrates positive/negative relationships. During the 1930s, designs were primarily arranged perpendicular to their borders and took the form of letters of the alphabet. The shortening of big shirts occurred during the 1930s to make the tucking of the bottom portion into pants easier. Length: 37 inches. Collection of Sara W. Reeves and I.S.K Reeves V. (Photo: Beverly Brosius)

was once sacred has become secularized or lost. Traditional knowledge has lost much of its influence today. As designs are passed around, they are invariably altered, resulting in a broader interpretation of the original. When traditions are modified, "meanings must be invented anew."[24] This act of reinvention becomes necessary for a culture to claim a recognizable image as an emblem. Consequently the meanings more recently given to designs could be attempts to "assert a new identity or reassert an old one."[25] Patchwork more than identifies the Seminoles; it represents their pride in their heritage. Women usually make patchwork. Although Betty Mae Jumper said that one of the best patchworkers she knows is a man who learned from his mother, for the most part it is a women's art form. There are many contributing factors as to why this is the case. Traditionally, men were out hunting or farming away from the home. Women were responsible for domestic affairs, including making clothing for the family. When there are children around, it is more convenient to have a craft that can easily be put down and picked up at will. As with most Native American cultures, there were traditional sex roles and division of labor. However, the twentieth century has turned many traditional roles on their heads. Both men and women can participate in making patchwork, but they must be taught, usually from their mother or grandmother. It is rare for a man to be the instructor. Bobby Henry said that he would not know where to begin, nor would he attempt to make patchwork, even though his wife and daughter do. According to Betty Mae Jumper, "Women work independently, but in groups, enjoying small talk and gossip."[26] Women have always exchanged ideas and consider copying a form of flattery. In keeping with oral tradition, women do not write down, draw or document their innovations; rather they remember them and keep samples.[27]

When Connie Gowen was a little girl, her mother, Jane Tiger Motlow, taught her how to sew (Figure 6). She said, with pride, that her mother used to make the turbans for the "Crowning of the Chief" ceremony at the Florida State University's Homecoming.[28] Since her mother passed away, Gowen has taken over her turban making responsibilities. She shows her own work at festivals and powwows, and museums ask her to help set up exhibits. She makes shirts, skirts, potholders, dolls, beadwork, wall-hangings, and more. Usually, when she shows at a festival, she demon-

Figure 6. Connie Gowen of Hollywood, Florida. This photo was taken at the 16th Annual Native American Heritage Festival in Tallahassee, Florida, on September 28, 1997. (Photo: Diana Roman)

strates patchwork. She says there are trends within the Seminole artistic community. Currently, what are known as "the fire colors" are popular; white, black, red, and yellow. This is convenient for her commissions from Florida State University fans because, not coincidentally, their school colors are garnet and gold, shades of red and yellow.

Like the others, Diane Billie was quite young when her mother and grandmother taught her how to sew. When asked about the patterns on her clothing, she said that the designs were independent creations with no meanings at all. Her mother did not teach her how to do specific patterns; she just observed, copied what she liked, and made up some of her own. Even some of the more "traditional" patterns that once carried meanings do not, currently. When she comes to the festivals, she only brings a few of her own creations to sell. Mostly she sells for other people. Billie said that now the popular design is "rainbow colors," which can be seen in much of the clothing at the Heritage Festival.[29]

Powwows, festivals and art shows have made the availability of Seminole designs to non-Indians widespread. Some Seminoles think it is okay for others to study patchwork, but they should not create it. They consider patchwork to be a cultural copyright of the Seminoles.[30] However, Jumper believes that those who are interested should be able to try it. She sells how-to books and hands out personal samples for construction study. Ironically, tourism has played an important role in providing Seminoles with economic opportunity. Yet, there is a price that both sides pay for the commercialization of traditional arts. In the early twentieth century, for the Seminoles, it was their "authenticity" that was sold by marketing agents in the form of commercial Seminole camps. These places were set up by businessmen, putting the lifestyles of the inhabitants on display. Tourists watched Seminoles create arts and crafts which were then sold to them as souvenirs.[31]

Today, the Seminoles are in control of their own economic activities. Powwows, art shows, and heritage festivals provide places for exchanging ideas and for selling their creations. The intricate designs of patchwork are not confined to clothing. At the Seminole Cultural Center in Tampa, patchwork adorns baseball caps, oven mitts, blankets, dolls and even key chains. In a fashion show held in January of 1993, at an annual powwow, patchwork decorated denim jackets and mini-skirts. Ready-made cloth with designs already printed on it is incorporated into the designs of the patchwork, like the calico of the 1800s. Cartoon characters can be found in the background cloth of children's clothes today.

Women are able to support themselves financially with the arts that they sell. Connie Gowen's year is full of festivals, powwows and art shows that take her all around the state of Florida, sometimes into southern Georgia. Orders for custom-made objects that she takes now will not be filled for up to six months because of her full schedule. She recently made a patchwork wall hanging for her son's office, which has led to requests for many more wall hangings.[32] Tourists want innovation, but artists are constantly creating new styles for themselves as well as the rapidly-changing world. This is a natural process of co-evolution between traditions and trends that keep customs alive.

The debate over when patchwork came into being and its symbolic nature reflects the Western academic need for strictly-defined terms and boundaries. To own the intangible, scholars have always tried to capture the "facts" passed down through oral traditions. Whether these "facts" are actual is not the point of a cultural narrative. Cultural meanings are transitory, constantly redefined to account for new experiences and information. Patchwork continues to be created by the Seminoles, because of the Seminoles. If there were no tourists, they would probably still make it for themselves as they did a hundred years ago. In the modern world, patchwork has become almost synonymous with Seminole identity.

1 David M. Blackard, *Patchwork and Palmettos* (Fort Lauderdale: Fort Lauderdale Historical Society, 1990) 9.

2 James A. Maxwell, *America's Fascinating Indian Heritage* (New York: Reader's Digest, 1978) 105.

3 Blackard 10.

4 Blackard 11. Technically, the Seminoles never surrendered to the US government.

5 Blackard 12.

6 Blackard 16.

7 Keith Reeves, personal communication, November 17, 1997.

8 Blackard 45-46. Seminole "big shirts" have a loose-fitting skirt, body and sleeves which were gathered and attached to a tighter fitting waistband, yoke and cuffs.

9 True Jackets for sale at the 16th Annual Native American Festival on September 28, 1997 in Tallahassee, Florida.

10 Blackard 48.

11 Dorothy Downs, *Art of the Florida Seminole and Miccosukee Indians* (Gainesville: U of Florida P, 1989) 114.

12 Diane Billie, personal communication to Ashley Remer, Fall 1997.

13 Betty Mae Jumper, personal communication to Page-Leiberman, Spring 1997.

14 Downs 98.

15 Downs 90.

16 Bobby Henry, personal communication to Page-Leiberman, Spring 1997.

17 Beverly Rush and Lassie Whitman, *The Complete Book of Seminole Patchwork* (Seattle: Madrona Publishers, 1982) 8.

18 Keith Reeves, personal communication, November 17, 1997. (Special thanks to Keith Reeves for his help in providing additional information.)

19 Rush 26.

20 Betty Mae Jumper, personal communication to Page-Leiberman, Spring 1997.

21 Connie Gowan, personal communication to Ashley Remer, 1997.

22 Connie Gowan, personal communication to Ashley Remer, 1997.

23 Merwyn Garbarino, *The Seminole* (Chicago: University of Illinois, Chelsea House Publishers, 1989) 37.

24 Sidney Littlefield Kasfir, "African Art and Authenticity: A Text with a Shadow." *African Arts* 25 (1992) 47.

25 Nelson H. H. Graburn, *Ethnic and Tourist Arts* (Berkeley: U of California P, 1976) 32.

26 Betty Mae Jumper, personal communication to Page-Leiberman, Spring 1997.

27 Downs 116.

28 Connie Gowan, personal communication to Ashley Remer, 1997.

29 Diane Billie, personal communication to Ashley Remer, Fall 1997.

30 Bobby Henry, personal communication to Page-Leiberman, Spring 1997.

31 Jay Mechling, "Florida Seminoles and the Last Frontier." *Dressing in Feathers* (Colorado: Westview Press Inc. 1996) 149-155.

32 Connie Gowan, personal communication to Ashley Remer, 1997.

Navajo / Diné Pictorial Weaving

Rebecca McNeil

Navajo weaving is a means of artistic expression in a medium which has been employed by the Navajo—or Diné people—for over 300 years. Originally, weavings served primarily utilitarian purposes. Among other uses, they were worn as clothing, served as saddle blankets, and were used as wall coverings. Contemporary weavings, especially pictorials, have entered a new realm where they seem most appropriate hung on walls as prestigious art objects, usually the walls of museums or of collectors rather than those of the weavers. Navajo weavings are still commonly referred to as "rugs," a term left over from the late nineteenth century when weavers thickened their weavings to accommodate the demands of trading posts for floor rugs. However, a contemporary weaver, Rena Mountain, told me she always puts borders around her work because they are pictures, and that she could not imagine anyone putting her weavings on a floor.[1]

Figure 1. Marie Nez in her sister's home in Many Farms, Arizona. (Photo: Rebecca McNeil)

The designs on both pictorial and geometric weavings are motifs which represent a variety of subject matters. They range in size from mere inches in width and height to some which are large enough to cover an entire wall. One weaver commented that a large rug can take her up to ten months to make.[2] "Pictorials" are distinguishable from geometric weavings in that they include or are dominated by naturalistic representations. According to Charlene Cerny, in 1976 there was about one pictorial design made for every ninety-nine geometric weavings.[3] I could not help noticing during a visit to numerous Arizona trading posts in August of 1997 that the number of pictorials being produced seems to have increased significantly. It would seem logical that this increase is a response to the growing popularity of pictorials, although Marie Nez, a weaver from Many

Figure 2. Rena Mountain seated at her loom. (Photo: Rebecca McNeil)

Farms, Arizona, in Chinle, explained that the market is becoming flooded, making it difficult to sell any of her work (Figure 1). This has been especially detrimental to her because weaving is her only source of income.[4]

On the other hand, Rena Mountain, a prolific weaver who lives in Cedar Ridge near the Grand Canyon area, has little diffi-culty selling her rugs (Figure 2). In fact, she receives requests for specific designs in advance which are essentially sold before they are even finished.[5] It is interesting that her reputation was founded on awards she has received for weaving almost all geometric designs except for one Yei rug (a design that is discussed later in this paper). However, one of the designs which she is commissioned to weave most often is the "Tree of Life" pictorial. "Tree of Life" rugs usually have either a tree or cornstalk which runs the length of the weaving, surrounded by birds (Figure 3).

The dichotomy between these two weavers' successes could seem, at first, to be a reflection of the greater tourist industry in the Grand Canyon area. Rena Mountain is most closely associated with trader Bill Malone of Hubbell Trading Post near Chinle. Because Rena Mountain is so busy weaving requested designs, she never has the opportunity to experiment with other types of pictorials.[6] Maria Nez, on the other hand, weaves only designs which come from her imagination, and then seeks out buyers.[7] Among her favorite designs are rodeos, Navajo scenescapes, and dance ceremonies.

Collaboration between traders and weavers has been an issue since the genesis of trading posts and is not always necessary for successful sales. An interesting, contemporary example of this trader / weaver dynamic is the relationship between Florence Riggs (daughter of Louise Nez whose work is exhibited here) and Bill Foutz of Shiprock Trading Post. Riggs was quoted in *Navajo Folk Art* as saying, "The colors come to me as I go along. I use colors that seem right. Bill Foutz likes bright colors but he doesn't like yellow. Too bad! I do!"[8] Scholars such as Amsden and James have questioned the "authenticity" of pictorials as opposed to geometric weavings, arguing that they are not a "traditional" Navajo art form.[9] Cerny raised an important point in stating that although the subject matter of pictorials may often reflect the colonial or post-colonial environment, "the designs themselves reflect the sensibilities of the individual weavers who produced them."[10]

The Origins and Development of Navajo / Diné Weaving

The route by which the Navajo (in their native tongue, *nihokáá dine'é* or just *dine*) traveled to the Southwest and the date when they arrived there are still being disputed by scholars.[11] According to Navajo myth, they entered this world through the sacred mountains.[12] Today, many Navajo live on the reservation spanning from the northeastern corner of Arizona and northwestern corner of New Mexico to the southeastern corner of Utah.[13] This Athapaskan-speaking group (linguistically and culturally related to the Apache) were once primarily hunters and gatherers. However, the Pueblo peoples of New Mexico are thought to have taught the Navajo farming and later, perhaps, some stock-raising techniques.[14] It is possible that the Pueblo people taught the Navajo to weave prior to 1680 (the year of the Pueblo Revolt) when some moved in with the Navajos to avoid Spanish retribution.[15]

If, in fact, the Navajo were taught weaving by the Pueblo people, then an interesting transition occurred.[16] Pueblo weavers were almost entirely men while Navajo weavers are almost entirely women.[17] That would imply that Pueblo men taught the Navajo women to weave, but to cross sex lines in art is rare. It may be that the Zuni Pueblo, where both sexes weave, were also responsible for teaching the Navajo.[18] According to Navajo legend, Spider Woman taught the Navajo to weave and Spider Man told them how to construct their looms. The art of weaving was then passed on from mother to daughter.[19]

The Navajo use a portable, vertical loom and employ a type of weaving known as the plain-weave tapestry process.[20] The design emerges from the bottom of the loom to the top as wefts (horizontal strings) are woven into the warps (the vertical strings).[21] In geometric weavings there may be a small diagonal line in a section of color. This technique is known as a "lazy line" and is mostly used by the Navajo. Lazy lines are mainly for convenience on very large weavings where the women may work small sections before moving to another area of the rug. (An example of a lazy line may be seen in the Yei rug from this exhibition: Figure 4.) On a pictorial, there are no lazy lines because the break occurs where the colors change, forming the shapes necessary for the overall design.[22] The plain-weave tapestry process has been compared to the process of creating a painting.[23]

Navajo weaving may be divided into four major periods: The Classic Period, 1650 to 1865; the Transition Period, 1865 to 1895; the Rug Period, 1895 to around 1950, and The Recent Period, 1950 to the present.[24] During the Classic Period the Navajo wove wool and cotton blankets with banded, geometric designs.[25] These weavings

Figure 3. Rena Mountain and Bill Malone with one of her award-winning "Tree of Life" rugs. Photo courtesy of Rena Mountain.

Figure 4. Yei Rug: Corn with Holy People, 38 x 52.5 inches, Private Collection, Los Alamos, New Mexico. (Photo: J. Teilhet-Fisk)

were mainly used as saddle blankets and garments by both sexes.[26] One of the most popular and common blanket types from this period is known as the chief's blanket. The term "chief" is probably indicative of the Plains people who could afford this type of blanket since the Navajo did not have chiefs.[27] Another uniquely Navajo weaving from this period is known as a serape, often with triangle and diamond shapes. A limited number of natural dyes were used until the five-year captivity of the Navajo (1863 to 1868) at Fort Sumner, where the Transition Period began.

During this period, weavers were supplied with commercial yarns of wool and cotton in a larger variety of natural and aniline dyes.[28] In 1822 the Santa Fe Trail opened, encouraging the sale and trade of Navajo goods with an outside market.[29] Weavers were exposed to new designs such as the Mexican Saltillos. By the 1870s, horizontal bands became increasingly vertical and began to include zigzags and jagged diamond motifs.[30] Such motifs contributed to the rise of "eyedazzler" blankets made from Germantown yarn.[31] Weavers were encouraged by traders to appeal to the outside market not only in their choice of designs, but in the type of weaving.[32]

The very end of the nineteenth century and first half of the twentieth century marked an increasingly commercial orientation for weavers. As demands for floor rugs grew, weavers responded with thicker weavings suitable for such use.[33] During this period, weaving became almost exclusively for outside sale. Regional styles began to develop which were sometimes associated with traders or trading posts in collaboration with the weavers.

The first pictorials are often associated with the arrival of the Santa Fe railroad in 1882.[34] Weavers depicted trains and buildings, often in a horizontal banding design, and also included some plants and animals into their geometric weavings.[35] Aboard the trains which came through Navajo land were varieties of yarns as well as tourists who purchased rugs. More importantly, the trains symbolize the changing Navajo world in greater contact with the rest of the country.

The earliest-known Navajo pictorial weaving was taken from the body of a Cheyenne chief following the Sand Creek Massacre

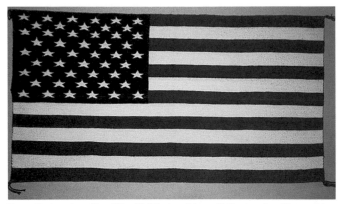

Figure 5. *American Flag*, 27 x 48.5 inches, Private Collection, Los Alamos, New Mexico. (Photo: J. Teilhet-Fisk)

of November 27, 1868, in Colorado.[36] The design was predominantly geometric except for four tiny ducks.[37] In ensuing years, imagery of the Navajos' surrounding environment eventually came to dominate the design space in a seemingly random placement; weavers thus abandoned the strict symmetry of geometric weavings. Pictorial weavings are thought to be the first naturalistic art form of the Navajo.[38] Early traders did not encourage naturalistic pictorials and they rarely included them in the catalogues. When they were sold they were labeled "curiosity pieces."[39] It is perplexing that weavers persisted in creating pictorials when the traders did not originally encourage it. The following examples of pictorials drawn from the exhibition provide a glimpse of the genre through popular as well as unique imageries.

Corn with Holy People

One form of pictorial weaving did meet with some success in the trading posts. These pictorials are generally known as Yei or Yeibichai rugs (Figure 4). *Yei* (Yé'ii) is the term referring to supernaturals or Holy People while *Yeibichais* refers to Navajo dancers portraying Holy People.[40] Although this type of rug did not gain popularity until about the beginning of the twentieth century, they first appeared in the late 1880s.[41] The demand for Yei and Yeibichai rugs was due in part to the belief that they held ceremonial and religious significance. As Parezo notes:

> The idea that these were traditional prayer rugs was probably the fabrication of a trader who was attempting to increase their value and hence increase sales, for it was evident that Anglo customers would pay more for a rug or object which is felt to be religious or symbolic.[42]

Yeis are based on sacred sandpaintings also known as drypaintings. Drypaintings, or *'ikááh*, are created as part of a sacred curing ceremony. If they are created properly, they are said to be representations of supernatural beings.[43] The drypaintings are thought of as powerful, potentially dangerous and intended as strictly impermanent ritual constructions. For that reason, the representation of a drypainting on a rug was controversial and remained so despite the fact that weavers would change the designs slightly and use colors uncharacteristic of the originals.[44]

The three figures represented in the anonymous artist's Yei are female and may be identified as such by their square face masks. Males are depicted with round masks that cover the entire head.[45] There are two corn plants flanking the central figure that allude to the use of corn in Navajo ceremonies.[46] Corn is sacred to the Navajo. The group is protected from negative forces by an elongated figure known as the Rainbow Guardian seen stretching to frame three sides.

American Flag

American Flag rugs appeared as early as the 1870s and are among the first asymmetrical weavings done by the Navajo (Figure 5).[47] The American Flag design is not, according to the definition, technically a pictorial, nor can it be classified as a Navajo geometric design. However, the design itself is not too removed from the chief blankets of the Classic Period. Although the example in this exhibition (also by an anonymous artist) has an accurate number of 50 stars and 13 stripes, weavers often take liberties in altering them to meet different sizes and aesthetic preferences, a practice they established long before Jasper Johns.[48]

As Toby Herbst and Joel Kopp have noted, Native American use of a symbol which signified an oppressive government "has always seemed curious and contradictory."[49] It was clear to Native Americans that the flag had protective powers for those who displayed it. The flag was seen marking military forts, being carried into battle, and later flown over schools.[50] It is not unusual that the Navajo would want to appropriate such a protective symbol, especially one which is banded with stripes of red, a color which signifies protection in their world view.[51] According to Reichard, "white garments are indicative of purification, readiness to undertake contact with divinity," and blue represents "the fructifying power of the earth."[52] With the establishment of trading posts, the flag weavings would have become an appealing item for sale to tourists.

Figure 6. Pictorial Tapestry, 1960, length 153 cm. Courtesy of the School of American Research, Santa Fe, New Mexico. (Photo © School of American Research)

Navajo Scenescape

Navajo scenescapes encompass a diverse array of objects seen in Navajo daily life (Figure 6). Commonly depicted elements are rock formations, trees, automobiles, clouds, animals such as sheep, horses and cattle, buildings, and even the weavers themselves. In this example, the weaver has included elements from both the "old" and "new" worlds. At the bottom of the picture plane is a truck and a car which have come to replace the horse or donkey as pictured just above them. The sheep are especially important to the Navajo because they provide economic security and are considered to be family. They also provide the wool with which the rugs are woven. In the middle ground there is a loom with a pictorial weaving in progress. The design appears to be rock formations cleverly mirroring those in the background of the overall rug. While artists frequently include a rug within their scenescapes, it is unusual for it to be a pictorial design. An important element in this weaving which transcends the boundaries of the "old" and "new" worlds is the *hogan* pictured in the background. A *hogan* is a Navajo dwelling and ceremonial space. Because of its ceremonial significance, even families who live in European style homes have a *hogan*.[53]

Home Sweet Home, Country Road

This weaving presents a humorous play on the American saying "Home Sweet Home" and the John Denver song "Take Me Home, Country Road" (Figure 7). It is not unusual to find words in English on Navajo weavings because they are often trying to appeal to an English-speaking market. The anonymous weaver has taken liberties with the colors of the cows and houses, making this piece a colorful and inviting scene. It is typical of what one might see driving through the reservation where the roads are often only two lanes, and there are *hogans* right next to European style homes with livestock grazing nearby.

There is one element which unifies most, if not all, of the objects represented in these three scenescapes: the central role of women in the organization of property-owning and residential groups within traditional Navajo society. The land on which their homes are built is provided by the women's families. The women manage the *hogans*. Livestock, including sheep, whether "owned" by men or women collectively belong to larger kinship groups of families linked together through the female line in the complicated property rights and inheritance system of Navajo society.

Women own the blankets which they weave and all of the profits from their sales.[54] These rugs are not only a glimpse of the Navajo home front, but of those things which Navajo women may call their own.

Dinosaur Rug by Louise Nez

Figure 8, a fanciful dinosaur scene woven in 1991 by Louise Nez depicts a prehistoric landscape with active volcanoes in the background. Louise Nez was the first to weave a dinosaur scene and her depiction predates *Jurassic Park*.[55] Other weavers, among them her daughter, Florence Riggs, have also woven dinosaur scenes which have become a novelty in light of the recent motion picture. The design was originally inspired by a coloring book which belonged to Louise's grandson.[56] Although far removed from any "traditional" or Classic style weaving, this work has a tripartite division created by the volcanoes in the background. The number three is also repeated in a set of rock formations in the middle ground. It is possible that a tripartite organization is an aesthetic from when weavings were worn on the body. The weaver would have had in mind what would appear on the back as well as on each side.

This scene may seem to be simply a fanciful representation of a prehistoric landscape, but it also recalls a Navajo myth concerning the development of this world. There are four sacred mountains that define the boundaries of Navajo land, from which emerged the first humans.[57] Twin sons were born to a woman who lived in the mountains. Their destiny was to conquer the monsters below, making the land inhabitable for humans. As the monsters were destroyed, their blood flowed out as lava and became landmarks which are still identifiable today, like Shiprock. The impact of their fall caused earthquakes and the earth was left in an unstable state. Whenever a victory is achieved over an enemy, prayers and offerings should be made to the earth.[58]

Navajo pictorial weavings are creative and often humorous representations of an unlimited variety of subject matters. Some provide a glimpse into the Navajo world, depicting scenes from the Navajo homefront and excerpts of daily life. The scenes are

Figure 7. *Home Sweet Home, Country Road,* 20.5 x 31.25 inches. Private Collection, Los Alamos, New Mexico. (Photo: J. Teilhet-Fisk.)

Figure 8. *Dinosaur Rug* by Louise Nez, 43 x 49 inches. Courtesy of the Museum of Northern Arizona, Flagstaff, E9622.

often playful as in the *Home Sweet Home* rug, but also itemize those things most closely associated with women. Other imagery, such as the *Dinosaur* rug, appear to be multilayered, colorful and fantastic while recalling Navajo mythology. For the Navajo, weaving is an old tradition which is not confined to any canon. Pictorial weavings are a testament to weavers' persistence in pursuing new ideas and pushing the limits of creativity.

1   Personal communication August 10, 1997.

2   Personal communication with Rena Mountain, August 10, 1997.

3   Charlene Cerny, "Navajo Pictorial Weaving," *American Indian Art Magazine* 2.1 (1976): 46.

4   Personal communication August 8, 1997.

5   Personal communication August 10, 1997.

6   Personal communication August 10, 1997.

7   Personal communication August 8, 1997.

8   Chuck and Jan Rosenak, *The People Speak: Navajo Folk Art* (Flagstaff, AZ: Northland Publishing Co., 1994) 142.

9   Susan Brown McGreevy, "The Image Weavers: Contemporary Navajo Pictorial Textiles," *American Indian Art Magazine* 19.4 (1994): 51. The definition of the word "authentic" in reference to art, specifically the "tribal arts" is, in and of itself, a debated issue. Sidney Littlefield Kasfir, in "African Art and Authenticity: A Text within a Shadow" has effectively refuted the fallacy that "authentic" art is somehow contingent upon its production in a "traditional society." Here, "traditional society" means pre-colonial and untouched by foreign patrons, an idea which assumes a "social-evolutionary notion of disappearing cultures." Kasfir, *African Arts* 25 (April 1992): 42.

10 Cerny 49.

11 Gary Witherspoon, *Language and Art in the Navajo Universe* (Ann Arbor: U of Michigan P, 1977) 35; David M. Brugge, "Navajo Prehistory and History to 1850," *Handbook of the North American Indians Southeast* 10 (1983): 489.

12 Gladys A. Reichard, *Navajo Religion* (Arizona: U of Arizona P, 1983) 18.

13 The Navajo originally settled in northwestern New Mexico. Over time, they migrated west into the Arizona region, but were relocated during the Long Walk to Fort Sumner at Bosque Redondo in east-central New Mexico in 1864. It was not until June of 1868 that they were allowed to return to Arizona. (Brugge 496, 512, 520.)

14 Marian E. Rodee, *One Hundred Years of Navajo Rugs* (Albuquerque: U of New Mexico P, 1995) 3.

15 Kate Peck Kent, *Navajo Weaving: Three Centuries of Change* (Santa Fe: School of American Research Press, 1985) 8.

16 The Pueblo tribes include the Hopi, Zuni, Acoma, Laguna, Piro, Tompiro, Northern and Southern Tiwa, Tano, Pecos, and Jemez.

17 Kent 8.

18 Kent 8.

19 Anthony Berlant and Mary Hunt Kahlenberg, *Walk in Beauty: The Navajo and Their Blankets* (Boston: New York Graphic Society, 1977) 39, 41.

20 Originally, the Navajos employed the Wide Loom and weaving techniques taught to them by the Pueblos. Kent 24-27.

21 Charles Avery Amsden, *Navajo Weaving, Its Technique and History* (Albuquerque: U of New Mexico P, 1949) 37-45.

22 Kent 27.

23 McGreevy 53.

24 Ann Lane Hedlund, *Reflections of the Weaver's World* (Denver: Denver Art Museum, 1992) 17.

25 Hedlund 17.

26 Rodee, *One Hundred Years* 12.

27 Rodee, *One Hundred Years* 12.

28 Kent 11.

29 Marian Rodee, *Old Navajo Rugs: Their Development from 1900 to 1940* (Albuquerque: U of New Mexico P, 1981) 2.

30 Hedlund 18.

31 Rodee, *One Hundred Years* 19.

32 Hedlund 18; Nancy J. Blomberg, *Navajo Textiles* (Tucson: U of Arizona P, 1988) 4.

33 Hedlund 18.

34 Brugge 522.

35 Blomberg 5.

36 Cerny 49.

37 Cerny 49.

38 Tyrone Campbell, Joel Kopp, and Kate Kopp, *Navajo Pictorial Weaving 1880-1950: Folk Art Images of Native Americans* (New York: Dutton Studio Books, 1991) 10:199.

39 Campbell 10.

40 Campbell 85.

41 Campbell 85.

42 Nancy J. Parezo, *Navajo Sandpainting: From Religious Act to Commercial Art* (Tucson: U of Arizona P, 1983) 42.

43 Parezo 1.

44 Campbell 85; Parezo 45.

45 Campbell 85.

46 Campbell 86.

47 Campbell 71.

48 Campbell 71.

49 Toby Herbst and Joel Kopp, *The Flag in American Indian Art* (Los Angeles: Perpetua Press, 1993) 15.

50 Herbst 16-17.

51 According to Reichard, red may also signify blood, flesh, danger, war, and sorcery. Reichard 197-200.

52 These are among the many color symbolisms about which Reichard gives a lengthy description, 180-203. Reichard 188, 192.

53 Clyde Kluckhohn and Dorothea Leighton, *The Navajo* (Cambridge: Harvard UP, 1974) 88.

54 Raymond Friday Locke, *The Book of the Navajo* (Los Angeles: Mankind Publishing Co., 1976) 17.

55 McGreevy 54.

56 McGreevy 54.

57 Reichard 20.

58 Reichard 21-22.

"Continuity and Change"—the Deer Motif within the Easel Painting Tradition of the Southwest

Faye Elizabeth Hunt

The deer is an important Native American symbol found in the easel paintings of the Southwest and should be evaluated as an image that represents both "continuity and change."[1] In order to understand the extent to which the deer, like the buffalo, bear, and eagle, has been a major figure in the historic struggle between traditional and modern subject matter and Native American style, the following categories will be discussed: early Native American painting traditions; the Modern School of American Indian Painting, which traces the development of easel painting in the Southwest and introduces the deer motif; the establishment of the Studio of the Santa Fe Indian School, which discusses the institutionalization of easel painting and elaborates upon the deer motif; and the "Bambi School of Native American Art," which pertains to how the deer made so popular by the Walt Disney studio in the late 1930s may have possibly been invented by Native American artists before Disney's animated film *Bambi* was ever conceived.[2]

Early Native American Painting Traditions

The concept of American Indians possessing a painting tradition all their own is not a "contemporary" development. From the ancient Anasazi of the Southwest to the nineteenth century, Native American painting has appeared on practically every medium: wood, rock, hides, baskets, pottery, and kiva walls. The Mimbres artists of the Mogollon district achieved unique perfection in ceramic painting, which incorporated both figurative and geometric elements.[3] Throughout the Pueblos of the Southwest, the mural form was developed by way of pictographs, both painted and pecked. In these murals figurative imagery predominated, although ranging from significant abstraction to comparative naturalism.[4]

The forerunners of the modern movement of Native American painting got their start in the Great Plains region.[5] Prior to Euroamerican contact, nearly every buffalo-hide tepee bore vivid figures of horses and men in battles; women painted geometric designs on household goods and clothes; and warriors painted their visions on shields as a form of recordskeeping.[6] The greater naturalism found in Plains painting after 1840 coincides with direct contact between Plains peoples and Euroamericans in Washington, D.C., where several prominent Plains warriors and leaders had their portraits painted as well as Euroamerican artists' visits to the Plains tribes.[7] By 1880, the buffalo had been almost completely exterminated; military conquest saw the Plains groups being placed on reservations; and the production of painting de-

creased considerably.[8] However, painting did find new outlets in foreign media: during this transition from the nineteenth to the twentieth century, Native American artists were being exposed to European-introduced materials such as ledger paper, crayons, pencils, ink, watercolor, canvas, and muslin, often obtained from proprietors of trading posts, schools, and prisons.[9] Although not recognized as such, the painting done in non-Native media in the closing decades of the Plains era was a precursor of the "Kiowa Five" and program at Bacone College, Oklahoma. The ancient designs in kivas, and in rock art are also precursors of the Modern School of American Indian Painting, the apellation of Dorothy Dunn.[10]

The Modern School of American Indian Painting

The beginnings of the Modern School are not definite, but one can speculate that it formally began in the early years of the 1900s, spanning from 1910 and continuing throughout the Santa Fe Indian School years, finally ending in 1962, at which point the Contemporary Indian Art Movement evolved. The artists of this newly-developed Modern School "taught themselves to paint new subjects in new media for a new audience, using what they could from older traditions of both the Pueblo and the Euroamerican worlds."[11] Before the School was initially formed through the works of its "founder" Crescencio Martínez (Ta'e, San Ildefonso, 1879-1918), the Pueblo Indians and the Navajo of the Southwest were observed using paper and experimenting with color around the turn-of-the-century. Pueblo works are mentioned as early as 1881, and three Navajo / Diné artists, Choh (c. 1856-unknown), Apie Begay, and Big Lefthanded (Klah Tso), were recorded in the late 1880s / early 1900s.[12] The fact that most of the work was sporadic and created with perishable material (i.e. wrapping paper and cardboard box ends) resulted in its being overlooked by the Euroamerican art world.[13] Esther Hoyt, a U.S. Indian Service teacher at San Ildefonso Pueblo Day School, distributed watercolor paints and paper to her pupils in 1900, encouraging her students to make pictures of Pueblo ceremonial dances.[14] Despite these diverse precursors of the Modern School, its official development is brought into focus with the works of Crescencio Martínez of San Ildefonso Pueblo.

As early as 1910, Dr. Edgar L. Hewett had given paper and watercolors to Crescencio Martínez.[15] By 1914, Martínez was collaborating with his wife, Maximiliana Martínez, who made ceremonial ollas while he painted them. In 1917 he was working intermittently for Dr. Hewett, then Director of the School of American Research. Hewett commissioned Martínez to produce 23 ceremonial watercolor paintings which illustrated the summer and winter moieties of San Ildefonso Pueblo, and these paintings were considered to be the official beginnings of the Modern School.[16] Martínez was a self-taught artist who was followed by several prominent artists also originating from San Ildefonso Pueblo. They were the leaders in the development of this new painting tradition and were part of what has been alternately termed the "San Ildefonso School:" Julián Martínez (Pocano, 1897-1943), Tonita Peña (Quah Ah, 1893-1949), Romando Vigil (Tse Ye Mu, 1902-1978), Oqwa Pi (Abel Sánchez, 1899-1971), and Awa Tsireh (Alfonso Roybal, 1898-1955).[17] There were also artists outside of San Ildefonso Pueblo who contributed to the Modern School, particularly Velino Shije Herrera (Ma Pe Wi, Zía Pueblo, 1902-1973).

Watercolor was the main medium used for the production of paintings and continued to be used throughout the duration of the School. The pigment was both transparent and opaque, and though tempera, nearest the consistency of native earth tones, was favored, transparent paints seem to have been the most available.[18] In addition to the convenience of commercially-produced watercolors, it was also a medium which complimented Native American painting. The School's compositional focus was on the formal arrangements of objects (i.e. the ceremonial dances dictating the composition) rather than modeling, foreshortening, or perspective.[19] Contour lines ranging from pencil-gray to dead black were employed, and motifs taken over from pottery accompanied some of the paintings (such as terraced and semicircular cloud

Figure 1. Awa Tsireh (Alfonso Roybal), *Deer Dance*, 1918-1919, 28 x 10 1/2 inches. Courtesy of the School of American Research. (Photo © School of American Research)

Figure 2. San Ildefonso Deer Dance, January 1985. (Photo: J. Teilhet-Fisk)

motifs, bird figures, abstract plant forms, and rainbow bands).[20] The depicted figures were flat, straightforward, and were usually created with unmodelled watercolor, which gave them a sense of simplicity of representation.

The establishment of easel painting was mainly born out of access to commercial materials and a Euroamerican art-buying public willing to commission paintings.[21] For example, Crescencio Martínez initially began his easel painting career because Dr. Hewett provided him with materials and because the School of American Research of Santa Fe commissioned the works. Encouragement of secular painting by Native Americans occurred only in the Santa Fe region, probably because influential Euroamericans had already been instrumental in stimulating a craft revival in that

area with pottery.[22] Inevitably Native American paintings were produced for an outside market. However, the issue of artist-desire is also a factor. Though the works were commissioned or purchased in the main by Euroamericans, Native Americans, from an indigenous aesthetic, often chose their own elements.

It was during the Modern School that the deer motif emerged in the easel painting tradition of the Southwest, later gathering momentum in the Studio of the Santa Fe Indian School. The deer motif, originally found on the walls of sacred kivas and ceremonial ollas (especially from Zuni and San Ildefonso Pueblo), was now being depicted in easel paintings in two main forms: deer represented in nature and deer personified by men in the Deer Dance ceremonies (Figure 1).[23]

The depiction of deer from the pre-contact era to the present, is an indication of the respect that Native Americans have toward these game animals which once contributed substantially to subsistence in the Southwest. Deer served as a major supply of protein for Native Americans; deer were easily harvested during periods when large herds moved between higher and lower elevations. It is noted that around 1840, the mountains were well-stocked with deer during the spring and especially the fall.[24] The hunting of deer can be considered a religious activity as illustrated by Joe Hilario Herrera (See Ru, Cochití Pueblo, 1923-):

When we go hunting...as we reach the mountain, and before we actually hunt, we meditate and throw corn meal to the deer. We say to them, 'Excuse me, my brother, I have come for you, to take you home. I apologize that I must slay you. Forgive me. I need you'...This is because we do not hunt the wild animals for sport as is done by other people. We use every part of the deer.[25] (Figure 2)

According to Herrera, the Deer Dance indicates that "the deer are part of the universe, that they are part of us, that we are in harmony with that deer, and that we convey a lot of respect during the time of the hunting season..."[26] The Deer Dance is a human petition for bountiful wildlife which involves a human deer figure, or dancer, with forces-of-nature symbols on his personal raiment:

Here, the figure wears the actual head of a deer, with feathers attached to the tips of the antlers. Turkey feathers radiate over the back. The dancer's face is painted black and the hands white. He wears a white shirt, openwork leggings (usually crocheted of cotton), and moccasins with pieces of skunk fur at the heels. His kilt is black, decorated with symbols, and wrapped around his waist are a string of bells and a rain sash, its long fringe hanging down symbolizing streaks of falling rain. . .he leans on two foreleg sticks. As he walks, he lifts his legs high in the graceful movements of the deer.[27] (Figure 3)

Crescencio Martínez is best known for his watercolor paintings of the "first version" of the deer motif, personifications of the Deer Dance by human impersonators.[28] In *Deer Dancer* (c. 1918), Martínez depicts a man dressed in ceremonial deer attire. The figure is in timeless profile; there is no apparent ground line or background which might underscore the ephemeral nature of the dance, occurring only at specific times of the year. Because the ceremony is not frozen in time with detailed backgrounds, it demonstrates Martínez's concern with projecting the transient quality of the Deer Dance, illusions of real-world dimensionality, and action within a shallow picture space, as indicated by the deer dancer's position of feet, arms, canes, and head.[29]

Other early modern painters who were known to depict this "first version" of the deer motif were, Alfredo Montoya

Figure 3. Oqwa Pi (Abel Sánchez), *Deer Dance,* c. 1930, watercolor, accession # 67.16.1. Philbrook Museum of Art, Tulsa, Oklahoma.

Figure 4. Romando Vigil (Tse Ye Mu), *Thunderbird and Deer,* c. 1930, watercolor on posterboard, 18 1/4 x 25 7/8 inches. Philbrook Museum of Art, Oklahoma.

Two Lady and Two Man (1920-21), she depicts two male deer dancers and two female participants. The painted symbols found on the dancers' kilts are extremely detailed, perhaps indicating the interest a female artist would have in the embroidery work,[34] thus adding a "feminine" touch to the work.

Around the same time Deer Dances were being painted, the "second version" of the deer motif emerged: the actual animal in a stylized, leaping, and / or doe-eyed depiction. Romando Vigil,[35] Oqwa Pi,[36] Velino Shije Herrera, and Awa Tsireh are noted for incorporating this particular version within their works (Figure 4). Tsireh was an artist of the Modern School who followed his uncle, Crescencio Martínez, into a career of easel painting. By 1917, Alice Corbin Henderson, a Santa Fe poet and sponsor of Native American paintings, had commissioned Tsireh to execute paintings for her. He was then commissioned by Dr. Hewett and eventually hired to work for the School of American Research.[37] Tsireh implemented the compositional technique of combining animal and / or human imagery framed by abstract shapes that can be read as wide-arching rainbows with cloud terraces. This combination has its roots in pottery motifs, as Dunn has pointed out: "not only the stylization and ingenious composition, the outlines and flat color areas, but the actual designs were often adopted from ceramic art."[38] *Bear with Fawn,* c. 1925, demonstrates the merging of two different traditions: Euroamerican artistic forms (such as illusions of three dimensionality and real-world space on two dimensional surfaces) with Pueblo artistic forms (such as deeply-rooted, abstract visual metaphors).[39] Specific metaphors or symbols used within this painting are an arching rainbow, the sun as an entity with a face, rain, a bear, and a deer. The bear is depicted as two-dimensional and flat while the deer is depicted as three-dimensional (Figure 5).

Velino Shije Herrera was another early modern painter who was hired by Dr. Hewett to work for the School of American Research and had a successful career in easel painting. Herrera's *Zía Deer Dance,* 1926-30, captures the mood and the costume

(Wen Tsireh, San Ildefonso, 1890-1913),[30] Julián Martínez,[31] and Tonita Peña. Tonita Peña was the only female painter recognized during the establishment of the Modern School. Prior to 1900, Native American women primarily produced and ornamented utilitarian art such as pottery.[32] Painting was considered a masculine art form and was therefore practiced by men until they left art in favor of agriculture, decorating pottery, or wage work which paid better.[33] Peña's work reflects the home scenes of Pueblo life and the ceremonial dances of the local village. In *Deer Dance—*

of the Deer Dance in its totality. However, some of his most remarkable works, such as *Deer and Mountain Lion, 1940-1950,* depict the deer in nature, making symbolic use of sky, field, and forest, where stylized plants and animals exist in a purely imaginary world. By painting a human figure participating in a ceremonial Deer Dance and subsequently depicting the actual animal in a stylized form, Herrera reiterated the importance of the symbol, thus illustrating that the deer motif is neither static nor meaningless, but rather forever changing.

The early 1900s to the 1920s can be considered the formative period of Native American easel painting. The painters discussed within the Modern School thus far have embodied the transformation of Native American art from decorative forms on kiva walls and ceremonial ollas to easel painting. As illustrated, the deer motif was prevalent in early easel painting of the Southwest, but its main importance at the time lay in the religious depictions of deer dancers despite the birth of the conventionalized, naturalistic, and even stylized deer forms of Romando Vigil, Oqwa Pi, Velino Shije Herrera, and Awa Tsireh. It was not until the establishment of an art department within the Santa Fe Indian School that a noticeable demand for the deer motif in a stylized form became apparent (Figure 6).

The Studio of the Santa Fe Indian School

The Studio of the Santa Fe Indian School was established in September of 1932 in an effort to encourage the development of Modern Indian Arts after the federal government and Santa Fe business associates had already built the Santa Fe Indian School (whose primary objective was to bring Native American children into acculturation and assimilation). This art department is more commonly referred to as "the Studio."[40] The Studio began an immediate campaign to bring attention to Southwestern Indian art.[41] Dunn, the founder of the Studio, persevered and her goal was that, through this newly-developed art department, young Native American students could express their imagination, home life, and cultural heritage via art. She helped bring together local and national movements that would improve Native American education, develop a new Native American painting genre, and foster a market for Native American painting. Dunn also transformed Native American education from a militaristic discipline designed to suppress Native American cultures to curricula that valued and promoted their different traditional heritages.[42] Painters of the Studio were directly influenced by the early artists of the Modern School of American Indian Painting who incorporated into their works the "traditional" style of painting found throughout the School.[43]

The Studio of the Santa Fe Indian School proved to be commercially viable. The paintings of this period, particularly the stylized deer figures, were made for economic gain. Nevertheless, they carried social meaning for the artists even though they were commercially successful among Anglos. According to J. J. Brody:

The earlier generation of Indian painters had no philosophical problems beyond the very basic one of whether secular painting was acceptable. Art for them was a relatively uncomplicated thing; most of the time it involved recording a familiar scene or reordering a series of familiar ceramic design patterns onto a two-dimensional surface. Its purpose was commercial...[t]he children at the Santa Fe Studio...were told [by Dunn] that art

Figure 5. Awa Tsireh (Alfonso Roybal), *Bear with Deer, c. 1925,* watercolor, 11 x 14 inches. Denver Art Museum. Gift of Anne Evans and Mary Kent Wallace.

Figure 6. Oqwa Pi (Abel Sánchez), *Three Deer,* 1928-1935, watercolor. Courtesy of the School of American Research, Santa Fe, New Mexico.

could and should be something more than a commercially successful activity, that it could have personal and social values that transcended description and decoration.[44]

Artists trained from this school who are known for depicting the painted deer motif, include: Gerald Nailor (Toh Yah, Navajo, 1917-1952);[45] Quincy Tahoma (Navajo, 1920-1956);[46] Harrison Begay (Haskay Yah Ne Yah, Navajo, 1917-);[47] Andrew Van Tsinhnahjinnie (Yazzie Bahe, Navajo, 1916-);[48] Pablita Velarde (Tse Tsan, Santa Clara Pueblo, 1918-);[49] and Merina Luján Hopkins, otherwise known as Pop Chalee (Taos Pueblo, 1906-1993). Their works reflect the distinctive painting style developed at the Studio from 1932 to 1937, which incorporates disciplined brush work (especially control of a firm and even contour line) and the use of flatly-applied, opaque, water-mixed paints.[50] San Ildefonsans had dominated early modern painting, but it was Navajo students like Nailor, Tahoma, Begay, and Tsihnahjinnie who developed a specialized subject matter, often relying heavily on the stylized, idealized deer forms (Figure 7).[51]

Pablita Velarde is an artist whose paintings of deer are unique in that they were inspired from oral legends handed down from her father. This is another way in which the deer motif was accessible to artists throughout the Southwest. Velarde states that she "was one of the fortunate children of [her] generation who was probably the last to hear stories firsthand from Great-grandfather or Grandfather."[52] Descriptions of these tribal legends that were handed down to her have been preserved in a book she wrote, *Old Father Story Teller.* Each legend is individually illustrated, and Velarde specifically describes the story behind the Deer Dance Ceremony, which was her inspiration for drawing the painted deer motifs found throughout the book.

Figure 7. Andrew Van Tsinhnahjinnie, *Male Sand Painting,* c. 1954, oil on canvas board, 18 1/4 x 17 7/16 inches. Philbrook Museum of Art, Tulsa, Oklahoma.

The Bambi School of Native American Art

In analyzing the importance of the deer as a traditional Native American symbol and following the development of its various versions throughout the easel painting genre of the Southwest, one cannot help but be drawn into the dialogue concerning the so-called "Bambi School of Native American Art" and the role of Pop Chalee within it. Chalee is best known for her paintings of animals and forest scenes, which were inspired by her childhood days of walking through the forest near Taos. Because

of such subject matter, the "Bambi Style" label has hung over her. According to Tryntje Van Ness Seymour, some critics have accused Chalee of painting in the "Bambi Style" because it seems as though she copied the cartoon characters and style of Walt Disney:

"In fact," says Pop Chalee, "it was the other way around. Bambi was born here—Walt Disney bought one of these paintings of the forest scene, and he made Bambi out of one of the deer. The way we met was that he came to Santa Fe to recruit some of the Indian artists to work in his studio because they work in fine detail. And so he came up to my studio and saw my painting, and he went to Gerald Nailor's and Allan Houser's—but nobody would go in for his work. And while he was here he bought a forest scene. So the idea for Bambi came from here."[53]

Chalee's most notable works consist of delicate forest scenes with lace-like trees and fanciful animals, especially deer. She exploited this style of painting to its fullest after 1937 and developed it while she attended the Studio along with other artists who adopted similar subject matter. *Black Forest* (n.d.) is just one variation of the numerous paintings Chalee has created in this style. This painting on paper is an idealized landscape with stylized trees, fluttering birds, bear cubs, young rabbits, squirrels, and leaping deer executed in a flat style (Figure 8).

The "Bambi Style" label emerged after the Hollywood animated cartoon became popular. Walt Disney had begun preparatory work on the full-length cartoon film, *Bambi,* as early as 1937. By 1939, the film was under production, and it was not until August 13, 1942 that the film was finally released. Great emphasis was placed on naturalism in the making of the movie, and because of the detail involved in personifying Bambi and his forest friends, it is evident that there is a connection between Native American depictions of deer and Disney's animators.[54] An additional connection can be made in evaluating thematic issues. For example, *Hounds Chasing a Deer,* by Chalee was created between 1934 and 1936, before Bambi was ever conceived. This painting's theme is concerned with vulnerability, as are the scenes of chasing and running found in *Bambi,* specifically the one in which Faline, Bambi's mother, is being chased by vicious dogs while running away from a forest fire. *Bambi*, the animated feature, is based on Felix Salten's book which focused on the hunter's invasion of the forest, bringing terror and destruction to the animals who live there.[55] The thematic connection seen here may serve as an analogy for the relationship between Native Americans and Euroamericans, alluded to in works such as Gerald Nailor's *Eagles Chasing Deer* of 1934, Velino Shije Herrera's *Deer and Mountain Lion* of 1940-50, as well as in *Lion and Deer* of 1940, by the later institutional painter Hoke Denetsosie (Kiya Ahnii, Navajo, 1919-).

After Dunn's departure from the Studio in 1937, and especially after Bambi went public, Chalee (like other Native American artists of the time) continued to paint deer well into the 1970s. Navajo artists who were trained at the Studio of the Santa Fe Indian School and / or elsewhere, elaborated upon this style of painting: Hoke Denetsosie; Charlie Lee (Hush Ka Yel Ha Yah, Navajo, 1924-);[56] Franklin Kahn (Navajo, 1934-);[57] Stanley Battese (Kehdoyah, Navajo, 1936-);[58] and Beatien Yazz (Jimmy Toddy, Navajo, 1928-).[59] Their deer paintings, like those of Chalee, were based on a need for cultural response, the demand of the Anglo art market, and efforts made by some Anglos to "recover" a lost world for Native Americans.

In general, *Bambi* was well received—the image of innocence, charm, and cuteness that Disney conveyed with this film was attractive to the American public.[60] Thus, the persona of Bambi prevailed but at some cost to the traditional Native American symbol of the deer. The "Bambi School of Native American Art" denies the true origin as well as the traditional and symbolic meanings of the

Figure 8. Pop Chalee (Merina Luján Hopkins), *Black Forest*, n.d. Courtesy of the School of American Research, Santa Fe, New Mexico.

deer, thus perpetuating a misconception. This label continues the Euroamerican art world's long tradition of Eurocentric value judgements. For example, Native American paintings with stylized, leaping deer may be discounted as touristy curios and therefore not truly connected to any "significant" Native American artistic traditions. Also, negative connotations are created by this label because it does not account for the possibility that both Native Americans and the animators of the Walt Disney Studio could have been in dialogue with one another.

Conclusion

It is important to reconstruct the history behind the easel painting tradition of the Southwest in order to understand the growth and development of the deer motif within this genre. As described, this painted motif has been seen in virtually every medium, from the walls of kivas to the easel painting of the Modern School, the Studio, and into the present. It has developed two

main versions, supposedly having evolved into a "Bambi style" of Native American painting. This misconceived label disregards the notion that this style of painting may have been created by Native Americans themselves or that it was a stylistic result of the interplay between animator Walt Disney and Native American artists. In fact, Brody believes that the wide-eyed animals made so popular by the Walt Disney Studio may have been invented by Studio painters, but as illustrated, they were first established by early modern painters and later refined by Studio artists.[61] Overall, the varied forms of the motif, namely human impersonators in Deer Dance ceremonies and leaping deer in nature, have attested to the notion that "while traditional ways [are] to be encouraged the innovative must be recognized, that art is dynamic and that Indian art, like all art, has always been and must always remain a part of a living and breathing culture."[62] The fact that the deer has been valued as a sacred and useful animal and that its image has persisted in the easel painting of the last one hundred years demonstrates that "even from the very beginning, the more creative Indian artists have continually brought new and fresh insights into the iconography of and about native peoples."[63] Thus, the deer motif is one that is continually changing.

The Southwest easel paintings throughout this exhibition are examples of an assimilated fine art. The development of paintings for the Anglo art market has been a way for Native Americans to become recognized by the art world while being commercially successful.[64] Up until the Contemporary American Indian Art Movement, easel paintings of the Southwest primarily existed in a category apart from the fine arts and, like other Native American art forms, belonged in ethnographic institutions or museums of mankind.[65] However, through the development of the Modern School and major art exhibitions, art historians have finally begun to place this form of Native American art "among the American fine arts."[66]

There has been an ongoing effort on the part of art historians to establish an exact definition of what imagery is truly Native American and what imagery is the result of the influence of European aesthetic mannerisms on Modern, Studio, and later institutional painters of Native American art. To conclude that authentic Native American art is art which only incorporates those formalistic qualities found within the Modern School of American Indian Painting and the Studio is to ignore the art of American Indians today, which has developed beyond the style of the painted deer motif. Contemporary artists themselves challenge the dominance of the "Bambi Style" of much Native American tourist painting in order to refine and restate the overall traditional symbolism of the deer. Nevertheless, the painted deer remains one of the most important Native American symbols within Native American art because it is still highly valued as sacred and useful. It is a symbol of "continuity and change," joining together what is considered to be "traditional" painting with more contemporary Native American painting and painters.

[1] "Continuity and change" is a phrase of Rennard Strickland. Rennard Strickland, "Where Have All The Blue Deer Gone?" *American Indian Art Magazine* (Spring 1985): 41.

[2] The deer's position in the historic struggle between traditional and modern subject matter and Native American style is extensively discussed by Rennard Strickland (Strickland 41).

[3] Dorothy Dunn, "The Development of Modern American Indian Painting in the Southwest and Plains Areas," *El Palacio* 58.11 (1951): 333.

[4] Dunn, "Development" 333.

[5] Dorothy Dunn, "America's First Painters," *National Geographic Magazine* 107 (March 1955): 349.

[6] Dunn, "America's" 349. Lydia L. Wyckoff, ed., *Vision and Voices: Native American Painting From the Philbrook Museum of Art* (Tulsa: Philbrook Museum of Art, 1996)19.

[7] Wyckoff 20.

[8] J. J. Brody, *Indian Painters and White Patrons* (Albuquerque: U of New Mexico P, 1971) 45. Dunn, "Development" 338.

[9] Julia M. Seton, *American Indian Arts: A Way of Life* (New York: Ronald, 1962) 230. Wyckoff 20. Prior to Euroamerican contact, the main sources of pigments were clays, sandstones, and ores (Dunn, "Development" 336).

[10] Dunn, "Development" 339. Dorothy Dunn, *American Indian Painting of the Southwest and Plains Areas* (Albuquerque: U of New Mexico P, 1968) 186. The Modern School of American Indian Painting refers to the post-contact era, which includes the duration of the Studio of the Santa Fe Indian School. This era was the time in which easel painting was begun by a group of self-taught painters. European-introduced materials were utilized and Native American artists were being trained by Euroamerican instructors.

[11] J. J. Brody, *Pueblo Indian Painting: Tradition and Modernism in New Mexico, 1900-1930* (Santa Fe: School of American Research, 1997) 4.

[12] Brody, *Pueblo* 73.

[13] Dunn, *American* 187.

[14] Brody, *Pueblo* 3.

[15] Brody, *Indian* 81.

[16] Wyckoff 26.

[17] The "San Ildefonso School" is a term used by Jeanne O. Snodgrass. Jeanne O. Snodgrass, *American Indian Painters: A Biographical Directory* (New York: Heye Foundation, 1968) 205. Wyckoff 27. It refers to the large group of self-taught artists from San Ildefonso Pueblo that were the early Modern painters of the Modern School of American Indian Painting.

[18] Dunn, "Development" 342. It is important to note that for centuries before Euroamerican contact Native Americans had been using and making watercolors by mixing native earths, minerals, and vegetable pigments with water. The usual process for preparing pigments consisted of separating the color substances from impurities, grinding them, and then combining them with water, fat, or adhesive agents (Dunn, "Development" 336). However, during the Modern School, watercolors were being commercially made by Euroamericans; this enabled Native Americans to begin their paintings immediately rather than having to prepare the pigments themselves (Seton 230).

[19] Dunn, *American* 216-217.

[20] Dunn, "Development" 342.

[21] The development of easel painting within the Southwest was a development of an assimilated fine art. According to Nelson Graburn, assimilated fine art occurs when "conquered minority artists have taken up the established art forms of the conquerors, following and competing with the artists of the dominant society. These are characteristic of extreme cultural domination and hence a desire to assimilate." Nelson H. H. Graburn, *Ethnic and Tourist Arts: Cultural Expressions from the Fourth World* (Berkeley: U of California P, 1976) 7.

[22] Brody, *Indian* 83.

[23] For example, see paintings depicting deer on the kiva walls from Jemez Pueblo of 1849. Clara Lee Tanner, *Southwest Indian Painting: A Changing Art* (Tucson: U of Arizona P, 1973) 47. Also, see *Deer Design, c. 1914*, collaboration of Maximiliana Martínez and Crescencio Martínez on a ceremonial olla (Dunn, *American* 106). See *Zuni Pottery Drum Jar*. Rene D'Harnoncourt and Frederic H. Douglas, *Indian Art of the United States* (New York: Museum of Modern Art, 1969) 107. The deer is an animal much favored by the Zuni and therefore is frequently depicted on Zuni pottery. Zuni pottery bowls are known to contain the "House of the Deer" device. This is a prominent device in which a deer with white rump spot and traditional breath-of-life line from mouth to heart stands within a scroll-decorated semicircle (Dunn, *American*101).

[24] Alfonso Ortiz, ed., *Handbook of North American Indians: Southwest 9* (Washington: Smithsonian Institution, 1979) 111.

[25] Tryntje Van Ness Seymour, *When the Rainbow Touches Down* (Phoenix: Heard Museum, 1988) 191.

[26] Seymour 192.

[27] Seymour 171.

[28] There are two versions of the deer motif discussed within this publication. The "first version" of the deer motif in easel painting refers to depicting human deer dancers as opposed to the "second version" of the deer motif which refers to depicting the actual animal in a stylized, leaping, or doe-eyed manner, usually found in a natural setting. The term "doe-eyed" refers to the anthropomorphized eyes found in certain Native American paintings, which have a pleading appeal.

[29] Brody, *Indian* 80; Brody, *Pueblo* 61.

[30] According to J. J. Brody (Brody, *Indian* 81), Alfredo Montoya was the first modern adult San Ildefonso painter. He may have been painting as early as 1900 and was a brother-in-law of Crescencio Martínez. Clara Lee Tanner (Tanner 85), quotes Dutton as saying that Montoya was perhaps "the young man from San Ildefonso who initiated modern pueblo painting." Montoya recorded the local dances and ceremonial modes of life of his people by portraying deer and antelope dancers until his death in 1913. Dorothy Dunn (Dunn, *American* 195, 198) acknowledges Montoya as being an earlier artist than Martínez but acknowledges Martínez as being the "founder"

of the Modern School because it was during his painting career that the School became formally recognized. Therefore, it is with Crescencio Martínez's paintings that I concentrate on the appearance of the "first version" of the deer motif.

31 Julián Martínez painted geometrically stylized figures and ceremonial figures as well. Although his watercolors were minor in comparison to his pottery achievements in collaboration with his wife, María, he had an immense impact on other Pueblo artists due to his popularization of a San Ildefonso "Deer Dance" style. *Hunter and Deer, c.* 1925, is the epitome of this style in which the dancers are shown in forward-bending attitude, usually with one foot swinging out backward. The figures are drawn in an extremely sure, incisive manner, the snow-white shirts outlined with fine, unwavering brush lines (Dunn, *American* 211).

32 Margaret Archuleta and Rennard Strickland, *Shared Visions: Native American Painters and Sculptors In the Twentieth Century* (New York: New Press, 1991) 74.

33 Brody, *Indian* 83, 88.

34 This inference is made because the details are very geometric and patterned; techniques found in weaving and in the production of pottery—two activities that traditionally have been performed by women. According to Brody, "more realistic representations are likely to be by men and to have ritual utility, while the more abstract ones are likely to be made by women and to have household uses" (Brody, *Pueblo* 19).

35 Romando Vigil began painting around 1918 and incorporates, like Velino Shije Herrera, stylized renderings of deer within his paintings. For example, see *Thunderbird and Deer*, 1930 (Wyckoff 279).

36 Oqwa Pi is another artist of the Modern School who participated in this same deer motif tradition; see *Three Deer* of 1928-35 (Brody, *Pueblo* 171).

37 Snodgrass 11. Brody, *Indian* 85.

38 Dunn, "Development" 342.

39 Brody, *Pueblo* 13.

40 Brody, *Indian* 126. Dorothy Dunn, "The Studio of Painting, Santa Fe Indian School," *El Palacio* 67 (1960): 16. Wyckoff 29.

41 Dunn, *American* 224.

42 Bruce Bernstein, "With a View to the Southwest: Dorothy Dunn," (1996). This article was found at the following Uniform Resource Locator in association with the Museum of Indian Arts and Culture of Albuquerque: http://www.collectorsguide.com/fa/fa044.html

43 "Traditional" painting in this context refers to Modern Painters (of the Modern School of American Indian Painting) utilizing the formalistic qualities of painting discussed previously. These formal qualities are considered "traditional" and the Studio of the Santa Fe Indian School used these "traditional" qualities in order to develop a style unique to the Studio. One of the main objectives of the Studio was to "study and explore traditional Indian art methods and productions in order to continue established basic painting forms, and to evolve new motifs, styles, and techniques only as they might be in character with the old, and worthy of supplementing them" (Dunn, "Studio" 19).
It should be noted that Dunn's Studio with its "traditional" style had its detractors. Edwin Wade's definition of "Bambi Art" emphasizes artistic rebellion: "Bambi Art—a term of derision applied to the Oklahoma and Santa Fe Studio schools of easel painting in the 1950s and 1960s by younger artists seeking to free themselves from the constraints of the established styles." Edwin L Wade, ed., *The Arts of the North American Indian: Native Traditions in Evolution* (New York: Hudson Hills Press, 1986) *Glossary.*

44 Brody, *Indian* 130-131.

45 See Nailor's *Eagles Chasing Deer,* 1934 (Brody, *Indian* 145) and *The Quiet Way,* 1938 (Strickland 37). *Eagles Chasing Deer* depicts leaping deer with scalloped necks and spidery legs which beautifully enhance the decorative effect. The delicately painted deer are among abstract plant forms and Navajo sand painting symbols, which are also incorporated in *The Quiet Way.* Nailor, a Navajo, is known for his interest in symbolism and his masterful use of color. His favorite subject was traditional Navajo life, which indicates the deer's value in this culture.

46 See Tahoma's *Deer and Fawns,* 1937 (Brody, *Indian* 118) and *A Sign of Spring,* 1953. Tahoma, a Navajo, was a lover of nature, which explains why his paintings of animals are usually realistically depicted, lifelike and honed to anatomical perfection. His devotion to and keen observation of nature are obvious within both paintings.

47 See Begay's *A Fawn and Rainbow* (n.d.) and *Desert Dwellers and Migrants Passing By* (n.d.). Begay's brush work is sensitive, expressive, and exquisitely fine. He makes his animals appear realistic and lifelike. His paintings have exerted greater influence on Navajo artists than any others (Tanner 80, 311).

48 See Tsinhnahjinnie's *Male Sand Painting,* 1954 (Wyckoff 268). "Everything he undertook to draw flowed into a thing of grace and beauty under his brush. He seemed never to find enough time to state all he had to say—spirited ceremonial dancers, fleeting deer and racing horses. . ." (Dunn, *American* 271). The spelling of the artist's name also appears as Tsinajinnie.

49 See Velarde's graceful, lyrical painting of three leaping deer on page 19 of her book, *Old Father Story Teller* (1989). Velarde, of Santa Clara Pueblo, has gone from direct watercolor portrayals of everyday pueblo life to more abstract work using pigments made from ground rock. According to *When the Rainbow Touches Down* (1988) by Tryntje Van Ness Seymour, her subject matter has never varied: "I am what they call 'traditional'. . .I have painted subjects from memory: the ceremonial dances, the home life, animals and birds, and things with a story to them. Why? Because I love my people and I wanted to keep some records of their way of life" (Seymour 165).

50 Brody, *Indian* 134.

51 Though there was some encouragement of genre scenes and subjects relating to home-life, any suggestion of social commentary was dismissed as caricature, and as a result, the contents of many Studio paintings are idealized and asocial (Brody, *Indian* 134).

52 Pablita Velarde, *Old Father Story Teller* (Santa Fe: Clear Light, 1989) 5.

53 Seymour 166.

54 Special art classes were instituted; real deer were kept on the studio lot; books of photographic studies were compiled; and thousands of feet of live-action material of deer were used for reference. Christopher Finch, *The Art of Walt Disney: From Mickey Mouse to the Magic Kingdoms* (New York: Abrams, 1995) 209.

55 Finch 208.

56 See *Friendship* (n.d.) by Charlie Lee. This painting depicts a fawn who looks extremely similar to the portrayal of Bambi in Disney's film (Tanner 337).

57 See *Spring in the Mountains* (n.d.) by Franklin Kahn (Tanner 395).

58 See *Curiosity* (n.d.) and *Blue Fawn* (n.d.) by Stanley Battese. Linzee W. King Davis, "Modern Navajo Water Color Painting," *Arizona Highways* 32 (1956): 29.

59   See *Deer in Forest* (n.d.) by Beatien Yazz (Davis 10-31).

60   *Liberty Magazine* described Disney as being "Hollywood's Rembrandt;" Richard Hallet's "The Trail of *Bambi*" in *Colliers* and Janet Martin's "Bringing *Bambi* to the Screen" in *Nature* praised the film for its forest setting and its realistic portrayal of animal behavior. Kathy Merlock Jackson, *Walt Disney: A Bio-Bibliography* (Westport: Greenwood, 1993) 179.

61   Brody, *Indian* 144.

62   Strickland 37.

63   Strickland 41.

64   Throughout the history of the painting traditions of the Southwest, there has been a major lack of credit given to original Native American artists because of the issue of "signature." It was not until post-contact that specific Native American artists actually received recognition for their artistic achievements.

65   J. J. Brody, *Anasazi and Pueblo Painting*, 1st ed. (Albuquerque: U of New Mexico P, 1991) 12.

66   Janet Catherine Berlo, ed., *The Early Years of Native American Art History: The Politics of Scholarship and Collecting* (Seattle: U of Washington P, 1992) 192.

Joseph Henry Sharp, *Chief Two Moons (Cheyenne)*, c. 1899, oil on canvas, 14 x 10 inches. Courtesy of The Butler Institute of American Art, Youngstown, Ohio.

III. MISCONCEPTIONS: THE AMERICAN INDIAN

Osceola's Public Life: Two Images of the Seminole Hero

Shari Addonizio

Osceola's public debut as a romantic, heroic figure in American culture occurred in 1834. Continuing until his death early in 1838, this phase of his life consisted of a period of only three years and three months. However, during those years his reputation as a resistance leader was established in the minds of both whites and Indians as he argued against removal to the West. Images of Osceola have been translated into a variety of media in the intervening one hundred and sixty-three years. Paintings, drawings, and engravings produced in the antebellum era were constructed to portray the celebrated Seminole as a leader of his people who resisted domination and rebelled against oppression. Most of these images portray him in full dress and regalia in static heroic poses appropriate to an elder stateman. Representations of Osceola in the second half of the nineteenth and the first half of the twentieth centuries varied widely in content and style, as well as in historical accuracy. In the second half of the twentieth century, images of Osceola became associated with Florida State University athletics. Today the public image of Osceola is alive and well in Tallahassee as the personification of Florida State football. Every fall thousands of spectators are treated to the victory cries of the "Spirit of Osceola," a personification of a warrior, dressed in Seminole garb and mounted on a horse, as he circles the field accompanied by the cheers of thousands of fans.

This exhibition examines some of these diverse representations as they convey meaning to the dominant white culture in which they originated and as they interact with that culture. As this white hegemony exercised its dominance to define and use such imagery, Osceola served to fill the needs of the culture, especially in the South. Patricia R. Wickman, whose book *Osceola's Legacy* is the foundation for much of this essay, puts forth the view that white perception has always shaped Osceola's public persona.[1] Moreover, according to Theda Purdue, as the personification of "the war hero, the worthy opponent, and the 'savage' past," Osceola represented a multi-faceted symbol to white Americans who understood him within the boundaries of their own cultural limitations.[2] Furthermore, according to Joel W. Martin, the American public fascination with Osceola, whom he calls "the real-life incarnation of the noble enemy," may be attributed in part to the active participation of Blacks in the Second Seminole War. This prolonged conflict contradicted the stereotypes constructed by whites for both Blacks and Indians during the antebellum period.[3] Finally, this essay leaves the antebellum south to jump ahead to the second half of the twentieth century where Osceola's public image became metonymic to Florida State

University's athletic prowess, an identification which evolved into more appropriate representations in the 1980s and 1990s as public attitudes toward racial stereotyping began to shift away from an uncritical acceptance of such images, and as the Seminole Indians began to exert some influence over the definition and use of the persona of Osceola. As a subject of fascination for his white American public, Osceola's image has been distributed geographically far beyond the relatively small scope of his life. Anglo-American writers and artists have variously taken antagonistic, romantic, or sensational stances toward Osceola and his exploits. Indeed, whites accorded him a higher status than did his peers. The Seminoles, for the most part, have confined themselves to oral traditions; perhaps their own cultural bias has made them reluctant to discuss Osceola and their traditions with non-Natives until recent years.[4]

During the 1830s Florida newspapers were full of rumors, reported sightings, and eventually, stories about the depredations of the Seminoles. Osceola was soon featured by writers who avidly traced his movements across the state.[5] His exploits were played out against the backdrop of hostililty between the Seminoles and Anglo-Americans which characterized the first half of the nineteenth century, gaining him high visibility among the Native Americans and notoriety among the whites.[6] He could speak persuasively, demonstrating passion in his beliefs and conveying a certain power or influence which has been characterized as charismatic. About five feet ten inches tall and slender, he was said to be a handsome man with delicate features. Both whites and Indians took note of his ego and apparently he did little to restrain it, being fond of both boasts and finery.[7]

The first decades of the nineteenth century were rife with complaints of African and Indian depredations from Florida settlers. Southern planters loudly voiced their objections to the loss of their human property to the Seminoles and demanded the return of their slaves. In order to further the President's own political ambitions by opening the new Florida terrritory for white settlement, the Jackson administration put forth the Indian Removal Act of 1830.[8] At first many Seminoles were adamantly against the proposed relocation to the West among the hated Creeks, some of whom had joined Jackson's forces against them in the Creek War of 1813-14 and in the so-called First Seminole War. However, the pressures favoring relocation were profound and diverse. In addition to military pressures put forth by the United States government, localized depredations by whites against the Indians and their cattle and hog herds occurred, as well as

Figure 1. George Catlin, *Osceola, Chief of the Seminoles*, 1838, oil on board, 29 x 24 inches. American Museum of Natural History, New York. (Neg./Transparency no. 33771, Courtesy Department of Library Services, American Museum of Natural History.—Photo: J. Kirschner)

91

outright appropriation of Indian lands. Much of the Florida territory given to the Seminoles in earlier treaties was incapable of supporting economic survival, and the devastating drought of 1831 caused widespread suffering among their people. By the early 1830s, therefore, some of the Seminoles seemed ready to listen to offers of a tract of their own far away from encroachment by the whites.[9]

Osceola, who had left his Muskogee (Creek) hometown in Alabama at age ten to begin a semi-nomadic existence with some of his family members in Florida (Andrew Jackson had signed the Removal Act in 1830), was living in the Big Swamp, near Fort King, by 1834. In October of 1834 his vehement refusal to leave Florida, and his determination to exhort others to resist removal, first became known to whites at the Fort King council. He was quickly singled out as a resistance leader by Indian Agent Wiley Thompson, who spent the next ten months trying to flatter and placate him with gifts. However, Thompson soon lost his patience with what he considered to be Osceola's inflammatory attitude. In June of 1835 Thompson had Osceola jailed, a humiliation that was evidently too much for Osceola to stand. He began a series of calculated and daring moves. In the following month, he arranged a traditional ball game at Fort King, which he used partly to consolidate his leadership image among the Seminoles and partially to secure ammunition from the military.[10]

In November he led the party that executed Charley Emathla, the most vocal member of the pro-emigration faction. In December he successfully ambushed a military baggage train, using the guerrilla warfare style traditionally waged by the Seminoles and adopted by their African allies, thereby beginning the conflict with the United States military which lasted seven years. Agent Thompson was eliminated, shot by Osceola himself, in December. On the 31st of that month Osceola led the first full display of Indian force at the Battle of Withlacoochee, where he was reportedly wounded in the arm while defiantly wearing a United States Army uniform. At the end of 1835 Osceola was probably at the peak of his power, commanding as many as 250 followers.[11]

Throughout 1836 Osceola played a visible part in military encounters. However, by 1837 reports indicated his force had dwindled to about eight warriors and he was said to be sick, probably having contracted malaria late in 1836. Eventually he was captured under a flag of truce on the orders of General Thomas Jesup. On October 21, 1837, he was imprisoned at St. Augustine and was later moved to Fort Moultrie in Charleston Harbor, South Carolina.[12]

At Fort Moultrie Osceola's celebrity status continued unabated as South Carolinians, who had been entertained by reports of his exploits in the local newspapers, flocked to see him. Artists were eager to paint his portrait. George Catlin, commissioned by the War Department, closed his New York studio and took a steam packet to Charleston. Catlin joined artists already at the fort in making portraits of Osceola and the other Indians.[13]

In 1844 Thomas W. Storrow described the setting and the circumstances of such endeavors for *Knickerbocker Magazine*. After consenting to sit for his portrait, Osceola spent a good part of the day carefully choosing his attire. Two artists each worked at opposite ends of a room where Osceola sat or stood at the center. The room was usually full of visitors who watched him as he sat placidly or moved about to exercise his legs. Osceola reportedly was very pleased with the portraits that these sessions produced.[14]

One of these works, a full length oil portrait by Catlin, is titled *The Black Drink* (Figure 1). The title is a reference to a loose translation of Osceola'a name: the Black Drink Singer.[15] Wearing his customary finery, the famous warrior stands proudly erect, one hand folded against his hip, the other firmly clutching his rifle. His countenance is open and relaxed as his eyes gaze calmly into the distance. Although Osceola's feet are firmly planted on the ground, his environment is ambiguous. Catlin presents Osceola standing alone without the distractions of a specific setting, thereby giving his subject the attention and respect due him as a heroic figure.

Here was an Indian whom white antebellum America could understand. In the early part of the nineteenth century, many Anglo-Americans were bewildered by what they considered to be the Native Americans' lack of motivation and their reluctance to adopt "civilization." Intensive efforts to convince the Indians to leave their "primitive" state had largely failed; most Native peoples did not accept the vaunted superiority of the white culture and steadfastly refused to embrace white customs, beliefs, and mores in lieu of their own. Indeed, the Indian people's recalcitrance stood in the way of the "progress" that an aggressive, expanding Anglo-American culture demanded. However, Osceola, due to his publicized exploits and his often discussed and presumed white paternity, had acquired a reputation for decisiveness and defiance, unusually positive qualities for an Indian in the minds of white Americans. As a "man of action" fighting for his homeland, Osceola was at least comprehensible to many in the white population. Moreover, his military leadership was more understandable than the seeming inaction of Chief Micanopy who was a hereditary leader to the Seminoles. Micanopy's authority held less attraction for Anglo-Americans than Osceola's daring, colorful feats.[16]

Such a mindset was intensified in the 1830s by the dominance of Andrew Jackson, the country's first national hero since George Washington. President Jackson, whose stature in the minds of some white Americans only increased during the Seminole Wars, was the regaled hero of the Battle of New Orleans. Setting the antebellum standard for heroic behavior in some quarters, Jackson had a reputation for not following the rules and rebelling against what he perceived to be overly restrictive regulations. Thus, although he would not have been compared favorably to Jackson by any means, many white Americans saw Osceola as representing a role that Jackson had premiered, according to Purdue.[17]

Jackson, however, was also partly responsible for a disturbing contradiction which Osceola helped to resolve. Unlike the guerrilla war that was waged in the Florida swamps, where an army of thousands of well-trained and expensively equipped United States soldiers fought against small bands of underfed and poorly armed Indian men, women, and children, the Battle of New Orleans, where Jackson and his troops had faced the British Army as equals, had been perceived as "glorious and honorable." Also, as Wickman has recently noted, the English were the social and cultural heroes of American whites, while the Indians were not. The dominant culture's code of honor, especially prevalent in the South, required that opponents be equal. The Second Seminole War, therefore, would have seemed particularly ignoble to white antebellum America. But with Osceola's image in place as the military leader of the Seminole nation, the combatants became better matched and the conflict more honorable.[18]

Osceola, constructed and represented as the heroic and colorful "chief" of the Seminoles, could also be used as pro-slavery propaganda. As the worthy opponent, his image bolstered white honor, but the free, romantic, warlike Indian also served as a foil to the African slave, whose captivity needed to be justified. The Second Seminole War disrupted this scenario and caused a conceptual crisis. Active participation by African Americans alongside Indians undercut the image of Blacks in antebellum literature as docile and obedient, happily submissive to the southern racial system, according to Martin. The romantic image of a rebellious, proud Osceola provided a dramatic and a necessary contrast to the captive Africans for the members of the southern hegemonic class.[19]

In the years after Osceola's death, images

Figure 2. "Spirit of Osceola." (Photo: Florida State University Photo Lab)

of the Seminole warrior were used to represent the defeated and "vanishing Indian" to many Anglo-Americans. Native peoples were considered part of the past, and this widespread conviction held that a "civilized" society could not coexist with a "savage" culture. Recalling the Aristotelian "triumph of civilization,"[20] the white American discourse of the day postulated that, since farmers destroyed the forests on which the Indians depended for vital resources, the former was certain to triumph over the latter. Furthermore, according to received wisdom, the resistance of the Native peoples to the pressures of white expansion merely accelerated their inevitable defeat at the hands of a numerically and technologically "superior" population. According to Purdue, Osceola's capture and death in 1838 represented the end of "savagery" in the eastern part of the country and confirmed the belief of white America that the ultimate result of the failure to accept "civilization" was death, no matter how heroic or romantic. This view

provided further justification for removal of the Indians to the frontier of Oklahoma where the Native peoples theoretically would be protected from extermination while they were given another chance to adopt white culture.[21]

Cultural perceptions continue to call up images of dead Native Americans and apply them to new, but parallel, social venues. In this regard, this exhibition examines some of the images of the Seminole hero as they were first used by Florida State University to promote its football program. Soon after the end of the Second World War, on May 7, 1947, the institution that had been known as the Florida State College for Women became The Florida State University. In that same year, the name "Seminoles" was selected by the student body in a campuswide competion, winning over other epithets, such as Crackers, Statesmen, Tarpons, and Fighting Warriors. The Seminoles' first home football game was played on October 18, 1947, against Stetson University in Deland, Florida.[22] In the earliest days of the "FSU Seminoles" there was some effort made to be true to traditional culture. For example, during the late 1940s / early 1950s the student newspaper, *The Florida Flambeau*, carried a logo in its masthead illustrated with the profile drawing of a Seminole man in turban and kerchief. Likewise, for a couple of years in the early 1950s the FSU cheerleaders wore knee-length patchwork skirts made by members of the real Seminole tribe of Florida. This was not to last long.

The rivalry between FSU and UF that developed in the succeeding decades is well known, of course. Early characterizations of this intense competition showed a simple cartoon image of FSU's Seminole (often nicknamed "Sammy Seminole") meeting UF's Gator, who is seen welcoming the FSU team and fans to Gainesville. Images of the Seminole warrior, it seems, continued to be conceptualized and employed by the white culture. In this case, a fledging football "dynasty" required an exciting and exotic "mascot" to fuel the flames of rivalry, an image to be evoked by publicists and imitated by fans. Moreover, these symbolic images emphasized the widely perceived unvanquished history of the Seminoles.[23]

In the 1950s, 1960s, and 1970s, reductive images of Native Americans were disseminated by university athletic programs, as well as by professional franchises. These representations ignored Native Americans as flesh-and-blood beings in specific historical contexts and emphasized the perjorative nature of stereotypical representation. Martin, deploring the use of "Braves" for the Atlanta major league baseball team, characterizes the nickname as an invitation to view Indians as "ignorant fools and bloodthirsty savages." Often these "mascots" were presented as comic characters, visual symbols which transmitted another level of meaning to viewers. Such representation reflects what Martin calls the "non-native preference for fantasy over reality,"[24] whereby the Native American is depicted as both an object of ridicule and a cuddly, non-threatening image which both reassures the white culture of its presumed superiority and further subverts the perception of the multivalent consequences of conquest and domination.

Florida State University was among the first to try to remedy the negative imagery of American Indians associated with athletic teams that take Indian names. In the late 1960s, the reigning mascot for basketball games was a character named "Chief Fullabull." According to Anthony Paredes, who was then faculty advisor for the campus organization American Indian Fellowship, opposition to Chief Fullabull received national attention in the Native American press, and by late 1970, the Fellowship in alliance with other campus groups and off-campus Seminole people were successful in eliminating Fullabull and having him replaced with a "spirit chief" dubbed "Yahola" at basketball games, wearing distinctive Seminole garb."[25]

Despite the change in basketball, the somewhat less offensive "Sammie Seminole" continued through most of the 1970s as the football mascot. Perhaps inspired by the Fullabull episode a few years earlier, a new representation of Seminole Spirit rode onto the football field on September 16, 1978, at the FSU-Oklahoma football game. During the 1980s, FSU athletic boosters tried to return to more ethnographically correct Seminole images. This rudimentary incarnation of the Florida State "warrior" on horseback was the idea of Coach Bobby Bowden and Seminole booster Bill Durham who owns and named the horse and who conceived of the horse and rider as a means to foster school spirit. By October 10, 1980, *The Florida Flambeau*, the student daily newspaper, referred to the rider as "Chief Osceola and his mighty Seminole steed Renegade" who "dispenses complete ecstasy and enthusiasm to FSU fans and football players alike"[26] (Figure 2).

Patricia Wickman currently writes about the accuracy of the clothing:

> by about 1984 or 1985, while I was the Senior Historian for the state (at the Museum of Florida History), I was approached by Lane Green, Director of the Tallahassee Junior Museum and an active member of the FSU Alumni Association, and asked to provide research that might (finally!) get FSU's "Osceola" into proper historical dress. . . . But FSU has not revisited its interpretation of the Seminoles because of Seminole tribal opinions alone. It is predomi-

nately because of the changes in social attitudes toward "ethnic minorities" among their Euroamerican peers that FSU has begun to "refine" its "Seminole" image.[27]

In the early 1990s, various national Native American groups began objecting to latter-day uses of Indian imagery by FSU. One of the most widely publicized critics, Michael Haney, is a member of the Seminole Nation of Oklahoma. According to Paredes—who has remained fairly close to the issue on campus and off—non-tribal protest groups might have helped to "get the attention of the administration" in being more careful to monitor the way in which Indian people and culture are portrayed. But, perhaps more important, in the 1990s the FSU administration has become increasingly concerned that it follow the correct protocol and extend proper respect to the governments of the Seminole Tribe of Florida, The Miccosukee Tribe of Indians of Florida, the Seminole Nation of Oklahoma, and other sovereign tribes as well. At the moment, the FSU administration appears to have good official relationships with all the interested tribes. Meanwhile, individual protestors still picket football games declaring their opposition to any use of "Indian mascots."

Through much-heralded success in many fields, including the grand opening of their own tribal museum in August 1997, the Seminole Indians are denying the widespread idea in popular white culture that the only "real" Indians are historical Indians. Florida State University, by turning its back on the stereotypical cartoon-like images of Native Americans of the 1970s and by participating in a dialogue with the Seminole Indians, has demonstrated its willingness to entertain Native concerns about representations of their culture. The public images of Osceola, the Seminole hero whose ethnically diverse background seems to foretell the multi-cultural focus of the 1990s, continues to have strong appeal to late-twentieth century viewers. As a symbol of courage and resistance, he represents leadership and the fighting spirit, qualities valued by many Americans, whether their ancestors came from Europe, Africa, or Asia, or were native to this continent.

[1] Patricia R. Wickman, *Osceola's Legacy* (Tuscaloosa, Alabama: U of Alabama P, 1991), xv, 30. This work on the artifacts and representations of Osceola furthers the scholarship of a relatively short article by John M. Goggin, "Osceola: Portraits, Features, and Dress" *Florida Historical Quarterly* 33 (January-April 1955): 25-32.

[2] Theda Purdue, "Osceola: The White Man's Indian" *Florida Historical Quarterly* (1991): 488.

[3] Joel W. Martin, "'My Grandmother Was a Cherokee Princess': Representations of Indians in Southern History" in S. Elizabeth Bird, ed., *Dressing in Feathers: The Construction of the Indian in American Popular Culture* (Boulder, Colorado: Westview Press, 1996) 135, 139.

[4] Wickman xv, 30.

[5] Wickman xxiii.

[6] Wickman xxiii.

[7] Wickman xxii.

8   Kevin Mulroy, *Freedom on the Border* (Texas UP, 1993) 27. According to Wickman, the purpose of this legislation was two-fold: The Removal Act was meant to rid the territory of Native Americans and to put a stop to treaty making as an end in itself (personal communication, 1997).

9   Mulroy 27, and Wickman personal communication.

10   Wickman xxi-xxii.

11   Wickman xxiii, 38.

12   Wickman xxiii-xxv.

13   Wickman 55.

14   Thomas W. Storrow, "Osceola, the Seminole War-Chief," *Knickerbocker Magazine* 24 (November 1844) 444-45. Quoted in Wickman 56.

15   Wickman 14, 60.

16   Perdue 481.

17   Perdue 482-83.

18   Perdue 484, and Wickman personal communication.

19   Martin 139.

20   Wickman personal communication.

21   Perdue 484-85.

22   Martee Wills and Joan Perry Morris, *Seminole History: A Pictorial History of Florida State University* (Jacksonville, Florida: South Star Publishing Co., 1987) no pagination.

23   The "tradition" that this opposition evokes was captialized upon by the white tourism industry and in no way reflects a Native cultural heritage. In fact, alligator wrestling was reportedly invented and taught to the Seminoles by the family who owned Coppinger's Tropical Gardens, Alligator Farm, and Seminole Village in Miami in the 1930s. Although alligator wrestling was not a part of the Seminoles' social repertoire, they were encouraged to perform these acts by their white employers who recognized the powerful symbolism such contests represented. See Dorothy Downs, "Coppinger's Tropical Gardens: The First Commercial Indian Village in Florida," and Patsy West, "The Miami Indian Attractions: A History and Analysis of a Transitional Mikasuki Seminole Environment" *Florida Anthropologist* 34 (1981): 227; 207. See also Jay Mechling, "Florida Seminoles and the Marketing of the Last Frontier" in Bird 154, 161.

     The Seminole economy relied instead on alligator hides to provide cash; Seminoles also earned tips from the tourists who visited these attractions. The spectacle of a wild animal being subdued (with appropriate difficulty) by an equally "wild" Seminole recalls and perpetuates the topos of Native Americans as "primitive" members of a vanishing race, a myth that was pervasive in the nineteenth century, as we have seen.

24   Martin 144.

25   "Yahola," according to Patricia Wickman, is the "word *yá hola*, from the Maskókî [Muskogee] root, *yaha*, meaning 'wolf.' Yahola is the cry, or 'song' that is delivered by a chosen individual at the introduction of the Black Drink (a 'medicine' drink), during the Green Corn Ceremony. The word has nothing to do with victory *per se*" (Wickman personal communication). The next year, the Student Senate allocated $1,450.00 to the American Indian Fellowship to fund an American Indian week in order to "bridge the gap between myth. . .and reality. . .to present the Indian in his true cultural perspective." See *The Florida Flambeau*, "Indians Upset over Name of Spirit Chief," 12 October 1970, "Basketball Chief Chooses Yahola as Indian Name," 14 October 1970, and "Red Pride," 26 February 1971.

26   Initially the rider was referred to as "Savage Sam." "With a 4.0 and Ability to Ride, He Gets the Job," *The Florida Flambeau*, 17 November 1978 and "Seminole Spirit Personified," 10 October 1980.

27   Personal communication.

The Search for the "Real Indian"—Joseph Henry Sharp and the Issue of Authenticity at the Turn of the Nineteenth Century

Marie Watkins

"We are just waking up here in America to appreciating the big interests of our own country and to a sense of cherishing our original greatness. We are painting our plains, protecting our forests, creating game preserves, and at last—not saving the existence of the North American Indian, the most picturesque roving people on earth, but making and preserving records of them from an historical, scientific and artistic point of view."

Craftsman, March, 1906.

By the late 1880s government policy and public opinion reflected the belief that the so-called "Indian problem" was resolved. President Grover Cleveland addressed Congress in December 1886: "There is no such thing as the Indian frontier. Civilization, with the busy hum of industry and the influences of Christianity, surrounds these people at every point. None of the tribes are outside of the bounds of organized government and society."[1] Frederick Jackson Turner's famous elegiac essay followed in 1893, formally bringing down the curtain on the American frontier, emphasizing the finiteness of America's resources.[2] Increasingly, the lament for America's passing wilderness and its inhabitants enveloped the nation. A need to preserve the past for future generations took hold and manifested itself in conservation movements, archaeology, anthropology and the arts. The phrase "the vanishing American" took on new meaning as cultural extinction appeared to be looming ominously.[3] The cultural salvage operation with regard to Native America, however, did not intend to preserve native cultures themselves, but rather to depict them in words, paintings, photographs, and sculpture, i.e. documentation—not preservation—of a way of life.

Fearing the loss of "pure primitive" cultures, anthropologists departed for the field before the "real Indians" were all gone. Despite the concern of many individuals for contemporary Native Americans in a state of transition, intensive investigations producing ethnographic data took precedence. Prominent in these ethnographic salvage operations were the self-educated "old guard" in the Bureau of American Ethnology, including James Mooney, Frank Hamilton Cushing, William Henry Holmes, and Alice Fletcher; and the new university-trained professionals under Franz Boas, such as Alfred Kroeber, Paul Radin and Robert H. Lowie. For some social scientists, study of "primitive cultures" allowed modern man to see his own ancient past. For other ethnographers, the collection of raw cultural data not only contributed to overall knowledge but provided direction for successful government policy.

Artists, too, purposely went west in search of their subjects—to record and preserve the memory of the Native American peoples. In their turn-of-the-century desire to document the race they perceived as vanishing, these artists consciously sought to record, as well as recreate, the American Indian in a state untouched by white civilization. This they did, more often than not at the exclusion of modernity, expressing what they wanted the West and its inhabitants to be. Physical presence and artistic acumen, however, did not ensure accurate portrayal of Native Americans. The artists depicted their own beliefs in their documentation of other cul-

tures. Our vision of the American Indian is largely grounded in artists' works of the late nineteenth and early twentieth centuries, who froze the West and its inhabitants in time. Even in the 1990s, the imagery of the 1890s persists, especially of the "Wild West" genre of Frederic Remington, Charles Russell, Henry Farny, Charles Schreyvogel and William Leigh. Although less well-known today, another group of artists from the turn of the century stands out for their ethnographic contribution, including Joseph Henry Sharp, Elbridge Burbank, Grace Carpenter Hudson, De Cost Smith, Winold Reiss and Carl Oscar Borg.[4] Both groups of artists, however, are not unique in their desire to paint and document Native Americans, but part of a long tradition of Euroamerican fascination that essentially began with John White's sketches and watercolors of New World peoples and their way of life recorded on Sir Walter Raleigh's 1585-1586 expedition.[5]

Noble or Savage, but Vanishing

For the past five centuries, images of Native Americans have been subjects of artistic, historical and scientific inquiry. Europeans in the sixteenth and seventeenth centuries, finding native peoples on a continent that was previously unknown to them, believed these peoples lived in a state of nature. They called all of the natives "Indians," although these peoples manifested a diversity of languages and cultures. Another collective term given to these groups of people was "savage." Originally, the nomenclature referred to their alleged way of life. Later, however, it indicated the state of their souls.[6] Euroamericans further differentiated "savage" into *noble* or *ignoble*, a classification that continued well into the twentieth century. Artists accompanied the early exploring expeditions and created pictures of the inhabitants and lands they encountered, but their documentations often reflected European primitivist ideologies and stylistic approaches based on proportions and poses of classical sculpture.[7]

Euroamericans freely manipulated the image of the Indian to suit the political and philosophical climate of the time; their construction, "the noble savage" lived in primal intimacy with nature and took Euroamericans back to a more desirable, simpler place and time, a Golden Age. The "ignoble savage," however, had failed to progress from this primordial state, and according to the laws of nature, the "inferior Indian" could not obstruct civilization and was thus ultimately doomed to extinction. The noble savage, handsome in appearance and heroic in manner, extended welcome and hospitality to the settlers. Conversely, the ignoble savage was a bloodthirsty devil filled with deception and cruelty who betrayed and fought the civilized colonists at every turn. President James Madison's speeches demonstrate how easily the image of the Indian could change. In 1809 he was pleased that "our Indian neighbors" were living peaceably under our "just and benevolent system," moving toward civilization.[8] By 1813, the nation was battling the British, and Madison referred to his former "Indian neighbors" as "eager to glut their savage thirst with the blood of the vanquished and to finish the work of torture and death on maimed and defenseless captives."[9] The Native American image had not become more or less ignoble but was deployed as a pawn of political temperaments. It was becoming more apparent that the Native American and white civilizations were incompatible.

With the ending of the War of 1812 in 1815, the government turned its attention again to the "Indian problem." Each American Indian tribe constituted a sovereign power, and representative members of the tribes periodically came to the capital to negotiate peace and trade treaties. Charles Bird King was among the first to paint a series of Native American portraits in Washington, beginning with a delegation of sixteen Indians from the Kansa, Oto, Missouri, Omaha and Pawnee tribes in 1821.[10] Among his portraits was Petalesharro, a Pawnee warrior whom he painted in a feather bonnet, probably the first representation of this Plains Indian headgear that would become a ubiquitous trait of Indian peoples in later imagery.[11] Likely commissioned by Thomas McKenney, who was superintendent of Indian trade and later head of the Office of Indian Affairs, King steadily worked under government patronage until 1842, painting at least one hundred and forty-three portraits of visiting American Indian delegates. McKenney's desire to preserve the "likenesses of some of the most distinguished

Figure 1. Karl Bodmer, *Mato-Tope, a Mandan Chief*, drawn 1822-1834, printed 1840-1843, engraver Hurlimann, etching and aquatint, hand-colored, 24 7/8 x 18 1/8 inches. Courtesy of the Buffalo Bill Historical Center, Cody, Wyoming. Gift of Clara S. Peck.

among this most extraordinary race of people" because "this race was about to become extinct" resulted in a National Indian Portrait Gallery of which King's portraits were the nucleus; the National Indian Portrait Gallery became a popular tourist attraction until its almost complete devastation by a fire in 1865.[12] Praised for their accuracy and beauty, many of King's portraits in the National Indian Portrait Gallery filled McKenney and James Hall's

monumental publication, *History of the Indian Tribes of North America* (1836-1844).

Explorer Artists: Catlin, Bodmer, Miller

Around the time that King began to paint visiting Native American delegates in his Washington studio, the first artists were accompanying government expeditions and providing a record of western expansion in the early nineteenth century. Samuel Seymour recorded the first view of the Rocky Mountains in 1820 with figures of a Native American and white hunter separated by a river at the foot of the mountains in *View of the Chasm through which the Platte Issues from the Rocky Mountains.*[13] By the 1830s more and more artists began to explore the American West and brought back visual proof of a dramatic new frontier to an urban eastern population. They performed a heroic act in leaving the security and confines of the studio for the boundless West where they journeyed thousands of miles amidst perilous terrain and unknown native peoples. George Catlin, Karl Bodmer and Alfred Jacob Miller were among the best known of the artist-explorers.[14] Each artist shared a Romantic heritage but brought distinctive styles to their representations of Native Americans and argued over the veracity of their work. Miller flatly stated that "There is in truth. . .a great deal of humbug about Mr. George Catlin."[15] Bodmer called Catlin a charlatan.[16]

Supposedly inspired by a delegation of western Indians traveling through Philadelphia, Catlin in 1830 zealously set out under his own volition to paint members of "every tribe of Indians" in the "uncivilized regions of their 'uninvaded' country," believing he was lending "a hand to a dying nation, who have no historians or biographers of their own to pourtray [sic] with fidelity their natural looks and history."[17] The slapdash technique of Catlin implied his urgent sense of mission to record one more face and likeness for posterity; Catlin painted the individual, capturing his dignity of bearing, rather than "types," as if they were little more than carefully delineated mannequins in exotic dress. Catlin's artistic limitations are obvious, but his best portraits sympathetically capture the individual's humanity as seen in *Red Bear, a distinguished warrior*. Artist, scientist, showman, romantic, George Catlin devoted himself to the preservation of Native Americans at a time when many fellow Americans wanted to push farther and farther into Indian Country, regardless the cost to native cultures. Catlin also promoted the first national wilderness park,

> a magnificent Park, where the world could see for ages to come the native American in his classic attire, galloping his wild horse, with sinewy bow and shield and lance, amidst the fleeting herds of buffaloes! a nation's Park, containing man and beast, all in the wild and freshness of their nature's beauty.[18]

Prefiguring Buffalo Bill's Wild West, Catlin took his Indian Gallery of paintings, artifacts and sometimes American Indian performers on the road in America and Europe, and in his attempts to educate the public, he angered some Americans in his criticisms of Indian policy. Wielding as much if not more influence than his paintings were Catlin's publications, such as the two-volume *Letters and Notes on the Manners, Customs and Condition of the North American Indians*, published in London in 1841.[19]

In 1832, the twenty-four-year-old Bodmer accompanied his patron, the German gentleman-scientist of Humboldtian tradition, Alexander Philipp Maximilian, Prince of Wied-Neuwied, to document his explorations and observations in the upper Missouri country that Catlin had recently traversed. While Bodmer and Catlin's paintings shared similarities of peoples and places, Bodmer's superior European training produced more precise rendering of details of anatomy and colorful material culture, hence a greater impression of truth. Bodmer's representations were clinically executed records of the ethnological detail of human specimens, such as Figure 1 *Mato-Tope [Four Bears], a Mandan Chief [Formal Dress]* and *Pehriska-Ruhpa [Two Ravens], Hidatsa Man* to accompany animal and plant life, geology and geography of the Upper Missouri.[20] Directed by Prince Maximilian, Bodmer thoroughly recorded all aspects of their travels which resulted in the widely acclaimed scientific publication, *Reise in das Innere Nord-Amerika in den Jahren 1832-1834*. Both Bodmer and Catlin's paintings had a remarkable influence on other artists, not only in encouraging them to venture west and paint Plains Indians, but in becoming reference works for illustrators who never left their eastern studios but hastened to meet the popular demand for Plains Indian imagery.[21]

Miller left the comforts of a New Orleans' French Quarter studio on Chartres Street to journey fifteen-hundred miles from St. Louis to the heart of the Rocky Mountains. He travelled through partially uncharted areas with the Scottish nobleman Sir William Drummond Stewart in 1837 to record his adventures as a dashing nineteenth-century romantic figure. Depicting the frontier with European romantic sensibilities, Miller represented Native Americans as the idealized noble savage, such as *Crow Indian on the Lookout*, whom he described as "a subject of unconscious wit grace & beauty."[22] Miller often painted Indian women partially dressed or nude as playful, youthful, woodland nymphs who had the appearance of dark-skinned Caucasians. *Snake Girl Swinging* is openly erotic in the Rococo tradition of Watteau, while *Indian*

Girls Making Toilet, Scene on the River "Eau Sucre," Indian Woman Sleeping, and *Waiting for the Caravan* are sisters to the odalisque and harem scenes in the Orientalist paintings of Delacroix and Ingres, which Miller likely saw while in Paris in 1833-34.[23] Although contemporary women in openly alluring paintings that appealed to the male viewer, the works avoided censure because they were exotic and could be deemed ethnographic objects.[24] Miller's paintings convey little of the impending doom of Native cultures that he recorded in his diaries; rather, they depict a land of romantic adventure, filled with nature's innocence in which his patron cavorted and embraced.[25]

While the explorer-artists recorded their westward adventures, the government debated the fate of Native Americans and eventually adopted a policy of exclusion through seclusion, exemplified by the Removal Act of 1830 and the Trade and Intercourse Act of 1834.[26] Although doubtful the Indian tribes would ultimately survive, many Americans believed the chances of individual Native Americans staying alive would improve the further removed they were from contaminating white civilization. Eastern tribes battled both in the courtroom and on the battlefield against their forced removal to lands west of the Mississippi. They found some white support as Senator Peleg Sprague of Maine voiced his opposition to the removal bill on the senate floor: "Let us permit them to live out their days, and die in peace; not bring down their gray hairs in blood, to a foreign grave."[27] Many eastern tribes, however, were being decimated, and their days seemed numbered, as Ralph Waldo Emerson expressed: "We in Massachusetts see the Indians only as a picturesque antiquity;—Massachusetts, Shawmut, Samoset, Squantum, Nantasket, Narraganset, Assabet, Musketaquid. But where are the men?"[28] Their days in painting were also numbered; the Plains Indians imagery of Catlin and Bodmer would come to dominate what the public saw as an "authentic Indian," replacing the horseless eastern woodlands tribes who tracked Daniel Boone.[29]

Westward Expansion—Scenes of Conflict

With subsequent settlement of the West in the 1840s, it became obvious that the Indian was not vanishing as quickly as predicted and could not be isolated in the far reaches of the West from white settlement. It also meant culture clashes and a concomitant rise in pictures illustrating conflict and violence culminating in inevitable triumph of progressive white civilization. A classic theme was emigrant wagon trains, symbols of western expansion and progress, attacked by "wild Indians," as exemplified by Carl Wimar's 1856 rendition, *The Attack on an Emigrant Train*, which he painted while studying in Dusseldorf, Germany.[30] In the same violent vein, Charles Deas painted *The Death Struggle* (c. 1845). A Native American and frontiersman, both on horseback with knives drawn, are wrapped in a deathlock and hang precipitously upon a cliff, above an abyss, their weight miraculously supported by the frontiersman's grip on a small tree limb. However, mutual dependency and intertwined destinies overshadow their impending brutal death.

Wounded Knee calamitously and tragically sealed the end of the Indian Wars in 1891; the wars had essentially come to a close in the 1870s, although a few bands of Apaches resisted through the 1880s. American policy had to be reformulated. Now the dictum became if the American Indian was to be saved, he must become civilized. Assimilation replaced the policy of segregation. To inculcate the values of white civilization, that is, agriculture and private property, the Dawes Act of 1887 intended to divide the reservations into individual allotments so the tribal governments would be broken up and the individual Native American would become self-supporting through working the soil. America, however, was no longer an agrarian nation, and big business, mass production and commercialism were the order of the day, making farming an unlikely road to financial success. In essence the noble savage, vis-à-vis the good Indian, would embrace the open arms of civilization and become a productive, albeit a subservient, member, as envisioned by government bureaucrats, reformers and missionaries. On the other hand, failing to comply with government decree and to adapt the practices of Christianity, education and agriculture, the " ignoble savage" would remain a ward of the state until eventually dying off. Expectations were that this should only take a generation to accomplish. In the mid-1890s the government abandoned the severalty program, but by this time Indians had lost half their lands to land-allotment and railroad rights-of-way.[31]

Over the years, American Indian policy had been expected to culminate in elimination or assimilation, but the Native Americans stubbornly refused to vanish from the American scene. The image of the American Indian remained a revered symbol of America. From the first European allegorical images of America, the Indian maiden symbolized America; in 1856, Thomas Crawford's allegorical bronze statue of Freedom, bedecked in a feather headdress, crowned the dome of the U.S. Capitol; and in 1914, James Earle Fraser's buffalo nickels, with an Indian head in profile, jingled in Americans' pockets.[32]

On the brink of cultural extinction at the turn of the century, "ignoble savages," the ones who practiced the old ways and would not cooperate with government edicts, captured the imagination and interests of the nation. "The frontier has gone," Frederick Jackson Turner wrote, "and with its going has closed the first period of American history."[33] No other symbol stood more for America's recent past than the American Indian, and as the nation apprehensively contemplated the new millennium, it nostalgically looked backward at this momentous historical closure and romantically sealed the West and its inhabitants away.

"Wild West" Imagery: Remington, Russell, Buffalo Bill

The "Wild West School" of imagery was one side of the artistic coin, and in their day, no one considered their paintings less

than factual renderings. Remington and Russell serve as the quintessential examples, for their canvases are a meeting point for polemical visions of the West. Remington's theme was the winning of the West with the clash, conflict and courage played out on the western plains. *Captured* (1899), for example, depicts a traditional captive scene with a white cavalryman defiantly awaiting the grim fate planned by his stoic Indian captors, a sacrifice to western settlement; the action-packed *Downing the Nigh Leader* (1907) portrays a common western image of a host of galloping Indians attacking a stagecoach, a symbol of progress.[34] An urbane Easterner who capitalized on his sporadic western experiences, Remington captured the imagination of Easterners, stopping Western history in a time frame of the wild and unsettled frontier. As William A. Coffin wrote in 1892:

> It is a fact that admits of no question that Eastern people have formed their conceptions of what the Far-Western life is like, more from what they have seen in Mr. Remington's pictures than from any other source, and if they went to the West or to Mexico they would expect to see men and places looking exactly as Mr. Remington has drawn them.[35]

Moreover, a reporter in 1907 remarked on Remington's reliable reporting: "He is the most conscientious of historians. He has never 'faked' an action, a costume or an episode."[36] Yet while working on *Downing the Nigh Leader*, Remington recorded on 10 July in his diary "Jack English and some wellbred boys called and they take my pictures for veritable happenings and speculate on what will happen next to the puppets so ardorous are boys' imaginations."[37] For Remington, his works were recurrently fictional constructs that addressed evolutionary truths: the savage American Indian as antagonist to Anglo Saxon western progress.

For the Eastern establishment, Charlie Russell was Remington's successor; for Westerners, especially Montanans, Russell was the beloved "Cowboy artist" untainted by eastern art traditions, who painted the West as it was. "The effete east has her Remington," the Butte *Miner* devotedly reported, "but the glorious west has her Russell."[38] Montana was home for Russell and he came to know many Plains Indians personally and established a reputation as their friend. Distinguished as a documentary artist in the 1960s, a leading Russell authority affirmed:

> One feature that distinguishes Russell's work from that of all other artists who tried to paint the West is accuracy. Whether it was the beadwork on an Indian's moccasin, or the brand on a horse, the observer can be certain such

Figure 2. Charles M. Russell, *Mothers Under the Skin,* 1900, pen and ink, 14 x 22 inches. Courtesy of the C.M. Russell Museum, Great Falls, Montana.

Figure 3. Charles M. Russell, *Skunk Wagon*, 1907, watercolor, 7 x 11 5/8 inches. Courtesy of the Buffalo Bill Historical Center, Cody, Wyoming. Gift of the Charles Ulrick and Josephine Bay Foundation, Inc.

details were exactly as Russell had seen them. Russell's memory was infallible.[39] While Russell may have had an unfailing memory, he wrote to a friend in 1918 that he "always studied the wild man from his picture side."[40] Relying on artists' works, such as Remington, and Native American artifacts, rather than a firsthand witness, Russell established his authenticity through realism of ethnographic details as in *Squaw Travois* (1895) and *Returning to Camp* (1901), depicting gender roles and details of camp life.

Russell also painted contemporary Native American life in works like his emphatic rendering, *Mothers Under the Skin* (1900, Figure 2): he contrasts a homeless Indian mother trudging down the street with her child on her back, accompanied by her scraggly dog, to the white woman of leisure, her cradled baby, and her pedigree dog in the shade of a tree at her comfortable home. Known and treasured for his humor, Russell also depicted an amusing side of contemporary life in the *Skunk Wagon* (1907), with an American Indian couple on horseback, commenting on two white couples whose car is stuck in the mud, "White man's skunk wagon no good, heap lame" (Figure 3). Russell attempted to paint the Native American's point of view as well as his own disdain for technological progress. For Russell, whom Brian Dippie terms the supreme memorialist, the West was about loss, nostalgia and regret.[41] Much of the West that Russell and Remington lovingly painted so realistically, they had never witnessed. It had long disappeared with the pioneers of progress they now despised. "The west is still a great country," Russell wrote, "but the picture and story part of it has been plowed under by the farmer."[42]

In 1883, however, picture and story came together for William F. "Buffalo Bill" Cody as he gave breath and life to these images when his Wild West show opened and would successfully play to audiences throughout America, Canada and Europe for more than three decades. "It is not a circus, nor indeed is it acting at all, in a theatrical sense," The *Illustrated London News* reported in 1887, "but an exact reproduction of daily scenes in frontier life, as experienced and enacted by the very people who now form the 'Wild West' Company" (Figure 4).[43] Sioux, Cheyenne and Pawnee, some who battled in the past Plains Wars, performed in the Wild West, thrilling viewers as they watched recreated versions of

events in America's recent past, such as the capture of a scout, a raid on an emigrant train, the ever-popular attack on the Deadwood Stage, and Custer's Last Stand.[44] Debate still rages over the Indian stereotypes created by Buffalo Bill's Wild West and the numerous off-spring imitative shows, as well as the exploitation of the performers.[45] Although viewers thought they were catching the last glimpses of America's past and the Vanishing Race, they were actually witnessing Native Americans in transition. They had survived the "Winning of the West," and their cultures had endured.[46]

Relics of America's Past

Rather than being seen as "real people" in a period of arduous transformation, Native Americans became relics of the past because a "real Indian" had no place in America's progressive forward movement. White civilization concurred that a document of the Vanishing American and their fleeting moments had to be made, urgently, for posterity's sake; it seemed important for artists and scientists to preserve accurate details of a race soon to disappear in the amalgamation of white culture. Both artists and anthropologists searched for pure ethnic specimens—the "real Indian"—to paint on canvases and record in their notebooks. If the subject was not pure, s/he was of no use to the documentor. Essentially, the "real Indian" was what the Anglo was not, and was conceived of in terms of what s/he was not. Through stereotyping, identity became fixed and thus controllable. If individuals moved out of the identities fixed for them or beyond essentialized traits given to them, then they were no longer "authentic" for the dominant culture. Stuart Hall contends that "we fix that signifier outside of history, outside of change, outside of political intervention."[47] Documentors of the Indian only paid attention to those who fit their idea of authenticity. The others were discounted because they were no longer of use to their portrayers. When a native is "used to represent the point of 'authenticity' for our critical discourse," Rey Chow maintains,

> they become at the same time the place of
> myth-making and an escape from the impure
> nature of political reality.... We see that in our
> fascination with the authentic native, we are

Figure 4. Indians and tipis in the *Wild West* show arena, c. 1890-1910, photograph, 4 1/4 x 6 3/4 inches. Courtesy of the Buffalo Bill Historical Center, Cody, Wyoming.

Figure 5. Joseph Henry Sharp, c. 1915, photograph. Courtesy of the Buffalo Bill Historical Center, Cody, Wyoming.

actually engaged in a search for the equivalent of the aura even while our search processes themselves take us farther and farther away from that original point of identification.[48]

Thus the American Indian came to represent, and be defined by, what the Anglo-American was not.

This is the other side of the artistic coin—purposely to document vestiges of "true" tribal life and experience. Therefore, artists continued to work under the theory of the Vanishing American as had their predecessors fifty years earlier. With good intentions to paint precisely what they saw, these artists often turned a romantic eye to their subjects and recreated a recent past redolent of their "Wild West" precursers. Artists in their westward travels encountered many Native American tribes on reservations and selectively chose particular individuals and settings to make records on canvas for posterity, science, patrons, and the art market. What constituted an "authentic Indian" at the turn of the century cannot be monolithically characterized. However, a perspective into attitudes and conceptions of Native Americans can be derived through the examination of how they were represented.

Joseph Henry Sharp, Artist-Ethnographer

The artist Joseph Henry Sharp (1859-1953), more than any other artist, provides that vantage point because he was well respected by his contemporaries, that is, the public, fellow artists and anthropologists, for his authentic representations of Native Americans (Figure 5). During the first years of the twentieth century, the patronage of the distinguished Smithsonian Institution and of philanthropist and aficionado of anthropology, Phoebe Hearst, validated his work as important ethnological documents and conferred prestige upon Sharp.[49] Indeed, the names of the Smithsonian and Hearst became a litany in Sharp's prolific seventy-year career which resulted in more than 7,800 oils, watercolors, pastels, monotypes, and etchings of Native American peoples and themes.[50] His works appeared not only in art galleries but also in natural history museums, world's fairs, popular magazines, and scientific journals. No one, however, has considered the issue of authenticity in Sharp's works and how they came to bear that stamp of approval. Moreover, for his paintings to be authentic, Sharp himself must first take on the question of authenticity. He himself must first recognize and know the "truth" and then present that reality in his paintings.

To portray authentic Indian subjects, Sharp travelled and lived among the Native Americans predominantly in New Mexico and Montana. He typically made on-the-spot sketches, drawings and paintings, and often wrote notes, brief biographical sketches and anecdotes about many of his portrait sitters. Sharp, who was deaf, also learned sign language as a means of communication with Native Americans.[51] He took photographs and collected artifacts as well. From his firsthand experiences with various Indian peoples including the Crow, Blackfoot, Cheyenne, and Pueblos, Sharp filled his paintings with conspicuous ethnographic detail. In many ways, his life as an artist paralleled the methodology of the nascent field anthropologists; Sharp echoed the premises of the emerging discipline of anthropology, as well as the early artist-explorers before him, because he wanted to paint Indians before they were gone and to document their passing way of life. Preserving a record of the Native American in a pre-contact, that is, a pure state, was more important than depicting the degenerative condition of contemporary Native Americans because they had already turned the corner of assimilation and were no longer identifiable as "real Indians."

Sharp in the Southwest: "Return of the Adventurer from the Wilds of New Mexico"

Sharp's first experiences among the pueblos of Tesuque, San Juan, Pojoaque, San Ildefonso, and Santa Clara in 1893 made popular copy in his hometown of Cincinnati and also attracted the attention of *Harper's Weekly*, for whom Sharp wrote two articles with illustrations. The articles focused on the remoteness, the exoticism, and the ancient Native American customs. Newspapers hailed Sharp as an artist-explorer returned from the "land of the Comanche and Apache in the wilds of New Mexico. . .in places where few white men have ever ventured."[52] The Cincinnati *Times-Star* headlines announced: "Return of the Adventurer from the Wilds of New Mexico—Strange Customs and Superstitions of a Neglected Corner of America."[53] The rival Cincinnati *Commercial Tribune* published Sharp's account under the heading: "At the Pueblo Games. An Artist's Experiences in New Mexico. Life Among the People. Vast Opportunities for Studies, Though the Models are Wary—Unceremonious Customs in Domestic Life."[54] Although traveling in 1893, Sharp took on the guise of a pioneer / frontiersman leaving behind the comforts of the East for hardships, danger and gunplay in the West for the rewards of being amidst rugged landscape and "picturesque" Indians. Predicting that all of it would disappear in five years, Sharp brought back to Cincinnati as much of his Western experience and of the Indian as he could pack for future paintings, and Sharp would continue to paint Native Americans until his death in 1953.

In wide-eyed amazement, a reporter watched Sharp unpack upon his return to Cincinnati and regarded Sharp's leather trunk a veritable treasure chest of Indian artifacts:

> studies of Indian faces and dreary scenes of sage deserts and mountains. A hundred photographs covertly taken were scattered about, while war bonnets, dance bonnets, peace pipes, saddles, boots and spurs, pistols and guns, bows and arrows and quivers, buckskin dresses and long-fringed leggings, moccasins and war clubs, turquoise beads and bright bone necklaces,

Figure 6. Absarokee Hut, exterior, Joseph Henry Sharp Cabin, museum installation September 1992, Sharp Garden. Courtesy of the Buffalo Bill Historical Center, Cody, Wyoming. Gift of Mr. and Mrs. Forrest Fenn.

Absarokee Hut, interior, Joseph Henry Sharp Cabin, museum installation September 1992, Sharp Garden. Courtesy of the Buffalo Bill Historical Center, Cody, Wyoming. Gift of Mr. and Mrs. Forrest Fenn. Objects on loan from Mr. and Mrs. Forrest Fenn.

> purses woven of porcupine quills, gaily colored and solid silver armlets and rings were tumbled about.[55]

Upon seeing Sharp's studio, decorated with his recently acquired Native American objects to recall a distant mysterious world, a visitor noted:

> In Mr. Sharp's studio is vividly suggested his recent journey…in New Mexico. It would seem as if a whole tribe of Indians, not too large a one, could camp right in his front studio without bringing any baggage or even a change of clothing with them, and not miss many of the necessities for living. Exquisite robes of all kinds, hats and caps of the most ornate designs, pottery, bread bowls and baskets, bows and arrows, Indian dolls, moccasins, beads, instruments of war, and utensils for all purposes lie around in the richest profusion.[56]

Sharp derived a glamor of association with the objects, for they spoke of foreign peoples and adventures that were not at hand to the Cincinnati public.

The Native American artifacts also served the practical function of artistic props for future paintings. Factual accuracy was part of Sharp's art, and he utilized a backdrop of authentic Indian objects to prove it. Sometimes displaying his collection of American Indian curios among his paintings, Sharp readily used these detached objects again and again throughout his career. A familiar drum, hides, pots, and pieces of clothing turn up like old friends as a viewer looks at a collection of Sharp's works. The significance of the objects, however, lies more with the identity of the collector, because they were removed from their Native American function and context, and in his later years, he freely cobbled together artifacts from different cultures to create an "Indian setting." An important testimony to his presence among Native Americans, the objects were evidence of his authenticity in that he knew "real Indians"—but inevitably represented misleading ethnographic information when manipulated as a painter's studio-props in created settings.

In his eyewitness narratives, Sharp merged the role of artist and anthropologist and described southwestern peoples in tran-

sition, all the while lamenting the difficulties with Native American models.[57] Soaring Eagle was his favorite model, whom he described as "a pure type of Indian in face, beautiful in figure, stolid, and as inquisitive as a child in character. Sad to say, he had the prevailing weakness for whisky, though his generous nature prompted him to first divide his earnings with his squaw[58] before sending some one to get drink for him and his companions."[59] Soaring Eagle conformed to an "authentic" image of the American Indian for Sharp. Several of his anecdotes typified the nineteenth-century theory of vice and virtue, in which the Indian surrendered the native virtue of childlike innocence and acquired the vices of the white population, for example susceptibility to alcohol. Although he witnessed and described in his prose certain manifestations of extreme poverty, disease and alcoholism, he refused to paint such imagery because it reflected white contact and ultimate acculturation and thus doom for the "real Indian." Sharp wanted to preserve the "authentic" Native American, a noble image secure from white intervention. Moreover, the public wanted a "noble savage" to be noble.

In scenes such as *Apache Squaw's Tent*, a woman makes baskets in front of a tent pitched on the mesa. Placed in a setting without an historical referent, she is at one with nature in a desolate landscape unmarked by urban intrusion; Sharp made her a living ruin. A doctor introduced the Apache woman to Sharp, noting she wore the same dress she had had on four years ago. Appraising her as "authentic," Sharp described her as the "last nomad Apache I saw," because she, unlike the other Apaches, had left the reservation, no longer drew government rations, and had not abandoned traditional dress for store-bought clothes.[60] Sharp ruefully reported the Apache were agriculturists, an image of assimilation he would never paint. He would rather have painted the Apache he first met on his trip westward, whom he had labeled "the meanest Indian we have" and who "combined all that is ugly fierce and treacherous."[61] Once Sharp noted he could readily pick the Apache out "by his features and carriage, for his is cynical, overbearing, and vicious, and jeers at the priests."[62] Reconstructed into a tiller of the soil, the Apache had lost his menacing, warlike past and thus his exotic attraction; he was no longer romantic to Sharp or his audience.

Figure 7. "The Prairie Dog," Sharp's mobile studio, c. 1909, photograph. Courtesy of the Buffalo Bill Historical Center, Cody, Wyoming.

Sharp's paintings are not simple reflections of Native American cultures and people as they appeared in his time, but socially constructed and meaningful representations of the people as he preferred to see them. Although Sharp's travels and first-hand experiences in the West authenticated his writing and art, his views nonetheless corresponded to white Americans' idea of Indian cultures as exotic, timeless, and isolated. Removing his Native American images from the influences of white civilization, Sharp selectively chose images that he saw as "fast disappearing."[63] Sharp set his pictures in the present, but his subjects transcended time, becoming icons, which the public would view as "real" and "natural" interpretations of Indians for decades to come. His paintings of the southwestern peoples and cultures produced an appearance of this people's reality that viewers accepted as truly Indian. For Native Americans, there was a growing disparity between their common existence and their public image.

Sharp in the Northern Plains: "If I do not paint them no one ever will."

At the turn of the century, the fieldwork of anthropologists revealed that the native peoples of the southwest were not vanishing at all, but rather continuing much in their ancient way of life. Coming to the same conclusion from his personal observations, Sharp abandoned his work in New Mexico and turned north to the rapidly changing cultures of the Plains Indians. Speaking like an anthropologist, Sharp unequivocally stated that he was aware of the

> longevity of the southwestern Indian. I found that his northern prototype would soon become extinct and I decided to put into my canvases representations of their present day and time. I went north because I realized that Taos would last longer.[64]

With the ardor of a modern-day George Catlin, Sharp emphatically declared: "if I do not paint them no one ever will."[65] Documenting the disappearing Plains culture became an artistic mission, and Sharp set out to paint as many portraits as he could. He also painted Plains Indian customs, ceremonies and costumes that met with anthropological approval as these paintings also found their way into anthropology exhibitions and collections.

Sharp arrived at Crow Agency, Montana, in the summer of 1899 and witnessed a Crow Council deliberating over land cessions because the government wanted to purchase 1,080,000 acres of Crow land. Blackfeet, Cheyenne and Sioux also gathered at Crow Agency for the council meeting. Rather than seeing this as an opportunity to document a contemporary reality of political and social conflict on the reservation, Sharp instead saw with fascination the old Plains warriors gathered about, and he imagined and isolated them in a past he would paint as if historical documents. Looking with artist's eyes at the Native Americans, Sharp wrote that the tribal council "gives an artist great opportunities for old time things."[66]

Finding unique artistic opportunities at Crow Agency, Sharp decided to live on the reservation and successfully integrated art and life. This lifestyle paralleled the current emphasis on ethnographic fieldwork that Franz Boas articulated in opposition to "armchair" anthropology. Both artist and anthropologist responded to the same cultural stimuli. To the Eastern public, Sharp's willingness to leave the warm walls of a refined eastern studio and urban life for a perceived coarse existence in a "little house standing alone in the heart of a great western plain"[67] signaled his dedication to his subject matter and strengthened his standing as an accurate and truthful interpreter of Indian life.

Sharp built a rustic log cabin in 1905 to live year round on Crow Agency (Figure 6); he called his cabin "Absarokee Hut," which is derived from the Crow people's word for themselves, meaning "children of the long-beaked bird."[68] Although cabin architecture was an outmoded structure at this time in Montana, it symbolically harked back to the days of the early white settlers. Sharp also transformed a sheepherder's wagon, christened "The Prairie Dog," into a mobile studio to travel about the reservation, especially in winter months (Figure 7). Painting under pioneer hardships and travails, Sharp proudly told of working in subzero temperatures with freezing paints and using three overcoats, two rugs, and a foot warmer. No longer an Eastern tenderfoot, Sharp would paint under the harshest of conditions in order to bring authenticity to his work. Embracing a perception of Western veneer, Sharp legitimized himself in his own eyes as well as in the eyes of the public, in a certain way authentic like the "authentic" Indians he painted.

Sharp's initial visit to Crow Agency began an intensely productive period, especially in Native American portraiture. In his selection of Plains Indian subjects, Sharp preferred those of perceived historical value, and that usually meant those Native Americans who fought against Custer. Whereas warfare was a part of Plains Indians' history, the Battle of the Little Big Horn was a defining moment in both the Native American and white American cultures. Although the Battle of the Little Big Horn took place in 1876, interest in this fight peaked in the 1880s and 1890s. This fascination infected Sharp as it did the rest of the nation, and he painted portraits of 212 Indians who participated in the battle.[69]

In emphasizing this one battle as a selection criterion for many of his portrait sitters, what Sharp chose not to consider is perhaps more important: he chose not to consider Indian lives and their conditions since that pivotal battle. Nonetheless, Sharp did not paint war imagery like his contemporaries Remington and Russell. While continuing to paint portraits, Sharp told patron Joseph Butler, Jr., that he wanted to paint "compositions and pictures of the poetry and legends as well as the home life of the Indians."[70] Although Sharp privileged the warriors in portraiture,

Figure 8. Joseph Henry Sharp, *Wolf Ear (Sioux)*, c. 1900, oil on canvas, 14 x 10 inches. Courtesy of The Butler Institute of American Art, Youngstown, Ohio.

103

he chose to portray another side of Native Americans, a domestic side that revealed their humanity. Sharp also perpetuated the established tradition of Catlin, Bodmer and Miller, who focused on Plains Indians, to the extent that the Plains tribes essentially came to represent to the public the whole of the Native American population.

In such a myopic schema, what became of historical importance was the American Indian past only as it related to the white culture; skewed by this distortion, it was as if Native America had no history to speak of until white Americans came along. The painters' Native Americans were of commemorative value, like relics of the Wild West tableaux of the "Death of Custer and The Last Stand." The philosophical underpinings of this system held no future for Indian peoples because they were to be imminently assimilated and no longer possess a distinctive identity from non-Indian Americans. Re-inventing Native American history in the context of an inexorable Manifest Destiny, the identity of the American Indian now took on mythic proportions. The nation, in the throes of hero-worship for the defeated chiefs and warriors, praised and valorized them for their valiant and skillful war strategies. Portraits of Plains Indians were popular commodities for entrepreneurs compiling "Indian collections," which were in vogue, and the general public eagerly bought prints of famous Indian chiefs. Sharp's Indian paintings contributed to making Native Americans part of the mass culture.

Sharp painted portraits several times between 1900 and 1939 of one of his favorite models, Wolf Ear, a Sioux combatant at the Little Big Horn (Figure 8).[71] Several of the portraits of *Wolf Ear* exemplify Sharp's early style of Indian portraiture—a clean, frozen profile that ennobled his models. The rich colors of the head, executed in exacting detail, stand in contrast to the sketchier and softer edges of the body. The left side light highlights the model's features, especially along the nose and high cheekbones where Sharp wiped clean the red and brown color contrasts. Acclaimed for the ethnological value of representing "types" in his portraiture, Sharp captured the individuality of his subject and gave the portrait meaning—a meaning that coincided with the expectations of the public and his patrons.

Sharp came to know and like many of his models. Recalling his memories of Wolf Ear to his patron, Thomas Gilcrease, Sharp wrote he was "a strong character & councillor [*sic*], but pleasant and friendly."[72] As was his custom, Sharp often included a written statement on the back of his portraits which authenticated the first-hand experience, knowledge and intimacy he had with his subject, as well as revealing to us the turn-of-the-

Figure 9. Joseph Henry Sharp, *Custer's Scout "Curley" (Crow),* c. 1900, oil on canvas, 18 x 12 inches. Courtesy of The Butler Institute of American Art, Youngstown, Ohio.

Figure 10. Joseph Henry Sharp, *Curley,* photograph. Courtesy of the C.M. Russell Museum, Great Falls, Montana.

century ideal conception of the Indian sitter as well as, of course, his individuality. A portrait of Wolf Ear had the following label:

A Custer battle warrior of much prominence …Wolf Ear had a real sense of humor and very clever. He was much amused that I would pay him $2.00 a sitting to look at him and put spots of paint on canvas. Every rest period he looked at the painting—never criticized—they rarely ever did—another trait whites could emulate.[73]

Sharp, like many other white Americans, perceived Wolf Ear (and other American Indians) through the ideologies of his own culture. Through the written word and the enhancement of the image with anthropological details, Sharp gave Wolf Ear dignity and captured what was heroic to the artist, all the while consigning Wolf Ear to the past of the Battle of the Little Big Horn, creating for him an historical presence. By focusing on a unique, exotic and solitary event in Wolf Ear's long life, Sharp ignored his sitter's contemporary life on the impoverished reservation, a life Sharp had witnessed. Recording native peoples in both paint and words, Sharp intentionally created historical documents which he believed important and true to be saved for posterity. Yet the paintings were misleading and provided a selective image of contemporary Indian existence to the public.

Curley, a Crow scout for the U.S. Army (Figure 9), also posed for Sharp as he elatedly conveyed to a friend,

I have just succeeded in getting a portrait of Curley, Custer's famous scout, and the only one to escape that well known battle. I have been after him for three years, but he was harder to land than a salmon on a trout hook. He is a man of fine physique, but very morose and taciturn. It is difficult to get him into conversation and he will not talk of the battle.[74]

At the age of sixteen, Curley was a scout assigned temporarily to Custer. Dismissed shortly before the battle, Curley, who may have witnessed some of the battle, was the first to report to Generals Terry and Gibbon that the American Indians were victors on the field of the Little Big Horn.[75] For his supposed role in the Battle of the Little Big Horn, Curley was in demand as an authentic Indian portrait and Sharp painted at least seven oils of Curley. In addition to painting Curley from life, Sharp also took photographs of him. In some of the photographs, Curley appears seated in the agency store with stacks of blankets around him (Figure 10). Moreover, he holds a newspaper in his hands. In the oil portraits, Sharp carefully edited out traces of Curley's literacy and contamination with white contact that would reveal he was a reservation Indian. A feather has also been added to Curley's hair which did not appear in the photographs. For Sharp and his viewers, Curley could not remain a "real Indian" unless he appeared with the essentialized signifiers, and thus they denied Curley's complexity as an individual. Curley jumped out of the stereotypical box in the cloistered photograph, but his painted portrait reconstructed that box and is revealing of turn-of-the-century cultural assumptions.

Sharp also witnessed Curley's opposition to the government's desire to purchase land of deceased tribal members in the summer of 1899 and kept a translated copy of Curley's powerful speech. "I was a friend of General Custer," Curley began, to speak before Washington officials at a tribal conference.

> I was one of his scouts and will say a few words. The Great Father in Washington sent you here about this land. The soil you see is not ordinary soil—it is the dust of the blood, the flesh and bones of our ancestors. We fought and bled and died helping the whites. You will have to dig down through the surface before you can find nature's earth, as the upper portion is Crow. The land as it is, is my blood and my dead; it is consecrated and I do not want to give up any portion of it.[76]

Curley's words failed to block the land sale, but he impressed Sharp to tears, according to Fenn.[77] While Sharp may have had tears in his eyes, they had dried by 1907 because he too bought Indian land from Big Medicine, Old Horn, Crazy Crane, and Not a Pretty Woman of Crow Agency.[78] Turning over reservation lands for cash and out of Crow ownership was a divisive tribal political issue and one that Sharp would not translate to canvases. He, like the anthropologists, was too busy in his salvage operations to record the old ways and the old people, not the realities of modern existence. Sharp looked nostalgically back for the Plains Indians as he recollected that "twenty-five years ago this valley was the home of the Sioux Indians. Now the Crow Indians have it under cultivation."[79] Sharp preferred to paint the past rather than Indian on the road of assimilation, for he found the "younger generation of Indians are not so interesting or paintable."[80] The younger generation reservation Indians were not "real Indians" in Sharp's eyes.

Two Moons was another fighter at the battle with Custer and a popular subject with the artist who thought he had "splendid Indian features."[81] Sharp painted him at least twenty-five times. The Montana *Standard* reported that

> among his Indian heads is one of Two Moons, the famous Cheyenne chief, who led the onslaught on unfortunate Custer not two miles distant from the spot where he sat as a model only a few weeks ago. Two Moons was over at Crow Agency from Lame Deer, visiting friends. He stands more than six feet in his stockings and is straight as an arrow. He was attired in a

long Prince Albert coat and a derby hat about three sizes too small for him, but the face, the strong Cheyenne type was there and this is all that Mr. Sharp took.[82] The painting of Two Moons (Figure 11) was a half-length portrait bust with head slightly turned. Sharp modeled Two Moons' strong, fleshy face with light and color, casting a shadow on the right side of his face. With a seriousness and toughness of character, his life-like eyes pierce the viewer. Sharp wrote of Two

Figure 11. Joseph Henry Sharp, *Chief Two Moons (Cheyenne)*, c. 1899, oil on canvas, 14 x 10 inches. Courtesy of The Butler Institute of American Art, Youngstown, Ohio.

Moons' solid and big physique which he insinuated in the large chest and wide shoulders cropped by the canvas's edges. The body was sketchy, but the face was finished and carefully done, as was the highly-prized bear claw necklace that attested to the documentary nature of the painting valued by anthropologists.[83]

Although Two Moons typically wore store-bought clothing, Sharp chose to portray him in a hide shirt with the fierce, bear-claw necklace prominently displayed, an image that the public would construe as visibly "Indian."[84] In Sharp's representation of Two Moons in this way, we learn certain things—why he is popular and to whom he appeals. Two Moons is the noble, but savage, warrior who defeated Custer. He transcends individuality, becoming a symbolic image, both a stereotype *and* an archetype. Sharp had keen powers of representation, and his images produce visual knowledge that has ramifications in many arenas. The public did not question the image for its accuracy of information because it was naturalized. In 1901 a Cincinnati newspaper unquestioningly reported that Sharp:

> saw that when these old fellows should die there would be left none of the real warriors and characteristic men of the various tribes. An Indian in a sack cloth and derby is hardly an Indian at all, and there are few now that have not felt the influence of the white civilization. So he picked out the chiefs and the old men here and there, and the pictures that he paints are not ideal or as the subject might have been, but as the subject is.[85]

Despite the commendation of the newspaper report, Sharp clearly knew what the "real Indian" was and was not. After working among the Plains Indians he deemed the Pueblos "a mild type, peaceful Indians" who were "fine for figure compositions but very few have the interesting faces & history of the old plains fighters."[86] He wanted to paint "those old time fighters—they are dying rapidly—& the present generation haven't the force & characteristic features of the old timers."[87] The Alaskan tribes he totally dismissed as they "compare[ed] very poorly with the types to be found on the Plains."[88] They were too Asiatic. "The real, picturesque Indian is fast disappearing and seems to be going with this generation," Sharp lamented:

> The Government school on the reservation and at every pueblo is making this change. The small boys wear short hair and a shirt, while the girls are tidied up and in calico. It is heartbreaking to the artist, and particularly so if he has not had foresight to collect costumes and various articles which become more rare each year. [89]

Sharp continued that an American Indian in store clothes with hair cut, and without his blanket, was not picturesque.[90] Although Sharp emphatically supported the American Indians' right to retain cultural identity, he felt that in losing cultural distinctiveness, the Indians had less artistic value and ultimately less economic value as an artistic commodity to him.

Sharp had liked to attend festivals on the Montana reservations such as the Crow Agency Fair and Fourth of July celebrations among other Northwestern tribes where traditional customs and practices were celebrated; he could make sketches and paint another "head," as he liked to call his Native American portraits. But—as he wrote in 1909 to a friend who had asked his advice on where he could paint "real Indians"—he found the fairs were becoming disappointing and lacking in authenticity:

Figure 12. Joseph Henry Sharp, *Bill Jones (Gros Ventre)*, c. 1905, oil on canvas, 18 x 12 inches. Courtesy of The Butler Institute of American Art, Youngstown, Ohio.

> Too many tents instead of teepees. The dances at night are good. They had a sham battle between Crows & Cheyennes one day, & the whole thing was a ride around & come together in a bunch in front of a moving picture machine, fire off their guns & retire—all a pose for the camera, & heart breaking & disgusting to see. But please do not allow *any* of this to get in the paper or tell anyone—don't want the people around here to think I am a knocker, for they [sic] are others won't understand that I'm thinking & talking from a *painter's* standpoint. . . .[91]

In a follow-up letter Sharp advised that the fairs did not "compare to a Buffalo Bill show any more, so I'm cutting it all out & stick to models & landscapes. The Shoshone & Arapahos have no costumes at all, & their celebrations & dances are nothing."[92]

Sharp's Models: "He Understood What I Wanted."

From Sharp's aesthetic standpoint in terms of his professional livelihood, contemporary Native American subjects provided little interest unless they were performing ancient customs and wearing traditional hide clothing embellished with ornate beadwork. Sharp also found posing for the movie imagery exploitative, in that it failed to document the truth of those Native Americans who posed for his canvases. He believed he was painting and preserving the "real Indian" when he chose to paint them in romantic visions of the past, not their everyday ordinary dress and manner. "He understood what I wanted," Sharp said of the Blackfoot Big Brave, "and each time he came in a different make up—shirt, paint, head dress & etc."[93] That was what the public wanted to see as well and often saw when they came to the reservation.

Some of Sharp's models posed for tourists as he recorded on the portrait of Bill Jones, a Gros Ventre (Figure 12): "Medicine Man. Montana. Army Scout for many years. Has earth paint on his face and hair. Generally around the agency, painted and fixed up for tourists—snap shot—2 bits—intelligent and great sense of humor."[94] Bill Jones, like Big Brave and Sharp's other models, was an American Indian in transition, earning money in a restricted economy where role-playing an earlier historical persona, i.e. essentially as an actor, was one among relatively few choices. Sharp, however, avowed a distinct difference in the Native Americans who posed for him as opposed to their posing for tourists; in his mind, his models with face paint and feathers were authentic. Many years later Sharp remarked on the portrait of another model, Running Horse, whom he said was a "fine young brave— 25 yrs. ago before they began to paint and dress up with feathers & stuff for tourists. This fellow is a big fat 200 pounder & has a curio store!"[95] Running Horse had escaped reservation poverty and become a successful entrepreneur; to Sharp's disdain, acculturation had taken away Running Horse's Indianness. In some instances, acculturation took away Sharp's models. The Crow tribe's slowly increasing prosperity from dealing in horses and cattle made it difficult for the artist to obtain models, forcing him to paint the more available Native Americans in Taos.[96] By 1910 Sharp had resettled in Taos, although he would continue to return to Crow Agency for brief periods through 1920.

Sharp's models also negotiated their portrayals, within limits, appealing to a sense of authenticity and consciousness of the image they projected. The famed Sioux Chief Red Cloud (Figure 13) posed for Sharp on several occasions and the artist noted that the "last time I painted him, his eyes failing, anxious it would not show in pictures."[97] A Taos Indian, White Weasel, initially refused to wear a Crow hat explaining that Taos Indians did not wear hats and it would be "bad medicine" for him to put on the hat of a Crow Indian. Newspapers found the anecdote amusing and a critic commented that the finished portrait was that of a "decidedly angry and grumpy Indian."[98] The Arapaho and Shoshone puzzled Sharp also in their preference to be painted in their store clothes, rather than their picturesque buckskins. Even Sharp's models turned a critical eye to his portraits, as Crow Chief Deaf Bull (Figure 14) had the final say on their authenticity:

> I hung all my Indian portraits around the

walls—Deaf Bull happened in, went around,—stopped rather defiantly a bit, in front of each one—finally came to his own portrait, looked at it a bit pointing his finger at it, said, 'there is the only real Indian in the lot, the rest are cowards;' turned and stalked out.[99]

"The Indians as we see them today. . .have no significance either to historian or artist. . . ."

What indeed constituted a "real Indian" in this transitional generation? Both Native Americans and white Americans shared a nostalgia for a world that was slipping away from them, but white America was willing to accept the American Indians' cultural demise. They wished to preserve a picture of this romantic, picturesque world in the face of the evolving, modern, Indian nation undergoing concomitant changes in religious, social and economic practices. However, to the general Euroamerican public, Native Americans lost their identity as "Indians" whenever they were not exotic and possessed of distinctive features that conformed to a particular, picturesque stereotype.

A plethora of newspapers sang dirges to the Vanishing American on Sharp's canvases. "Ethnologically these portraits are of great importance as portraying in the most faithful degree the famous men and general types of a race whose primary characteristics and customs will soon be a matter of tradition," a Detroit reporter proclaimed in 1901. "If today we are interested in the portraits of these great chiefs because of their connection with events which touch us so nearly, how incalculable will be their importance a century hence."[100] In 1906 the New York *Herald* boldly announced in a banner headline: "Studio on Custer's Battlefield / How J. Henry Sharp is Perpetuating on Canvas at Close Range Human Documents of the Vanishing Race of North American Indians."[101] And even in 1927, one of Sharp's patrons, a Justice for the Supreme Court of Pennsylvania, explained he was purchasing the portrait of White Weasel

> because it tells its own story without any explanation being needed. The Old Chief is typical of the entire Indian race. He is old and passing away, as I am afraid the Indians, as a race, are also doing. The horses and horsemen depicted on the walls, representative, as they are, of the earlier life of both himself and the race, tell, all too truly, of the past to which both he and they are looking back with infinite regret.[102]

The "Vanishing Race" was defined by the attrition of traditions and attributes, not by population figures. Clearly the American Indian as a mythological subject deserving great attention was most appealing when he / she was vanishing. A contemporary critic was unequivocal about present reality when he stated:

> The Indians as we see them today. . .have no significance either to historian or artist, whereas the race from which they descended, the once rulers of the continent, were men of joy and spiritual contentment, of personal dignity and

beauty, and of wise simplicity of existence.[103]

Sharp helped define the American Indian for a commercial market, and the viewer willingly mistook the images for the real thing. The public in the first decade of the twentieth century certainly thought his paintings

> represent several Western tribes as Mr. Sharp found them in their own villages. He has lived among the Indians the greater part of the last five or six years. He has been privileged to camp with them and witness their ceremonies; he has been with them on the march and when after game; he has smoked the pipe of peace with them and enjoyed the confidence of their chiefs and their medicine men. His pictures present in realistic and faithful manner a phase of Western life which is fast disappearing.[104]

While Sharp did paint aspects of "real life" that he assumed were important, he constructed a simplified image that the public wanted to see—not the totality of their modern existence. Sharp's "Indians" were both ethnological specimens and living ruins who could never be allowed to exist outside of a picture frame; they could only be memories of America's past.

Figure 13. Joseph Henry Sharp, *Red Cloud (Oglala Sioux)*, c. 1899, oil on canvas, 18 x 12 inches. Courtesy of The Butler Institute of American Art, Youngstown, Ohio.

> Very few of the present generation know anything of the Indian, the romance, dignity & beauty of their life and care less," Sharp regretted in his declining years. "In a way, all these cowboy stunts with Indians or not makes it all kind of common & curio stuff—they have it in every town out west that has a hotel or place for trailers"[105]

In a way, very few of the present generation know anything of the Indian other than the romance, dignity and beauty of his life, as we are unraveling the cultural myths and influence of past generations' paintings of Native Americans.

Sharp's hard-earned credentials of life in the West among Native Americans, whether he had undergone everything the public believed or not, confirmed the truth of the exacting details of subject matter on the canvas. His collection of native arts also served him well, not only acknowledging his presence among Native Americans, but as a source of his aesthetic inspiration and truthfulness. It has long been (and often still is) a given that an objective of western art is accuracy, which ostensibly derives from factual research of detail. Sharp went to great lengths to promote

Figure 14. Joseph Henry Sharp, *Chief Deaf Bull (Crow)*, c. 1900, oil on canvas, 18 x 12 inches. Courtesy of The Butler Institute of American Art, Youngstown,

authenticity of his paintings, especially the portraits as he emphasized, "absolutely every one was painted direct from life at their homes on reservations or wherever I could contact them."[106] Sharp, however, would paint several versions of popular portraits, relying on photographs, sketches and notes. Unquestionably, Sharp captured the individuality of his sitters in his early years in Taos and Montana. Although he preferred the Plains Indians as models, he did paint portraits of southwestern and Alaskan Native Americans. Women, children and adolescents number among his portraits, with males forming the majority. Typically painted from the waist-up and in three-quarters view in broad, free brushstrokes, the portraits are usually vibrant, hearty and full of life—not images of a dying race. Many times the invariable adjectives "proud" and "noble" *do* come to mind. Without Sharp's portraits many faces would be lost to history, as well as to the families of his models.

In his later years while living in Taos, Sharp freely blended the imaginary with past observations, his paintings having a veneer of historical truth over typifying details. Likewise he tended to preserve all American Indians in a state before European contact. Tipis and Native Americans in traditional dress on horseback steadily appear in a pristine environment in his paintings. Sharp's reservation snapshots often included, however, the woodframe and brick homes that the Indians now lived in, wagons for transportation, store-bought clothing and utensils. Furthermore, in painting Pueblo people costumed in his collection of Plains clothing and surrounded by Plains artifacts, Sharp frequently cobbled cultures together to present his vision of the American Indian. He preferred the romantic and picturesque in his paintings, while his prose and photographs disclosed his consciousness of native peoples in transition.

Sharp's representations of Native Americans are an integral part of both turn-of-the-century western genre and ethnological documents. Sharp, his fellow artists and their American Indian subjects are long dead, but their art remains a visual record of attitudes and perceptions of the American Indian in this chapter of America's past.

---

1 Brian Dippie, *The Vanishing American: White Attitudes and U.S. Policy* (Middleton, Conn.: The Wesleyan UP, 1982) 141.

2 Frederick Jackson Turner read his essay, "The Significance of the Frontier in American History," in 1893 to the American Historical Association's annual meeting. The setting was the Chicago's World's Columbian Exposition,

whose theme was American progress; on the outskirts of the exposition, "Buffalo Bill's Wild West-America's National Entertainment" played to packed crowds with some visitors mistaking the entrance for the World's Fair. Both Turner's frontier thesis and Buffalo Bill's Wild West would influence and dominate interpretations of the West for generations to come.

3 Dippie considers the preservationist response in chapter fourteen of *The Vanishing American*, "Now or Never is the Time: Cultural Extinction and the Conservationist Impulse." Lee Clark Mitchell in *Witnesses to a Vanishing America. The Nineteenth-Century Response* (Princeton: Princeton UP, 1981) discusses nineteenth-century Americans awakening to the costs of empire building and their diverse responses to their culture.

4 Burbank was a Munich schoolmate of Sharp's who turned to Indian portraiture, notably under the patronage of his uncle, Edward Everett Ayer, president of the Field Museum of Natural History in Chicago. From 1897-1914, Burbank produced more than 1200 portraits representing over one hundred tribes; he is the most prolific artist of American Indian portraits. Unlike most of the artist-ethnographers, Hudson was not only a woman, but a *bona fide* Westerner from California. She specialized in the painting of the native Pomo children. Her realistic rendering of the children's dirty and ragged appearance impressed critics and the public alike, and she could not paint Pomo portraits quickly enough to meet public demand. Smith was a New Yorker who grew up near the Onondaga Indian Reservation and was initiated into the tribe. In 1884, Smith made his way westward for the first time and earned a reputation from both his paintings and articles on Plains Indians. Reiss and Borg were European immigrants from Germany and Sweden, respectively. Captivated by James Fenimore Cooper's and Karl May's novels, Reiss came to America in 1913 specifically to paint Indians and was disconcerted to find that they did not live in villages on the edge of America's cities. In 1919, he made the first of several trips to Browning, Montana, winning critical acclaim for portraits of the Blackfeet, Piegans and Crow. Borg was also a latecomer to the American West, but under the patronage of Phoebe Hearst, he went to live among the Hopi and Navajo tribes in 1916. Commissioned to photograph and paint these tribes, Borg felt a spiritual kinship with the native peoples, and his poems and writings of his relationship with the Southwestern Indians evoke primitivism. In addition to the previously discussed artist-ethnographers, the following is a rudimentary roll call of artists who recorded the Indians and their cultures at the turn of the century: Louis B. Akin, John D. Allen, Henry C. Balink, Ira Diamond Gerald Cassidy, J. Andre Castaigne, Charles Abel Corwin, Kate T. Cory, E. Irving Couse, Henry H. Cross, Charles Arthur Ellsworth, Robert E. Emerson, Jean Louis Theodore Gentilz, Nicholas de Grandmaison, John Hauser, Joseph A. Imhof, Wilfred Langdon Kihn, Robert Ottokar Lindneux, Fernand Harvey Lungren, Frank Sauerwein (Sauerwen), Joe Scheuerle, and Hubert Vos.

5 Few people actually saw John White's illustrations. However, through the engravings of Theodor de Bry, White's images reached a greater audience in the 1590 publication, *Grands Voyages*, and ensuing seventeenth-century images of American Indians were derived from de Bry's engravings. Jacques Le Moyne de Morgues is believed to be the first European artist to draw North American Indians from life on Rene de Laudonniere's 1564 Florida expedition. Although there are only two known originals, Le Moyne's work is best known through the widely-circulating de Bry's engravings.

6 Among the most extensive sources for imagery of Indians are Robert Berkhofer, Jr., *The White Man's Indian: Images of the American Indian from Columbus to the Present* (New York: Vintage Books, 1979) and Dippie, *The Vanishing American*.

7 For excellent discussions and sources of European images of America, see Rachel Doggett, ed., *New World of Wonders: European Images of the Americas, 1492-1700* (Seattle: U of Washington P, 1992), Karen O. Kupperman, ed., *America in European Consciousness, 1493-1750* (Chapel Hill: University of North Carolina, 1995), Hugh Honour, *The European Vision of America* (Cleveland: The Cleveland Museum of Art, 1975), Hugh Honour, *The New Golden Land: European Images of America from the Discoveries*

to the Present Time (New York: Pantheon Books, 1975), and Christian F. Feest, "The Virginia Indian in Pictures, 1612-1624," *Smithsonian Journal of History* 2.1 (1967): 1-30.

8   Dippie 6.

9   Dippie 6. Although painted prior to the War of 1812, John Vanderlyn's *The Death of Jane McCrea* depicts a similarly appalling image of frontier violence that supposedly took place during the Revolutionary War. Painted in neoclassical style, two Mohawk warriors modeled from Hellenistic sculpture savagely scalp a blonde white woman. The brutal Mohawks not only threatened colonial women but the very nation itself, thus vindicating their exclusion and possible annihilation from the civilized world.

10   Portraits of American Indian mediators had appeared as early as 1710, when John Verelst painted full-length portraits of four Mohawk chiefs visiting England, suggesting their recognition as heads of state. In 1735, William Penn's sons renegotiated their father's deed with the Delaware Indians. John Penn commissioned Gustavus Hesselius to paint the Delaware chiefs, Tiscohan and Lapowinsa, commemorating this negotiation, which came to be known as the Walker Purchase Treaty. Hesselius was the first Anglo artist to paint lifesize, bustlength portraits of Native Americans in colonial America. In 1790, John Trumbull painted portraits of Creek Indians who came to New York to sign a treaty with the United States government. In 1804, Charles-Balthazar-Julien Fevret de Saint-Memin, a French artist in exile from the French Revolution, painted twelve Osage men and two boys, the first delegation of Native Americans from beyond the Mississippi. Upon meeting the Osage, President Thomas Jefferson stated that the Osage men were "the most gigantic" and "the finest men we have ever seen" (John Ewers, "The Emergence of the Plains Indians as the Symbol of the North American Indian," *Smithsonian Report for 1964* ((Washington, D.C., Smithsonian Institution, 1965)) 532). A second Native American delegation from the West that included the young Pawnee, Pagesgata from the Platte Valley followed; Charles Wilson Peale, artist, naturalist and museum founder, cut silhouettes of them, which he sent to President Jefferson on February 8, 1806.

11   In addition to King's portrait of Petalesharro, John Neagle and Samuel F.B. Morse painted Petalesharro in a flowing feather bonnet. In Morse's "The Old House of Representatives" of 1822, Petalesharro is in front of the visitor's gallery. Petalesharro was also the inspiration for Hard Heart, the hero of James Fenimore Cooper's novel *The Prairie* (1827), which is his only novel set in the Great Plains. There are conflicting sources of Cooper's knowledge of Petalesharro. Howard R. Lamar ("An Overview of Westward Expansion," in the *West as America*, edited by William Truettner ((Washington, D.C.: Smithsonian Institution Press, 1991)) 4-6) writes that Stephen Long's accounts of the 1820 expedition to reach the Rocky Mountains, which included reports of a Pawnee warrior, Petalesharro, fascinated Cooper, and he drew on Long's discussion for his novel. John Ewers ("The Emergence of the Plains Indians as the Symbol of the North American Indian" 533) relates that Cooper met Petalesharro on his eastern tour where he received a hero's welcome because he had bravely saved a Comanche girl prisoner from being sacrificed to the morning star in the annual Pawnee ceremony. Cooper wrote that Petalesharro was an excellent example of a "loftinesss of spirit, of bearing and of savage heroism...that might embarrass the fertility of the richest inventor to equal." For further discussion of the Plains Indian imagery, see Ewers (531-544). From many nineteenth- and twentieth-century pictures, Plains Indian clothing and the tipi dwelling became standard traits for Native Americans of other cultures, with some Native Americans actually adapting the Plains' attire as well.

12   F.W. Hodge, "The Origin and Destruction of a National Indian Portrait Gallery," *Holmes Anniversary Volume, Anthropological Essays* (Washington, 1916) 190. On January 15, 1865, a fire destroyed many of King's and John Mix Stanley's portraits in the National Indian Gallery, which was housed in the Smithsonian. Henry Inman had copied many of Kings's portraits, which were used for lithographs in *The Indian Tribes of North America*, thus preserving likenesses of King's portraits.

13   Martha A. Sandweiss, "The Public Life of Western Art," *Discovered Lands, Invented Pasts* (New Haven: Yale UP, 1992) 121. Ironically, Seymour's watercolor, *View of the Chasm through which the Platte Issues from the Rocky Mountains,* was altered by the engraver illustrating the official painting of the Stephen Long expedition of which Seymour was the primary artist. In removing Seymour's figures of an Indian and white hunter, the picture is strikingly different. Perhaps a signifier of the prosperous fur trade or what may have been an initial friendly interaction between two cultures, the image was transformed into a mysterious and empty virginal landscape filled and overflowing with opportunities and promise of wealth. On a darker side, the revised image foretold the ultimate removal and eradication of the Indian from the West. See also Patricia Trenton and Peter Hassrick, *The Rocky Mountains: A Vision for Artists in the Nineteenth Century* (Norman: U of Oklahoma P, 1983) 20-30 for a discussion of the accuracy of Seymour's field sketches.

14   Other artist-explorers include Titian Ramsey, James O. Lewis, Charles Wimar, John Mix Stanley, Paul Kane, Seth Eastman, Richard and Benjamin Kern, Lee Clark Mitchell, *Witness to a Vanishing Race: The Nineteenth Century Response* (Princeton: Princeton UP, 1981) 122, 127-128. Mitchell includes the following artists in his list of survey painters: Samuel Carvalho, Gustavus Sohon, George Gibbs, Balduin Mollhausen, and Albert Bierstadt. Independent painters are: Felix O. C. Darley, George Winter, Rudolph Friedrich Kurz, Nicolas Point, and Frank Blackwell Mayer.

15   Ron C. Tyler, ed., *Alfred Jacob Miller: Artist on the Oregon Trail* (Fort Worth: Amon Carter Museum, 1982) 51; Brian Dippie, *Catlin and His Contemporaries: The Politics of Patronage* (Lincoln: U of Nebraska P, 1990) 301. Miller's statement was in reference to Catlin's *Letters and Notes;* however, he questioned the authority of Catlin's paintings as well. Dippie's book is revealing of the rivalries among the artist explorers, writers, and scholars, often taking on a soap opera format. The issue of accuracy also would follow the next generation of Indian painters. In 1903, Remington waged an all-out vitriolic attack on his rival, Charles Schreyvogel, whose work he viewed as feigned. Remington charged that Schreyvogel's painting, *Custer's Demand,* was, in short, "half-baked stuff" and filled with errors. He proceeded to list the faults: "pistol holders, ammunition belts, war bonnets, hats, boots, stirrup covers, saddlebags, saddle cloths, uniform colors, the height of Custer's horse." Remington regarded these details as wrong and, therefore, deemed the painting inauthentic. A newspaper battle erupted with Mrs. Custer, Theodore Roosevelt, Colonel Montgomery Schuyler, and John S. Crosby defending the authenticity of the painting. Crosby was actually present on that auspicious occasion with Custer; Schuyler's military trousers served as Schreyvogel's archetype; and who could doubt the word of the beloved Libby Custer and the President of the United States? The controversy ended with Remington expressing his regrets, although he "knew the West better than any other man."

16   Dippie, *Catlin and His Contemporaries* 367.

17   Dippie, *Catlin and His Contemporaries* 5, 17-18.

18   George Catlin, *Illustrations of the Manners, Customs and Condition of the North American Indian with Letters and Notes Written During Eight Years of Travel and Adventure among the Wildest and Most Remarkable Tribes Now Existing,* 9th edition., 2 vols. (London: H.G. Bohm, 1857), Vol. 1, p. 262.

19   *Letters and Notes on the Manners, Customs and Condition of the North American Indian* was reprinted five times within a five-year span. Additional written works by Catlin include *An Account of an Annual Religious Ceremony Practised by the Mandan Tribe of North American Indians* (1865), *The Breath of Life; or, Mal-Respiration* (1861), *Catlin's Notes of Eight Years' Travels and Residence in Europe, with His North American Indian Collection* (1848), *Last Rambles amongst the Indians of the Rocky Mountains and the Andes* (1867), *Life Amongst the Indians* (1861), *The Lifted and Subsided Rocks of America, with Their Influences on the Oceanic, Atmospheric, and Land Currents, and the Distribution of Races* (1870), *Memo-*

rial of George Catlin (1868), and *O-Kee-Pa: A Religious Ceremony; and Other Customs of the Mandans.*

20 Joseph C. Porter, "The Romantic Horizon in History & Ethnology" in *The West as Romantic Horizon* (Omaha: Center for Western Studies, Joslyn Art Museum, Internorth Art Foundation, 1981) 39-44. The ethnographic details reveal a history of Mato-Tope's life as a warrior. The red wooden knife in his hair signifies his killing of a Cheyenne chief in hand-to-hand combat; the colored wooden pegs indicate each musket wound received; the turkey wing feathers represent arrow wounds; the owl feathers (yellow with red tips) denote that he was a member of the Dog band of warriors; yellow stripes on his arms represent bravery on the battlefield; and the yellow hand on his chest signifies he captured prisoners. Mato-Tope knew both Bodmer and Catlin, but as smallpox almost decimated his tribe, he regretted and cursed the whites he had befriended in an eloquent last speech to the remaining members of his tribe before succumbing himself to the disease. See Porter, p. 44 for Mato-Tope's last address.

21 Ewers, "The Emergence of the Plains Indian" 535-538. Artists whose Plains Indian imagery relied on Catlin's and Bodmer's paintings include Felix O.C. Darley, Louis Maurer and Arthur Fitzwilliam Tait.

22 Joan Carpenter Troccoli, *Alfred Jacob Miller. Watercolors of the American West* (Tulsa: Thomas Gilcrease Museum Association, 1990) 39.

23 Joan Carpenter Troccoli, "Alfred Jacob Miller. Watercolors of the American West," *American Art Review* (Winter 1993): 114-115.

24 For a discussion of women in Miller's paintings, see Susan Prendergast Schoelwer, "The Absent Other" in *Discovered Lands, Invented Pasts* (New Haven: Yale UP, 1992) 143-155.

25 Miller wrote of the Kansas, whom King had been painted earlier in their noble state: "The Kansas Indians live pretty much now on the recollections of the past—the future for them is entirely hopeless—somewhat like the Beggars of Spain. . . . In a few, very few years, they will be swept from the face of the earth & the places that now know them, shall behold them no more-forever—the expression of their faces seems as if their sad destiny had already cause them to be hopeless & despairing." (Cited in Troccoli, *American Art Review* 113-114.)

26 Brian Dippie, "This Bold But Vanishing Race: Stereotypes and American Indian Policy," *Montana The Magazine of Western History* 23.1 (January 1973): 6.

27 Dippie, "This Bold But Vanishing Race" 8.

28 Dippie, "This Bold But Vanishing Race" 3.

29 Ewers, "The Emergence of the Plains Indian" 536-543.

30 Wimar painted two versions of *Attack on an Emigrant Train*, both in Dusseldorf in 1854 and 1856. Perry Rathbone (*Charles Wimar, 1828-1862: Painter of the Indian Frontier* ((St. Louis: City Art Museum of St. Louis, 1946)) 15-16) believes Wimar was inspired by French author Gabriel Ferry's episode in *Impressions de voyages et aventures dans le Mexique, la Haute Californie, et les regions de l'or* (1851). The 1854 version was the probable source of a popular color lithograph, *On the Prairie*, printed by Leopold Grozelier of Boston. J. M. Boundy's *The Weak Never Started* (1861) was most likely copied from the widely-circulating lithograph. See Richard H. Saunders, *Collecting the West* (Austin: University of Texas, 1988) 66-67 for further discussion of *Attack on the Immigrant Train*.

31 Frederick E Hoxie, *A Final Promise: The Campaign to Assimilate the Indians 1880-1920* (Lincoln: University of Nebraska, 1984).

32 The Indian-head penny was minted in 1859; Augustus Saint-Gauden's design of the Goddess Liberty in feathered bonnet for the $10 gold piece was issued in 1907.

33 Frederick Jackson Turner, "The Significance of the Frontier in American History," American Historical Association *Annual Report,* 1893 (Washington, D.C., 1894) 227.

34 In his later years, Remington would paint Native Americans with a more sympathetic and nostalgic brush, as in *With the Eye of the Mind* (1908).

35 William A. Coffin, "American Illustrations of Today," *Scribner's Monthly* 11 (1892): 348; Emerson Hough, "Texas Transformed," *Putnam's Magazine* 7 (1909-1910): 200. Hough wrote, "Buffalo Bill, Ned Buntline and Frederic Remington. . .It is something to have created a region as large as the American West, and lo! have not these done that thing?"

36 Brian Dippie, "Frederic Remington's West: Where History Meets Myth," *Myth of the West* (Seattle: The Henry Art Gallery, 1990) 111.

37 Alexander Nemerov, *Frederic Remington and Turn-of-the-Century America* (New Haven: Yale Publicatons, 1995) 196.

38 "Charles Russell, Cowboy Artist," Butte *Miner,* 11 October 1903.

39 Frederic G. Renner, *Paper Talk: Illustrated Letters of Charles M. Russell* (Fort Worth: Amon Carter Museum of Western Art, 1962) 68. Jane Meyer ["The Russell Gallery at Great Falls," *American Artist* 30 (1966): 26] declared Russell "was *the* documentary artist of the American West." Brian Dippie, *Looking at Russell* (Fort Worth: Amon Carter Museum, 1987) examines Russell as a documentary realist.

40 Charles M. Russell to Harry P. Stanford, 13 December 1918, private collection, in Brian Dippie, *Remington and Russell*, revised edition (Austin: U of Texas P, 1994) 9.

41 I am indebted to Brian Dippie and his 1996 seminar, *Remington, Russell and the Rest: Art and the Mythic West*, held at the Buffalo Bill Historical Center, for thoughts put forth in this essay.

42 Brian Dippie, *Charles M. Russell, Word Painter* (Fort Worth: Amon Carter Museum, 199) 3.

43 *Illustrated London News,* 16 April 1887.

44 Most of Cody's performers were Sioux from Pine Ridge agency.

45 See LG. Moses, *Wild West Shows and the Images of American Indians, 1883-1933* (Albuquerque: U of New Mexico P, 1996) for an excellent and illuminating discussion of the complexities of the imagery of "Show Indians." He examines the lives and experiences of the Native American participants from their point of view.

46 Moses 194.

47 Stuart Hall, "What is This 'Black' in Black Popular Culture?" *Stuart Hall: Critical Dialogue in Cultural Studies,* ed. by David Morley and Kuan-Hsing Chen (New York: Routledge Press, 1996) 472.

48 Rey Chow, "Where Have All the Natives Gone?" ed. Angelika Bammer, *Displacements: Cultural Identities in Question* (Bloomington, Indiana: Indiana UP, 1994) 139-140.

49 In December 1901, Mrs. Hearst purchased seventy-nine paintings from Sharp, fifty-six of which had been exhibited recently at the Pan-American Exposition in Buffalo. She proceeded to make a five-year contract, agreeing to buy fifteen paintings per year and established what would turn out to be a warm friendship with the Sharps. Purchasing the majority of the paintings for her newly founded Berkeley anthropology department, Mrs. Hearst eventually donated a total of ninety-six paintings.

50 Forrest Fenn, *The Beat of the Drum and the Whoop of the Dance. A Story of the Life and Works of Joseph Henry Sharp* (Santa Fe: Fenn Publishing Company, 1983) 308. Of the publications on Sharp, Forrest Fenn's book is the most comprehensive biography.

51 Joseph Henry Sharp Papers, owned by the Gilcrease Institute of American History and Art, Tulsa, Oklahoma, microfilmed by the Archives of American Art, Smithsonian Institution. Sharp wrote that White Swan, who was a scout for Major Reno at the Battle of the Little Big Horn, taught him sign language. Additionally, Sharp wrote of communicating with the Sioux Long Soldier in sign language.

52 Undated clipping from the Cincinnati *Times-Star*, "An American Crucifixion," in the Joseph Henry Sharp scrapbook, MS22, Joseph Henry Sharp Archives, Harold McCracken Research Library, Buffalo Bill Historical Center, Cody, Wyoming [hereafter JHSA].

53 Unidentified clipping, JHSA.

54 Unidentified clipping, JHSA.

55 Undated clipping from the Cincinnati *Times-Star*, "An American Crucifixion," JHSA.

56 Undated clipping from the Cincinnati *Enquirer*, JHSA.

57 Joseph Henry Sharp, "An Artist Among the Indians," *Brush and Pencil* 4.1 (April 1899): 1. "As a model the Indian is not a great success. After various tribulations to get him to pose, it is impossible to make him unbend. If it is his first attempt he will invariably take a pose of majestic an often ludicrous stiffness. Having used much persuasion, time, and patience in breaking one in, he soon becomes indifferent, often gets too familiar, goes on a strike for more pay, or stays away altogether; so at times one is tempted to take Dooley's advice, 'give him ten dollars, and let him go off and drink himself to death.'"

58 Although the word "squaw" is offensive and unacceptable to modern eyes and ears, it was common terminology at the turn of the century. The word is used in this paper in the context of historical quotes or titles and in no way should suggest that I accept or endorse this pejorative terminology.

59 Sharp, "An Artist Among the Indians" 1-3.

60 Sharp, "An Artist Among the Indians" 5-6.

61 Sharp, "An Artist Among the Indians" 5; clipping "At the Pueblo Games" from the Cincinnati *Commercial Tribune*, 1893, JHSA.

62 Sharp, "An Artist Among the Indians" 5.

63 Sharp "An Artist Among the Indians" 6.

64 Jon de Lack, "J. Henry Sharp—Painter of Indians," *Society* (6 November 1913): 11.

65 Laura Bickerstaff, *Pioneer Artists of Taos* (Denver: Sage Books, 1955) 86.

66 Joseph Henry Sharp, Curatorial Files, National Museum of American Art, Smithsonian Institution.

67 "Our Home Department," *Craftsman* (June 1906): 408.

68 Absarokee is a variant of Absalokee or Absalooka, children of the long-beaked bird. For further discussion of Sharp's cabin and works at the Buffalo Bill Historical Center, see Sarah Boehme, *Absarokee Hut: The Joseph Henry Sharp Cabin* (Cody, Wyoming: Buffalo Bill Historical Center, 1992).

69 Fenn 105, 281.

70 Joseph Henry Sharp [hereafter JHS] to Joseph Butler, Jr., 14 March 1904, Butler Papers, Butler Institute of American Art, Youngstown, Ohio.

71 Sharp's likeness of Wolf Ear was the cover of *Sunset* magazine in June 1903.

72 Joseph Henry Sharp Papers, Gilcrease Institute of American History and Art, Tulsa, Oklahoma.

73 Joseph Henry Sharp Papers, Gilcrease Institute of American History and Art, Tulsa, Oklahoma.

74 Clippings from the Cincinnati *Enquirer* January 1901; Helena, Montana *Record* 10 August, 1901; Seattle *News-Letter* 31 August 1901 JHSA.

75 Fenn 150.

76 Joseph Henry Sharp Papers, owned by the Gilcrease Institute of American History and Art, Tulsa, Oklahoma.

77 Fenn 130-132.

78 Copy of Warranty Deed, 6 May 1907, JHSA.

79 Clipping from the St. Louis *Post Dispatch* 30 November 1902, JHSA.

80 JHS to Mrs. Garbur, Parmly Billings Library, 18 April 1930, JHSA.

81 Fenn 149. Although Sharp called the Cheyenne chief Two Moons, his name was Two Moon. Writers also sought out Two Moons for his participation in the Battle of the Little Big Horn. See Hamlin Garland's discussion "General Custer's Last Fight As Seen by Two Moon," *McClure's Magazine* Vol. 11, September, 1898: 443-448.

82 Undated clipping from the Montana *Standard*, JHSA.

83 Joseph Henry Sharp Papers, Gilcrease Institute of American History and Art, Tulsa, Oklahoma. Sharp wrote, "The bear claws in necklace the largest I ever saw. Two Moons' stretched his arms up high & said the bear towered over him—he killed it with his knife." Both Sharp and Dr. Joseph Dixon, an anthropologist, coveted Two Moons' bear claw necklace and attempted several times to trade Two Moons for it, but they were unsuccessful. Later, Two Moons gave Sharp one of his bear claw armlets as "a sacrifice to a friend." Two Moons thus valued Sharp above Dixon; in his triumph, Sharp immediately showed his trophy to Dixon.

84 See also Fenn 149.

85 Clipping from the Cincinnati *Observer*, 9 November 1901, JHSA.

86 JHS to J.H. Gest, 15 June 1906. Archives, Cincinnati Art Museum, Cincinnati, Ohio.

87 JHS to Lorenzo Hubbell, 6 October 1908. J.H. Sharp File, Box 74, Collection AZ375, Hubbell Trading Post Record, 1882-1968, Special Collections, University of Arizona Library.

88 Clipping from the Seattle *Newsletter*, 10 August 1901, JHSA.

89 Sharp, "An Artist Among the Indians" 6.

90 Sharp, "An Artist Among the Indians" 6.

91 JHS, Crow Agency to Joe Scheuerle, 20 October 1908. Joseph Scheuerle Letters, owned by Thronton Boileau, microfilmed by the Archives of American Art, Smithsonian Institution.

92 JHS, Sheridan, Wyoming to Joe Scheuerle, 15 April 1909. Joseph Scheuerle Letters.

93   Joseph Henry Sharp Papers, Gilcrease Institute of American History and Art, Tulsa, Oklahoma.

94   Joseph Henry Sharp Papers, Gilcrease Institute of American History and Art, Tulsa, Oklahoma.

95   Joseph Henry Sharp, Curatorial Files, National Museum of American Art, Smithsonian Institution.

96   See Frederick E. Hoxie, *Parading Through History. The Making of the Crow Nation in America 1805-1935* (Cambridge: Cambridge UP, 1995) for a discussion of the Crow economy, especially pages 266-294.

97   Joseph Henry Sharp Papers, Gilcrease Institute of American History and Art, Tulsa, Oklahoma.

98   Undated clipping from the Cincinnati *Times-Star,* JHSA.

99   Joseph Henry Sharp Papers, Gilcrease Institute of American History and Art, Tulsa, Oklahoma.

100 Unidentified clipping from Detroit, 1901, JHSA.

101 Clipping from the New York *Herald,* 23 December 1906, JHSA.

102 Justice Alex Simpson, Jr., Supreme Court of Pennsylvania to JHS, 15 September 1927, JHSA.

103 William Truettner, "Science and Sentiment," *Art in New Mexico, 1900-1945, Paths to Taos and Santa Fe* (New York: Abbeville Press, 1986) 32.

104 Clipping from the Kansas City *Star,* 10 January 1909, JHSA.

105 JHS, Litchfield Park, Arizona to Joe Scheuerle, 15 April 1937. Joseph Scheuerle Letters.

106 Joseph Henry Sharp Papers, Gilcrease Institute of American History and Art, Tulsa, Oklahoma.

Edward S. Curtis, *Vanishing Race—Navaho, c.* 1907. Photograph courtesy of Sotheby's, New York.

IV. PHOTOGRAPHS DON'T LIE?

Gertrude Käsebier's Native American Portraits

Jennifer Sheffield Currie

During the late-nineteenth and early-twentieth centuries, American Indians were viewed as a vanishing race, a perception which not only moved many photographers to record the passing culture of the "noble savage" but also shaped their artistic vision with regard to this subject.[1] At this time, the Arts and Crafts movement was burgeoning, and photography underwent a reevaluation.[2] Many photographers were exploring the documentary uses for this medium while Alfred Stieglitz and his group of Photo-Secessionists were introducing its artistic possibilities through pictorialism, a style which rejected the sterile portraits of professional photographers who often employed artificial devices in their work.[3] Pictorialist photographers intended to produce pictures that combined emotional content with beautiful subjects, resulting in images that appealed to the aesthetic sensibilities in all respects. In the minds of these artists the "Indian way of life" was the ultimate connection to nature and a symbol of purity.[4] The photographer Frederick Monsen noted that the Native American was

> ...doubly helpless, because the smattering of artificial teaching that has been given has blunted his naturally keen and true perception and destroyed all his native feeling for beauty, and also because his own simple standards cannot stand for a moment against the arrogant assumption of superior knowledge on the part of the white man. Some day when it is too late, we may realize what we have lost by 'educating' the Indian, and forcing him to accept our more complex but far inferior standards of life, work, and art.[5]

These assertions were widely shared at the turn of the century, and this led to a great interest in preserving and recording what was thought to be a fading culture. As a result, Native American arts and crafts became the subjects for much interest in magazine articles, and many photographers embraced the Native American as an artistic subject.[6]

Gertrude Stanton Käsebier was among the group of leading pictorialists who founded the Photo-Secession, and she upheld the objectives of pictorialist art.[7] Like many of her contemporaries, she too photographed Native Americans, inviting various performers from Buffalo Bill's Wild West Show to come to her studio. The result of these sittings is a series of striking images characteristic of Käsebier's pictorialist style and heavily weighted with her own romantic notions regarding the "plight" of the Native American.[8] These photographs reflect her desire to shun artificiality or emotionless documentation; however, she transformed each of her sitters into a "noble savage," reflecting the beliefs that prevailed among her contemporaries.

It has been suggested that Käsebier intended to capture individual personalities while also representing an archetypal Indian, and Käsebier's photography has often been noted for her ability to capture the personalities of her sitters.[9] Unlike many of her photographs in which her subjects are vividly portrayed with emotional accuracy, a veil of separation can be detected throughout her Native American series. Pictorialists such as Käsebier were drawn to Native Americans as romantic subjects and were interested in capturing what they perceived to be the spirit of the culture by alluding to the primitive past and their pure nature.

Käsebier's images react against the documentary approach of photographing American Indians such as that practiced by Edward S. Curtis, one of her most well-known contemporaries, who focused on Native Americans as his primary subjects.[10] His goal differed greatly from that of pictorialists in that he intended to create

> ...transcriptions for future generations that they might behold the Indian as nearly lifelike as possible as he moved about before he ever saw a pale face or knew there was anything human in nature other than what he himself had seen.[11]

The resulting images were intended to be aesthetic documentations; however, Curtis was more concerned with the mass appeal of such images than with their artistic value.[12] In his image entitled *Nayenesgani-Navaho*, 1904, he depicted a Native American in a headdress that does not reveal his face. The image addresses formal aesthetic concerns such as composition and lighting in order to create an intriguing image, but it does not express emotion or convey a message about the Native Americans as a people. This model is treated as a type and used as a prop for the traditional attire documented here. Curtis's images reflect his desire to document the practices and appearances of a culture, but his very different approach was also generated from the same prevailing belief that Native Americans were a vanishing race.

Differences in Curtis's photographic style also stemmed from his working method. Unlike Käsebier, who photographed within her city studio, Curtis was able to work in the field, observing and photographing Native American culture first-hand.[13] His photograph of *Nampeyo Decorating Pottery*, 1900, depicts Nampeyo sitting quietly in an interior surrounded by the tools of her trade. She is engrossed in her craft and pays no attention to the photograph that is being taken. Curtis made no attempt to connect with his subject; he simply photographed her involved in her everyday activity. In contrast, Käsebier's image depicting *Indians Drawing* in her studio, c. 1899 (Figure 1) shows traditionally-dressed figures who have been posed in front of a window revealing a cityscape. The seated figure holds his head high in a proud stance indicative of the "noble savage" while the other figure engages in an adopted craft of line drawing on paper. Unlike Nampeyo, who appears to be photographed while carrying out her daily routine, these figures are arranged, and the drawing is being produced at someone's request. Here, Käsebier tries to capture the disparity between the Native American spirit and the reality of their circumstances as a means of emphasizing their "plight."[14]

The people of the Sioux tribe photographed by Käsebier in the late 1890s were members of Buffalo Bill's Wild West Show that toured New York in 1898.[15] Buffalo Bill's troupe of cowboys, Indians, sharpshooters and other performers publicized their show by marching down the streets of Madison Square Garden where they were to perform. Käsebier saw the parade from her studio window and wrote to William F. Cody asking if "his Indians" could come sit for her.[16]

Buffalo Bill's Wild West was a popular, crowd-pleasing show that was one of the first recognized rodeos as well as a prototype of the Wild West. Cody hired various performers, including Native Americans, to enact events of Western life, ride in horse races, and demonstrate their abilities with rifles and pistols.[17] The Native Americans in the show received the most publicity due to their exotic nature, and Cody turned them into "show Indians," dressing them in grand regalia and making sure they had plenty of exposure.[18] Many of these Native Americans agreed to tour with the show because they saw it as a way to earn a living and care for their families, but their wages were low, and one position is that the show exploited their culture; other scholars may take a contrary view that such shows enabled Native Americans to retain and assert ethnic identity.

An account relates the promotional tactics used to generate sales for the dime novels about Buffalo Bill. In this particular story, Sammy Lone Bear, one of Käsebier's subjects was mentioned:

In the morning before the parade I would take out a stock on a wagon with Sammy Lone Bear,. . .and at every corner where there was a saloon Sammy would put on a war dance, sun dance, or mating dance of his nation, and then while he was inside. . .I would sell books. When the books were all gone I would put Sammy in the wagon and drive back to the lot.[19]

The photograph of Sammy Lone Bear taken by Käsebier removes him from this world and portrays him as a noble primitive, naïve and pure. Here, Käsebier conveys her own idealized views and concerns for the fading culture of the Native Americans rather than the personality of Sammy Lone Bear. When at one point Cody's employment of Native Americans was questioned by the Indian Bureau, he defended the practice, saying:

I thought I was benefiting the Indians as well as the government by taking them all over the United States, and giving them a correct idea of the customs, life, etc., of the pale faces, so that when they return to their people they could make known all they have seen.[20]

This statement reflects the way in which American Indians were thought of as wards of the government and a problem in need of a solution. Cody was seen as a teacher and an educator for those who did not understand fully the white man's way of life. The Native Americans were treated as children who needed guidance, and the Wild West Show offered what was viewed as acceptable care.[21]

Life with the Wild West Show was the reality that Käsebier's subjects experienced; however, we receive little, if any, sense of this world when viewing Käsebier's images. In her desire to capture what she saw as pure "Indian authenticity," she did the opposite of Curtis, who clothed his subjects in elaborate and sometimes inaccurate dress; she removed genuine ceremonial accessories from her sitters because she did not want to depict them as she perceived "show Indians" to be. It has been stated that these depictions of Native Americans concentrate on the personality of each individual sitter as a portrait would.[22] Käsebier stated that her objective in portraiture was

. . .to make pictures of real people, not maps

Figure 1. Gertrude Käsebier, *American Indian Portrait*, c. 1899, platinum print, 6 7/8 x 6 inches (17.5 x 15.2 cm.). The Museum of Modern Art, New York. Gift of Mrs. Mina Turner © 1997 The Museum of Modern Art, New York.

Figure 2. Gertrude Käsebier, *Iron Tail*, 1898. Department of Photographic History, National Museum of American History, Smithsonian Institution, Washington, D.C. Photo no. 81-9567.

of faces, but pictures of real men and women as they know themselves, to make likenesses that are biographies, to bring out in each photograph the essential personality that is variously called temperament, soul, humanity.[23]

Weston Naef suggests that oftentimes Käsebier's oratory did not coincide with her actual pictures, and regarding her Native American series, this rings true.[24] Here it appears that her main objective was bringing to fruition an idealized image created in her own mind. She said, "I want a real raw Indian for a change. . .the kind I used to see when I was a child."[25] Having grown up in Colorado, she associated Native Americans with her youth as well as with the sympathetic interest illustrated by many members of the pictorialist movement.

The "real Indian" that she sought was found in Chief Iron Tail, the oldest and most famous American Indian to visit her. He had reputedly fought in the Battle of Little Bighorn, and James Earle Fraser used him as a model for the Buffalo nickel.[26] Käsebier attempted to portray Iron Tail as an innocent primitive violated by

white civilization, and her photographic session was described by an observer who stated:

> Quite at random she selected Iron Tail, and proceeded to divest him of his finery. Feathers and trinkets were removed, and amid a dead silence she placed him before the camera and secured the most remarkable portrait of the whole collection. He never said a word, but obeyed instructions like a automaton. In the wonderful face. . .it is perhaps not fanciful to read something of the misery which he was really undergoing. For the truth was that every feather represented some act of bravery either on his own part or that of his ancestors. . . . When the portrait was handed to him some days later, he tore it in two and flung it from him. Luckily, however, an explanation and a second sitting in full regalia entirely restored his peace of mind.[27]

Because Iron Tail was often depicted in full regalia, Käsebier chose not to depict him in this manner.[28] She saw his garments as traits of a "show Indian," and they did not coincide with her idea of what a "real Indian" was. In stripping him of the garments he was so proud of, she neglected to connect with something of

Figure 3. Gertrude Käsebier, *Profile of Iron Tail*, 1898. Department of Photographic History, National Museum of American History, Smithsonian Institution, Washington, D.C. Photo no. 89-13428.

116

Figure 4. Gertrude Käsebier, *Willie Spotted Horse,* c. 1901. Department of Photographic History, National Museum of American History, Smithsonian Institution, Washington, D.C. Photo no. 83-903.

great importance to her sitter: the resulting image entitled *Iron Tail,* 1898 (Figure 2), gives us a view of a demeaned individual, one devoid of past pride or current celebrity. Käsebier's version of a "real Indian" conveys a deep sadness that translates through her eyes as a response to the devastation of the Native American culture. The expression of Iron Tail in this photograph alludes to a much greater issue, but in actuality he was disturbed at the loss of his traditional garments for the picture.

The second photograph of Iron Tail, entitled *Profile of Iron Tail with Headdress,* 1898 (Figure 3), depicts an equally idealized view of a Native American but in a much more romantic way.[29] In this picture, Iron Tail is shown in a very stately manner wearing his traditional garments. Both of these photgraphs portray eternalized images. One focuses on the emotional potential of the subject while the other creates an icon. In both, however, we are able to see Käsebier's artistic vision and Eurocentric viewpoint playing a dominant role, leaving the viewer with little sense of Iron Tail as an individual.

Throughout her Native American series, Käsebier tended to give her images varying titles, sometimes choosing the sitter's name and other times assigning more generalized titles. Photographs such as *American Indian Portrait,* 1898-1901, *Profile of a Sioux Man,* c. 1898, and *The Red Man,* c. 1900, represent iconic figures that present little sense of personality; rather they convey Käsebier's

idealization of the Native American—a quiet, pensive, noble man bearing a great tragedy both proudly and enduringly. Even in her images of Native American children, such as *Willie Spotted Horse,* c. 1901 (Figure 4), she captured an expression of sadness and separateness. It has been suggested that Käsebier's talent for putting children at ease, which is exhibited in many of her photographs such as *Lolly Pops,* 1910 (Figure 5), carries through to this image. However, the withdrawn and serious child seen here contrasts sharply with the charming, lighthearted children in her later image.

This romantic viewpoint carries through even in photographs of Zitkala-Sa, a highly educated Sioux woman who was an accomplished violinist and an advocate of Indian rights.[30] In a series of four portraits taken in 1898 (Figure 6), Käsebier depicted Zitkala-Sa in both Native American garments and contemporary dress, but in both guises we attain a similar sense of this woman as a romantic icon; her personality is not captured.

During the height of her career, Käsebier was a celebrated portraitist whose aim was to "make likenesses that are biographies, to put into each photograph. . .temperament, soul, humanity."[31] In many ways she achieved this goal and produced numerous portrait photographs of friends and acquaintances that capture their personalities beautifully. However, in her portraits of

Figure 5. Gertrude Käsebier, *Lolly Pops (Mrs. Hermine M. Turner and Children),* 1910, platinum print, 11 1/4 x 8 3/8 inches (28.6 x 21.3 cm.). The Museum of Modern Art, New York. Gift of Mrs. Hermine M. Turner © 1997 The Museum of Modern Art, New York.

117

Figure 6. Gertrude Käsebier, *Zitkala-Sa*, c. 1898. Department of Photographic History, National Museum of American History, Smithsonian Institution, Washington, D.C. Photo no. 85-7209.

Native Americans, Käsebier used these men and women as generic models for a series of romantic icons. In photographing people with whom she shared so few commonalities, she produced images that reflect her own personality and Eurocentric viewpoint more than the character of her sitters. It is accurate to view these photographs as a whole rather than as individualized portraits, for as a group, they exhibit Käsebier's belief in a tragic loss of culture translated as an emotional artistic statement.

1   Brian W. Dippie, "Representing the Other: The North American Indian," *Anthropology and Photography 1860-1920*, ed. Elizabeth Edwards (New Haven and London: Yale UP, 1992) 132-136.

2   Christian A. Peterson, "American Arts and Crafts: The Photograph Beautiful 1895-1915," *History of Photography* 16 (1992):189. The Industrial Revolution of the nineteenth century had fostered many of these changes, and during the early twentieth century various groups reacted to the more disagreeable facts of life such as tenement housing and urban congestion by looking back to nature and simplicity as an ideal. The American Arts and Crafts movement began in the mid-1890s and reflected this reform through its focus on beauty combined with utility.

3   Robert Doty, *Photo-Secession: Photography as Fine Art* (New York: The George Eastman House, 1960) 17-28. The Photo-Secession was estab-lished in 1902; however, prior to this Stieglitz and many of the other members of the Photo-Secession were working with photography as an artistic medium. It is the work of this group that has become most commonly associated with pictorialist photography.

Sadakichi Hartmann, "The Value of the Apparently Meaningless and Inaccurate," *Camera Work* 3 (July 1903): 18. Also reprinted in David Travis, Photography Rediscovered: American Photographs, 1900-1930 (New York: The Whitney Museum of American Art, 1979) 32.

4   Peterson 199.

5   Frederick Monsen, "The Destruction of Our Indians: What Civilization is Doing to Extinguish an Ancient and Highly Intelligent Race by Taking Away its Arts, Industries, and Religion," *The Craftsman*, 11 (March 1907): 689, reprinted in Peterson 199.

6   Peterson 199.

7   See Barbara L. Michaels, *Gertrude Käsebier: The Photographer and Her Photographs* (New York: Harry N. Abrams, Inc., 1992), and Naomi Rosenblum, *A History of Women Photographers* (New York: Abbeville Press, 1994) for more detailed information on Käsebier and a complete bibliography.

8   See Weston J. Naef, *The Collection of Alfred Stieglitz: Fifty Pioneers of Modern Photography* (New York: The Metropolitan Museum of Art; The Viking Press, 1978) 82-83 for more information regarding the pictorialist style and techniques.

9   Michaels 30. See also Peterson 199-201 and William Inness Homer, *Alfred Stieglitz and the Photo-Secession* (Boston: Little, Brown and Co., 1983) 62-64.

10 See Gerald Hausman, ed. *Prayer to the Great Mystery: The Uncollected Writings and Photography of Edward S. Curtis* (New York: St. Martin Press, 1995); Joseph Epes Brown, *The North American Indians: A Selection of Photographs by Edward S. Curtis* (New York: Aperture, Inc., 1972); and Edward S. Curtis, *The North American Indian*, Supplementary vol. 1, (1907-30).

11 Curtis 20.

12 Peterson 201. He describes Curtis as a documentarian with aesthetic concerns, but he points out that many of his images were produced with the public market in mind, and "the heritage evident in these photographs is not solely Native American."

13 Michaels 38.

14 Michaels 39-40.

15 Homer 62; Michaels 29-30.

16 Homer 62.

17 Sarah J. Blackstone, *Buckskins, Bullets, and Business: A History of Buffalo Bill's Wild West* (New York: Greenwood Press, 1986) 13; see also Don Russell, *The Lives and Legends of Buffalo Bill* (Norman: U of Oklahoma P, 1960), for a broader history and biography of William F. Cody and his Wild West Show.

18 Blackstone 85.

19 Russell 279.

20 Russell 262.

21 Blackstone 87. The Bureau of Indian Affairs set up guidelines that Cody had to abide by in order to take Native Americans from their designated

reservations. These included providing them with food, shelter, and medical care as well as managers who were to "protect them from all immoral influences and surroundings."

22   Michaels 30-33.

23   Mary Fanton Roberts, "Photography as an Emotional Art: A Study of the Work of Gertrude Käsebier," *Craftsman* 12 (April 1907): 88, reprinted in Marilyn F. Symmes, "Important Photographs by Women," *Bulletin of the Detroit Institute of Arts,* LVI (1978): 145-6.

24   Naef 83.

25   Michaels 30.

26   Michaels 30.

27   "Some Indian Portraits," *Everybody's Magazine* 4 (Jan. 1901): 7, reprinted in Michaels 30-32.

28   Michaels 33.

29   Michaels 33. Here she makes a much greater distinction between the two photographs, describing the first as an individualized portrait and the second as a more idealized icon. I interpret both of these images as having idealized and sentimental qualities.

30   Michaels 42. Zitkala-Sa was also known as Gertrude Simmons Bonnin and led a double life as a Native American and an accomplished lady of literature and music. She was also photographed by many other pictorialist photographers such as Joseph T. Keiley.

31   Käsebier 88; reprinted in Rosenblum 77.

"Questioning Good Intentions"[1]—
The Photography of Hulleah Tsinhnahjinnie

Susan Kloman

For years, Native Americans have had the parameters of their identity created for them as "named" objects.[2] The act of naming someone else, based on gender or ethnic parameters, then forces the named group or individual into another's definition of their identity. Photography was one tool that created and perpetuated a mythic American Indian identity for outsiders to Native culture. Times have changed. As subjects and creators of their own identity, Hulleah Tsinhnahjinnie and other Native American artists are now naming themselves. Tsinhnahjinnie, whose heritage is Seminole, Creek, and Diné (Navajo), is an artist who uses the media of photocollage and photography to challenge the practice of naming. Although she is of mixed heritage and was raised Navajo, Tsinhnahjinnie's photographs address a variety of Native American stereotypes so prevalent in the mind of Euroamerican culture. Her use of a collage technique refers metaphorically to the amalgamated identity that has developed both in representations of Native people and in their actual life experiences as a result of acculturation. As a Native American photographer, Tsinhnahjinnie defies the conventional definitions of what it means to be a Native American artist by subverting Euroamerican definitions and expectations.

Through artistic means, Tsinhnahjinnie composes an interactive dialogue between the past and the present. Focusing specifically on Native and Euroamerican cultural relations, her work evokes new questions. Are historical issues surrounding photographic myths of representation different from contemporary issues? Are we really living in a post-colonial age that respects diversity yet allows autonomy? Tsinhnahjinnie uses the media of photocollage and photography as critical vehicles for speaking out against what she calls the paternalistic "good intentions" of those "who have decided what is 'best'" for her.[3]

Photography symbolizes a new artistic independence within the category "Native American Art." The use of photography by Native Americans forces viewers to constantly redefine their concepts about artistic production by indigenous peoples. Tsinhnahjinnie's choice of photography as her preferred medium is a political statement because, in her words, "photography is not the instilled idea of traditional, marketable 'Indian Art'."[4] Moreover, photography was used as a tool by Euroamericans to define a singular Native American identity based on romantic notions of an idealized past. Edward S. Curtis is a famous example of a photographer who "documented" American Indians in order to "preserve" them for posterity. He photographed between the years 1900-1930, believing that photography was an art-science which legitimated his anthropological endeavors.[5] Photography, at the turn-of-the-century, was considered a truthful medium which revealed things "as they were." However, Curtis was not revealing true moments in time. He recreated a past based on many of society's own preconceptions and misconceptions about American Indian culture. His photographs function as foils to Tsinhnahjinnie's works because they are antithetically related.

The contemporary Native American art market typically revolves around established Euroamerican concepts and expectations of "evolved traditional" art forms. Objects considered to be in the traditional vein include ceramics, beadwork, woven baskets, and silverwork.[6] By the 1920s, paintings on paper were also incorporated into this "Indian Art" market even though these were not part of Native Americans' ancient artistic heritage.

Photography, therefore, as a technological and representational medium, did not have a place in the Native American art market. It is only within the last four years that the Santa Fe market opened photography as an acceptable category. As subjects of photographs created by the dominant culture, American Indians were written into the master narrative as myth. An American Indian identity was forged that conformed to Euroamerican expectations. The use of photography, which involved relatively new technology even for Euroamerican culture, was certainly thought to be an anachronism for so-called "real Indian" culture. The notion of "real Indians" is part of a romantic Euroamerican discourse that represents Native people as primitive and mystical without scientific or technological inclinations. Therefore, photography held virtually no economic viability for Native Americans within the often tourist-driven art market because it did not conform to the stereotype. Moreover, within the Native American community itself, photography was stigmatized. The camera, by the turn of the century, had become an intrusive element to tribal life. Both professional photographers and amateur tourist photographers disregarded the privacy and sanctity of American Indian ceremonial dances and festivities.[7] Furthermore, photographs of ceremonies were often used against the Natives by government officials (who found the practices offensive on religious grounds).[8] The suppression of photography by many tribal groups further delayed its acceptance as an artistic medium. Thus, without the benefit of community support, patrons, teachers, or available equipment, photography has only recently become part of the Native American artistic vocabulary.

Native American artist and writer Rick Hill asserts that with popular, prevalent images and ideologies created for American

Indians by television and film, the challenge today is to use their own voices to re-represent themselves.[9] They must dispel imposed myths. Hulleah Tsinhnahjinnie, as an artist and curator, asserts a Native-centered discourse. In her photocollages, she juxtaposes fragments to create a whole. However, the effects of this visual simultaneity do not leave the viewer with a sense of completion and satisfaction. On the contrary, the effects are ironic and unsettling.

Her collage titled *When Did Dreams of White Buffalo Turn to Dreams of White Women?* (1990) presents a rhetorical question (Figure 1). Responses to practices of acculturation did not occur in a single, nameable moment. The question of when Native American practices and ideologies changed is unanswerable because, like any living culture, Native American culture is in a constant state of flux and contextualization. It has never been a static entity. Moreover, the title confronts Euroamerican culture's proclivity for matching events with a specific moment in time. The linear narrative is incongruous with many Native American ideas of temporality. Time, in most American Indian cultures, particularly the Navajo and Pueblo, is perceived as being cyclical. Events reverberate beyond the moment in which they occur.

When Did Dreams of White Buffalo Turn to Dreams of White Women? addresses issues of cultural identity. The assertion of a cultural representation involves much more than the naming of the moment in which a culture was interrupted. Cultural identity is not about a single moment. Rather, it is involved in a process. It is many moments. The simultaneity of Tsinhnahjinnie's collage signifies this multiplicity of identity. Fragments coming together to form a whole represent Native American culture as it exists today.

Tsinhnahjinnie captures in her photocollage what Stuart Hall describes as the nature of post-colonial representation. This artistic representation is more than a retrieval of a so-called authentic past that has been "buried and overlaid."[10] Hall asserts that post-colonial representation is "not the rediscovery, but the production of identity." Identity is a synthesis of both being and becoming. "Being" assumes a shared history and ancestry among a cultural group. "Becoming" is the acknowledgement of difference in addition to the assumption of similarity.[11]

In this image, Tsinhnahjinnie synthesizes some of her previous photographs to create a re-contextualization of her own works. The woman in the upper right, the woman in the foreground, and the African Americans placed on the map of Africa are all taken from her other works.[12] The artist herself is not an immutable

Figure 1. Hulleah Tsinhnahjinnie, *When Did Dreams of White Buffalo Turn to Dreams of White Women?*, 1990, photocollage, 63 x 73.5 cm. Collection of the Artist.

persona. Likewise, her works change throughout time and within new contexts. By using her own photographic language, she asserts her own narrative. By quoting herself, she establishes truths based in her own reality.

In contrast to the turn-of-the-century premonitions of extinction, the contemporary Native American woman in the foreground presents a positive statement of survival. She is dressed in formal attire worn for powwows or ceremonies. Surrounding her are material objects symbolizing a living culture which has not forgotten its past. The contemporary Euroamerican furniture signifies acculturation. However, she also surrounds herself with "traditional" objects still made by women today. Tsinhnahjinnie asserts the continual interaction of the past and the present through these visual juxtapositions.

In *Oklahoma, the Unedited Version* (1990), the artist refers to how history and identity were constructed for Native Americans within master narratives of the dominant culture (Figure 2). In spite of television's negative effects upon Native American cultural identity, Tsinhnahjinnie, who was born in 1954, nevertheless embraces some aspects of television's impact in that she regards it as part of her generation's cultural heritage. Therefore, she inserts a photograph of an old Philco television as a signifier of the various media of communication and how they have been employed to objectify and stereotype Native Americans.

Oklahoma, the Unedited Version addresses mythic representations within mass culture in order to re-represent her version of history from a Native American perspective. Addressing issues of American Indian displacement and their consequent struggle for land rights, she places a map in the background. The map represents the counties of Oklahoma bearing the names of tribes who inhabited the area when it was considered Indian Territory. The Dawes Act of 1887 became a catalyst by which the territory became "free game" for settlement.[13] When Oklahoma Territory was admitted to the Union in 1907, the American Indian population within the area was only 5.3 percent. This small percentage diminished any claims Native Americans held to an area then so fully permeated by outsiders.[14]

The contemporary Native American woman inside the television screen gazes at the map as the horse grazes upon the grass. She is assessing the past. This woman, riding a pinto, then moves out of the television screen. She is wearing the traditional dress of the Plains culture as she rides, head down, into a new culture. She is not a passive Curtis-like object needing documentation; she is

Figure 2. Hulleah Tsinhnahjinnie, *Oklahoma, The Unedited Version*, 1990, B/W photocollage. Collection of Rennard Strickland.

not relegated to the past. Just as some previous photographic compositions by non-Natives were either altered or manipulated to hide any evidence of acculturation, Tsinhnahjinnie alters photographic contexts precisely to point out these elements.

In Edward Curtis's photograph *In a Piegan Lodge*, for instance, the original photograph contains a mechanical clock between the two men. For publication, the photograph was retouched. The clock, which served as a signifier of technology and contemporary Euroamerican time, was erased. Such manipulations were justified because Curtis felt that his was a noble cause, preserving the heritage of the indigenous people on their behalf.[15]

The woman in Tsinhnahjinnie's photograph rides forward, into the present, to confront the viewer as an active participant in her culture. The assertion of her presence counters Curtis's emblematic male Indians who ride into the metaphorical sunset, as shown in his *Vanishing Race—Navajo* from 1904 (Figure 3). Tsinhnahjinnie's juxtaposition of the past and the present suggests a dialogue prevalent in any living culture.[16] Moreover, it is her own Native American dialogue, not an imposed or stereotypical representation.

Tsinhnahjinnie's photographic series from 1993 titled *Creative Native* responds to the Indian Arts and Crafts Act of 1990, Public Law Number 101-644 (104 Stat. 4662). This series depicts Native American artists surrounded by text which labels them as "real Indians." The bold text signifies that their "label" or lineage takes precedence over individual selves or the meaning and importance of their artistic production.[17]

In this series of photocollages, Tsinhnahjinnie questions the implications and "good intentions" of the 1990 Act.[18] This act was passed, ostensibly, to protect the Native American arts and crafts industry. It is a multi-million dollar business, and, as such, it has been plagued by the presence of imported counterfeit merchandise. As stated by lawyer Jon Parsley, this Act, in its attempt to counter the "misrepresentation of products labeled 'Indian made' . . . [then] forces Congress to define who is and who is not an 'Indian'."[19] Tsinhnahjinnie's photocollages from the *Creative Native* series satirize the use of labels to define the parameters of artistic production. She examines the notion that these artists

must be labeled for the benefit of both outsiders and some Native groups, such as the Native American Arts Association, led by David Bradley, and insistence upon associating meaning with naming.[20] In essence, the law—not ancestry, not collective history, nor one's own sense of self—bestows identity.

Tsinhnahjinnie's use of bold labels begs the question: what is real Indian art? Forcing American Indians to prove their tribal heritage is the controversial part of this law. The law itself narrowly defines an Indian as an individual who is a member of a federally- or state-recognized tribe.[21] However, as Representative Ben Nighthorse Campbell acknowledges, many artists who consider themselves Native Americans cannot prove their tribal membership.[22] The reasons are varied. For instance, as artist Kay Walkingstick notes, the Cherokee tribe today acknowledges only those whose ancestors registered themselves with the federal government during the land allotment days.[23] Some tribes have been dissolved or have never been federally-recognized.[24] Variation in tribal standards for membership can also prevent someone who is a full-blooded Native American from being "officially" acknowledged as such.[25] Forcing Native Americans of mixed heritage to chose a tribal affiliation is yet another unjust ramification of this law's requirements.

In contrast to previously discussed works by Tsinhnahjinnie, the Native Americans portrayed in *Diné 007-A* and *Racially Pure* (Figures 4 and 5) are in contemporary American attire. Instead of interweaving the past and the present as in her other images, Tsinhnahjinnie portrays these artists as securely in the present. So what distinguishes them as Native Americans? Countering Edward S. Curtis's portraits, Tsinhnahjinnie does not alter her subjects' appearances. Their identity is not externalized through overt signs of "Indian-ness."

In *Racially Pure*, the artist Ed Singer wears a T-shirt, a tweed jacket, glasses, and a cowboy hat. He does not conform to constructed stereotypes or expectations which would have him wearing traditional Native attire. He is depicted as he has chosen to represent himself. A non-Native audience is then forced to re-evaluate its expectations.

Figure 3. Edward S. Curtis, *Vanishing Race—Navaho, c.* 1907. Photograph courtesy of Sotheby's, New York.

Figure 4. Hulleah Tsinhnahjinnie, *Diné 007-A*, 1993, photocollage, 30 x40 inches. Collection of the Artist.

Hulleah Tsinhnahjinnie, using the language of photography and photocollage, creates a Native-centered discourse surrounding issues of Native American identity and self-representation. Her text is double-voiced: she is speaking to both her own and to Euroamerican culture. The synthesized fragments of her photocollages create a circuitous narrative. She addresses issues of contemporary identity by simultaneously invoking and referring to the past.

Tsinhnahjinnie questions the very notion that identity can be defined by anyone other than one's self. James Clifford would describe these attempts to identify another as a situation in which "self-other relations are matters of power and rhetoric rather than essence."[26] The protean nature of identity defies the imposed, reductive definitions that surface when attempts are made to define someone's "essence." Tsinhnahjinnie's work, far from cultivating a singular Native American identity, uses both visual and metaphorical juxtapositions to show the irony of attempts to name and define, and thereby mythologize, another's life experience.

1   I refer to this phrase because the artist herself uses it to describe some of her artistic motivations. That is, she questions the good intentions of Euroamericans and policy makers who claim to be acting in the best interest of Native Americans. Hulleah Tsinhnahjinnie, "Artist Statement," in *Stand: Four Artists Interpret the Native American Experience* (Edinboro, PA: Bruce Gallery, Edinboro University of Pennsylvania, 1994) n. pag.

2   Mary V. Dearborn, *Pocahontas's Daughter: Gender and Ethnicity in American Culture* (New York: Oxford UP, 1986) 18. Dearborn is typically credited as the first to articulate the notion that naming another is an assertion of power. Naming another group forces them to negotiate their self-identities through another's imposed definition of themselves. The "namer" has power. Therefore, the "named" can empower themselves by re-naming themselves. They can create their own self-identity which is neither static nor monolithic.

3   Tsinhnahjinnie, "Artist Statement" n. pag.

4   Hulleah Tsinhnahjinnie, "Compensating Imbalances," *Exposure* 29. 3 (Fall, 1993): 30.

5   Christopher Lyman, *The Vanishing Race and Other Illusions: The Photographs of Edward S. Curtis* (Washington D.C.: Smithsonian Institute Press, 1982) 18-20.

6   Even works that are considered "traditional" are largely defined as such by Euroamerican culture. Hence, silverwork, which is an acculturated medium introduced by the Spanish, is included in the category of works considered to be indigenous to Native American culture.

7   Lucy Lippard, "Introduction," in Lucy Lippard, ed., *Partial Recall* (New York: The New Press, 1992) 29.

8   Lippard 30.

9   Rick Hill, "In Our Own Image: Stereotyped Images of Indians Leads to New Art Form," *Exposure* 29.1 (Fall 1993): 11.

10 Stuart Hall, "Cultural Identity and Diaspora," in Jonathan Rutherford, ed., *Identity: Community, Culture, Difference* (London: Lawrence and Wishart, 1990) 224.

11 Hall 223, 225.

12 The woman in the upper right is a fragment from a photograph titled *Idelia*, 1983, 76 x 51 cm., The Princeton Collections of Western Americana. The foreground image is from another photocollage, *She Has It All*, 1988, 20 x 24 inches. The photographs of the African Americans shown here also appear in the photocollage *Mattie Looks for Stephen Biko*, 1986 (re-worked 1990), Artist's Collection.

Figure 5. Hulleah Tsinhnahjinnie, *Racially Pure*, 1993, photocollage, 30 x40 inches. Collection of the Artist.

13 Angie Debo, *A History of Indians in the United States* (Norman, OK: U of Oklahoma P, 1970) 300.

14 Debo 309.

15 The two images of *In a Piegan Lodge* are reproduced in Lyman, *The Vanishing Race*, figures 82 and 83.

16 Tsinhnahjinnie defies the notion that so-called authentic Native American culture is dying. Like any living culture, it interacts with the present, simultaneously enriched by its past; Tsinhnahjinnie, in "Headcount," artist's statement for the "International Istanbul Biennial," (Istanbul Municipality Nejat F. Eczacibasi Art Museum, Halic Turkey, Oct. 17-Nov. 30, 1992) n.p.

17 Labels, which are disparagingly referred to as "pedigrees," are bestowed upon Native Americans by a federally-issued Certificate of Degree of Indian Blood, to which not all Natives are entitled. I address this topic later in this paper. M. Annette Jaimes, "Federal Indian Identification Policy: A Usurpation of Indigenous Sovereignty in North America," in *The State of Native America: Genocide, Colonization, and Resistance*, ed. M. Annette Jaimes, Race and Resistance Series (Boston: South End Press, 1992) 131.

18 Tsinhnahjinnie, *Stand* n. pag.

19 Jon Keith Parsley, "Regulation of Counterfeit Indian Arts and Crafts: An Analysis of the Indian Art and Crafts Act of 1990," *American Indian Law Review* 18.2 (1993): 487. Parsley also notes that a law was passed shortly before the 1990 Act that provided an alternative solution to the problems concerning the misrepresentation of counterfeit goods. The 1988 Indelible Marking Act forces those who are importing goods to mark these with an indelible mark of origin. This mark would replace the previous peel-off labels. However, this Act was not given time to go into effect before lobbying for the Indian Arts and Crafts Act began. It was part of the Omnibus Trade Bill, Public Law Number 100-418, for which the final regulations were released on October 18, 1990, one month before the Indian Arts and Crafts Act was signed into law; Parsley 511, ns. 193, 194. The 1988 Act would have forced the outsiders to identify themselves, as opposed to forcing Native artists to prove their ancestry; Parsley 511-512.

20 This group was highly influential in the passage of the 1990 Act. They state that their goal is to stop the misrepresentation of art created by non-Indians. However, they typically target domestic artistic production by other Natives rather than the actual perpetrators, who generally import these counterfeit goods. As Ward Churchill points out, this group, in its support of the law, appealed to the government's predilection for defining identity in order to eliminate much of the group's competition from people of Native American ancestry who do not meet the often arbitrary standards for tribal membership. Churchill, "Nobody's Pet Poodle," in *Indians Are Us? Culture and Genocide in Native North America* (Monroe, ME: Common Courage Press, 1994) 94-95.

21 Parsley 494 n. 69, 497.

22 Parsley 498.

23 Kay Walkingstick, "Democracy Inc,: Kay Walkingstick on Indian Law," *Artforum* 30.3 (November 1991): 20.

24 Jaimes 132.

25 Walkingstick 21.

26 James Clifford, *The Predicament of Culture: Twentieth Century Ethnography, Literature, and Art* (Cambridge: Harvard UP, 1988) 14.

James Luna, a scene from *Our Indians,* first performed March, 1996.

Contemporary Artists in the Contact Zone: Happy Meeting Grounds or Circle the Wagons?

Robin Franklin Nigh

The experience of finding humor or irony in the misconceptions of others, and being aware of the historical misconceptions of one's own cultural history is a familiar experience for those who travel outside of their own communities. As communities expand and become increasingly global, the likelihood of interfacing with multiple cultural groups also increases. Museums—whether fine art, natural history or ethnographic—provide "contact" with other cultures without the viewer having to leave his / her own community. Like other institutions in Western society, museums are products of societal perceptions and social memories, because museums are not only the receptacles for but the representations of cultural history. They may also be the sites of historical reclamation.[1]

There has been significant scholarship on the evaluation and development of museum exhibitions and displays.[2] In the United States, early twentieth-century museum displays of cultural groups were grounded in ideologies of primitivism and were most frequently conceived through colonialist sensibilities. There was and remains significant confusion about what constitutes a display of art, artifacts, and/or the living environment of a people.

In the visual arts, an energy or tension has emerged from the museum as a "contact zone."[3] In one sense, contemporary artists who display their works in fine arts museums or galleries, while simultaneously addressing notions surrounding the construction of ethnic identities and cultural systems become cultural brokers. They are exchangers of culture—cultural history, property and traditions.[4] They are also part of a larger dialogue that addresses issues of "border culture" (where two cultures come into contact with one another), and postcolonialism / postmodernism.

It is inevitable, and not without irony, for one to become entangled in language when discussing contemporary Native and non-Native artists and their work. All of the contemporary artists in this part of the exhibition are aware of these complexities, and are philosophically sophisticated in the discourses of contemporary art. They belong to the global art world. However, Native artists possess an awareness and experience of cultural history: they are literally and figuratively bi-lingual and bi- or tri-cultural. Unquestionably, this is a dimension unavailable to artists who are not Native. As one Native American artist Zig Jackson (Mandan / Hidatsa / Arikara), has said "Native Americans are never allowed to forget his / her race and the social stratification that accompanies it."[5]

Consequently, this awareness of cultural experience (and lack of participation in it) is where non-Native artists position themselves. Issues of cultural ownership can further complicate these artists' works, for how does one interpret with sensibility and accuracy, an ethnic identity that is not his? It is this type of appropriation that runs the risk of offending viewers depending on how a work is interpreted. However, what happens when an artist interprets his / her own cultural heritage and views about such things as what is primitive by using images from another culture?

This raises the question of what "primitivism" is as a concept to contemporary Native and non-Native artists. How it applies—or doesn't apply—to their work is dictated by a long history. "Primitivism" is a construct created and defined by the West. As a label, it has generally been used to describe a Western interest in, and / or reconstruction of, societies designated as "primitive" and their cultural artifacts.[6] It is not a school, a style, or a movement with any specific characteristics, but, rather, like modernism and postmodernism, is undergoing constant revision as scholars gain critical distance. Modernist "primitivism" is about "the gaze" and the history of looking at objects unidimensionally, not appreciating context. It is an appropriation without regard to place or meaning. Hence, what is defined as "primitive" depends on how one is exposed to the information. In our postcolonial world, transformations happen as artists take up the dialogue surrounding "primitivism" and import it into the museum. In this arena, the museum becomes a place where disciplines of art history, museology, and anthropology blend and collide. To be a "postmodern primitive" is to be fully aware of the historical, cultural and artistic traditions of prior conceptions and misconceptions of what is (and is not) primitive.

A prominent example of the museum as an arena in which the Euroamerican society observed what was then considered "primitive" (in the modernist sense) is the case of Ishi, the last tribal member of the Yahi in Northern California. Ishi, an older man, was alone and starving when he was "discovered" in Orville, California in 1911. The Bureau of Indian Affairs presented him with three options: he could return to the "wild;" go live on a reservation; or live in the Museum of Anthropology at the University of California in Berkeley. Ishi chose to remain at the Museum where he would be with, among others, Alfred Kroeber, one of the first individuals he met when he came into contact with the White man's world.[7] Until his death from tuberculosis in 1916, Ishi performed odd jobs in the museum and gave demonstrations for the viewing public. These demonstrations included such things as making bows and arrows and building a Yahi "house" in the back of the museum.[8] He was literally a "living diorama" and an anthropologist's dream, on site at the museum, providing Kroeber with significant first-hand information.

Whether it was the demonstrations of Ishi, or other Native Americans, the living dioramas and the notions of display overlap with the concept of performing.[9] Additionally, the frame—or location—that surrounds any individual is a key factor. Museum exhibitions, like photographs, present a certain cultural vision. This emphasis on location (context) is particularly heightened in the work of many performance artists and installation artists because within the very act of display, in the contradictory structure of spectatorship itself, there exists an ambivalence to the representation of cultural difference. This co-existence of opposing views can create a productive tension between the "borderline artist" and the "borderline curator."[10]

The notion of place or where one comes into contact with contemporary artists is a viable issue in works of James Luna (Luiseño). Some of his performances have parodied value-producing systems, such as museums, the art world, and anthropology. Luna acknowledges image prototypes from art history and anthropology and then re-invents them by positioning himself as an extension of the original. In this sense, Luna dispels the myth by replicating it. Yet Luna, who works in many different media, addresses the environment of the museum only when it is appropriate to the issues in a given work. He then subverts the language of the museum (the artifact) or the particular icon of art historical significance, as he did by alluding to James Earle Fraser's 1894 sculpture *The End of the Trail* with the parodic photographic pose "End of the Frail" (Figure 1), from the 1992 performance

Figure 1. James Luna (Luiseño), strikes a photographic pose entitled "End of the Frail" which he also incorporated in his 1992 performance *AA Meets Art History*. Photo courtesy of the Artist.

AA Meets Art History. Fraser's popular equestrian image depicts a romanticized, defeated American Indian. The rider's spear is down and his anthropomorphized horse emulates his posture; enlarged to monumental scale and exhibited at the 1915 Panama-Pacific Exposition in San Francisco, this sculpture was so popular that it was brought back and used as a promotional image for the Golden Gate Exposition in San Francisco in 1939. Luna strikes this same pose astride a sawhorse instead of a horse, and with a bottle of Jack Daniel's instead of a spear. This is a paradoxical use of images, one to confirm, the other to reject mythic representation. In performances such as *History of the Luiseño People*, Luna tautly interweaves issues of autobiography and cultural identity with a finely-tuned sense of anger and humor.[11] Most likely, a non-Indian will not understand all of Luna's references: "My appeal for

humor in my work comes from Indian culture, where humor can be a form of knowledge, cultural though, and perhaps to just ease the pain. I think we Indians live in worlds filled with irony and I want to relate that in my works."[12]

In his 1987 performance *Artifact Piece*, Luna chose the museum space to question the notion that if information is presented within an institution of authority, it must be true. The work functions in much the same way as the early photography utilized by amateur ethnographers to document their pre-conceived notions of a culture. In this performance, Luna became an artifact when he placed himself in a vitrine. He was "on display" with other personal artifacts that included college diplomas, divorce papers, childhood photographs, and almost clinical descriptions of how physical and psychological scars were received, etc. While *Artifact Piece* and the photographic pose "End of the Frail," are extensions of the dialogues surrounding museum displays and living dioramas seen in museums and world's fairs, Luna ultimately parodies and diffuses notions of "primitivism" and exoticism by reenacting and / or mocking social constructions.

Parody of the Western culture by Native artists has always existed, though perhaps it was not often seen, or written about, and it was documented even less.[13] Julius E. Lips, *The Savage Hits Back*, (New Haven: Yale UP, 1937):1.[14] One example of an early parodic commentary of the tourist encounter is Woody Crumbo's (Creek / Potawatomi, d. 1989) 1947 watercolor *Land of Enchantment* (Figure 2).[15] This work succinctly presents the notion that tourists are as often observed and criticized by the Natives as they are themselves observing of Native cultures.[16] In Crumbo's *Land of Enchantment* a well-to-do Anglo family inspects the American Indian goods of a woman and her daughter on a reservation in the Southwest.[17] The large woman tourist is the central focus.[18] Standing behind her, comically smaller in size, is presumably her husband. He holds a briefcase bearing the initials JPM (John Pierpont Morgan?). The contrast is stark, sympathetic to the Indian figures and simultaneously an editorial caricature revealing J.P. Morgan's legendary art acquisitiveness. Crumbo's humor functions to make the "tourists" appear ridiculously out of place. The title, *Land of Enchantment*, is an ironic description of the Anglo involvement with "exotic" culture, and of Native American life.[19] "Land of Enchantment" became the offical slogan for the State of New Mexico in the 1940s and is still used today to identify the State in tourist brochures. Native Americans have always reviewed

Figure 2. Woodrow (Woody) Crumbo (Creek / Potowatomi, d. 1989), *Land of Enchantment*, c. 1946, watercolor on paper. Collection of the Philbrook Museum of Art, Tulsa, Oklahoma. Gift of Clark Field.

Euroamericans' national and personal characteristics and dramatized actions, follies, and motives through art, performance, stories, and jokes.[20] There is also a contemporary irony in this image as the viewer (whose interpretation may depend on Indian or non-Indian orientation) critiques Crumbo who critiques tourists who are critiquing "real Indians."

Crumbo's parodic and sophisticated use of imagery may have been unknown to many or most of his contemporary non-Indian artists.[21] Idealistic response towards Indian cultures is a longstanding tradition of non-Indian artists. Many non-Indian artists had their own agendas and were looking for a "primitive" that was romantic, universal and even cosmic.

There has been a well-established European, particularly German, fascination with "America's Indians as well."[22] Two late twentieth-century German artists who have looked to Native American art and culture in creating their works are Joseph Beuys (d.1986) and Lothar Baumgarten.

Joseph Beuys performed *I Like America and America Likes Me* with Little John, a live coyote on May 21 through May 25, 1974, in the Rene Block Gallery in New York. Beuys, who considered himself a shaman, isolated himself and Little John in the gallery space for five days. One interpretation of Beuys' work is that the persecution of the coyote—considered a menace to Euroamerican ranchers, etc., but also an animal respected in Native cultures for its cunning ability—is analogous to the federal government's treatment of Native American peoples.[23] According to Heiner Stachelhaus, Beuys felt that "America is rich in minorities, but the Indians, as the aboriginal inhabitants, are a special case in the history of persecution."[24] His choice of laying down issues of *The Wall Street Journal* on the gallery floor for the "unhouse-broken," wild coyote is an intended commentary of Western capitalism. In most critical assessments, interpretation of this performance stops here. On one level, he may not appear to be making much of a statement about Native American conditions, but perhaps this performance can be interpreted differently if Beuys knew (which he probably did) that the coyote in many

American Indian cultures also represents the mythic figure of the trickster (*i.e.* he is clever, licentious, and lives by his wits). When this performance is discussed, the fact that it was held just one year after the 1973 Wounded Knee incident is also not mentioned. Though the performance was held and photographically documented in an art gallery, one is left to wonder if Beuys' choice—to be separated or "walled off" from the outside world—is a not direct allusion to the actual event at Pine Ridge in which American Indians "walled" themselves off for two months. Like the coyote, these individuals lived by their wits.

Lothar Baumgarten's art works have been criticized for improperly appropriating, and then not addressing, Native American issues. *The Tongue of the Cherokee*, 1985-1988, is a permanent installation located in the Hall of Sculpture at the Carnegie Museum of Art in Pittsburgh. In this work, Baumgarten, through a process of sandblasting, lamination, and painting, has isolated each of the eighty-five letters comprising Sequoia's syllabary of the Cherokee written language and distributed them among the glass panels of the expansive ceiling grid.[25] Their placement within the composition is not grammatical syntax, but based on design. The ceiling floats directly above a replica of the Parthenon frieze. This creates a visual association with a classical Western culture that is "dead." Subsequently, though Baumgarten's intent most likely was to honor the Cherokee, and also honor the peoples of the First Nations in the *Monument to the Native People of Ontario*, his combination of text-based works with Greek or Renaissance architectural motifs has been critiqued as essentially reinforcing the philosophical heritage of the Enlightenment (a rejection of anything not European). Hence, there is a sense of exclusion, and an example of the continued colonial practice of speaking *for* rather than *in* dialogue with Native peoples.

Some contemporary Native artists are suspicious of how Beuys and Baumgarten have used Native American issues in idiosyncratic artistic statements.[26] Though certainly not their intention

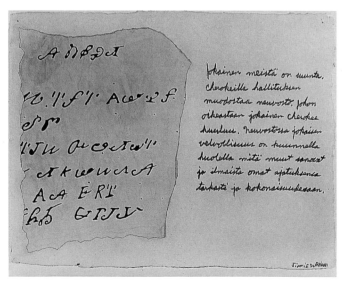

Figure 3. Jimmie Durham (Cherokee descent), *Not Lothar Baumgarten's Cherokee*, 1990, mixed media on paper, 17 x 20 1/4 inches (43.2 x 51.4 cm.). Collection of Whitney Museum of American Art, New York. Purchase, with funds from the Drawing Committee.

Figue 4. Phil Hughte (Zuni), "The Big Photo," from *A Zuni Artist Looks at Frank Hamilton Cushing*, Zuni, New Mexico, A:shiwi Publishing, © 1994.

to offend, both artists works may be read as inaccurate and perpetuating the stereotype of "primitivism." Jimmie Durham, an artist not without his own storms of controversy, has created a visual dialogue by directly responding to the works of the artists mentioned above.[27] Durham's *Not Joseph Beuys' Coyote* (1990), a mixed media sculpture and his drawing *Not Lothar Baumgarten's Cherokee* (1990) are visual, and personal reclamations. *Not Lothar Baumgarten's Cherokee* (Figure 3) is a text-based drawing written in Cherokee. It remains untranslated (and untranslatable?). Most of Durham's audience can look at the text and appreciate it for its formal qualities. However, unless one knows Cherokee, one is excluded. The work creates a very similar, though reversed, effect to Baumgarten's.

Another artist whose work reverses the postmodern gaze and reveals a finely-tuned sensitivity to living in two worlds is Phil Hughte (Zuni, d.1997). His work belongs to the tradition of editorial cartoons, and his 1994 series on the Anglo researcher for the Smithsonian Institution Bureau of Ethnography, Frank Hamilton Cushing (1857-1900) satirically presents the Smithsonian researcher through the eyes of the people he studied. Like many Zuni, Hughte "had a love / hate relationship with Cushing. They recognize the good that he did in recording many elements of their culture, but they also see him as a 'busy body, pushy person that told too much.'"[28]

Hughte often parodied well-known images of Cushing: *The Big Photo* (Figure 4), recalls the photograph of Cushing by John K. Hillers in which Cushing is posed in Zuni regalia, filling the entire frame.[29] There are no signs of props or even other individuals, but the portrait was carefully composed for the photographer. In Hughte's version, he makes it clear that Cushing is on a set or stage. He has widened the frame to show what is going on around Cushing while he has his photograph taken. Hughte's accompanying text describes the scene:

> Here Cushing is getting his portrait done. This is just an artist's perception of what I thought it might have looked like. And here, of course, are some Zuni kids making fun of him, and two Zuni ladies just admiring him the way he is standing.[30]

Juxtaposed to Hughte's text is a transcription of what was written by an ethnographer colleague of Cushing on the back of his photograph:

> Frank Hamilton Cushing in his fantastic dress worn among the Zuni Indians. This man was

the biggest fool and charlatan I ever knew. He even put his hair in curl papers every night. How could a man walk weighed down with so much toggery.[31]

Hughte's distinctive drawing style depicts hair hanging over the eyes of all his characters, whether male or female, Anglo or Zuni.[32] There was an undeniable humor in Hughte's works coupled with a painful honesty in addressing the unethical transgressions of white society. There are several artists, Native and non-Native, who critique these transgressions by individuals or by systems (e.g., anthropology and ethnography). Some of these artists and artworks have already been discussed. Certainly how one reacts to the history of ethnographic studies depends on which side of the exhibit case one occupies.

There are several Indian artists who have explored the anthropological discourse that surrounds Ishi. Frank Day (Maidu, d.1976), Jean LaMar (Paiute / Pit River), James Luna (Luiseño), and Frank Tuttle (Yuki-Wailaki / Konkow Maidu,) for instance, have all created art works about, or in response to Ishi. Hulleah J. Tsinhnahjinnie's (Seminole / Creek / Diné) *Ishi and Me* (1996) is a powerful work about assimilation and the recognition of "creating of presence by writing one's existence—in other words, realizing the impact of a written existence (where a Native presence exists)," she continues that "rather than have an anthropologist interpret my existence—I have taken control of how I am presented."[33] In this work, Tsinhnahjinnie has reconfigured an archival photograph of Ishi with one of herself, and has combed her hair like Ishi and copied his dress. Tsinhnahjinnie's emulation

Figure 5. Elaine Reichek, *Painted Blackfoot*, 1990, oil on b/w photo, wool, overall 79 x 73 inches. Courtesy Elaine Reichek, New York.

Figure 6. Mark Tansey, *Purity Test*, 1982, oil on canvas, 72 x 96 inches. Collection of the Chase Manhattan Bank. (Photo: Zindman/Fremont)

of Ishi's dress may recall Edie Sedgewick's emulation of Andy Warhol. However Tsinhnahjinnie's motivations are not of the same sensibility as the androgynous Pop artist groupie. Rather Tsinhnahjinnie's commentary is about assimilation by legislation. Tsinhnahjinnie has also incorporated a passage taken from The Bureau of Indian Affairs that details a dress code for the "savage."

Like Tsinhnahjinnie, Elaine Reichek also manipulates photographic material to address issues of identity, originality, and systems of knowing. However, Reichek is careful to position herself outside the frame, as a non-Indian. She is not attempting to speak for Native Americans, but rather investigates what is culturally inaccessible to her as a non-Indian.

In *Painted Blackfoot*, 1990 (Figure 5), Reichek, through her choice of materials, process and subject, purports to expose systems of anthropological and ethnographic study.[34] This work is part of a complex series in which Reichek adds pigment to a documentary photograph of a tepee and then knits a replica of the manipulated photograph, and creates a sophisticated statement about artistic choices and Western art-historical canons. For instance, the choice of color—red, yellow and blue—refer to Western viewing habits and Western vision, and a position that Reichek recognizes herself as occupying. Hence, Reichek is "pointing to the image as an aestheticized icon rather than a view of a tepee *in situ*."[35]

Reichek's sampler-inspired imagery exposes colonial associations (iconic in the cross-stitched sampler), juxtaposed against text that creates a paradox in medium and message. In *The Country Was...*, (1992) Reichek incorporates a quotation about land and boundaries by Heinmot Tooyaklet (Chief Joseph, Nez Perce) that becomes a searing indictment since listed below this quote in two columns separated by a small, cross-stitched church are 24 states implicated in evictions of Native populations and their dates of statehood.

Mark Tansey's art frequently exposes systems within the visual arts and art historical traditions. His *Purity Test*, 1982 (Figure 6), critiques modernist misinterpretations of the "primitive," depicting a group of Americans Indians on horseback viewing Rob-

ert Smithson's *Spiral Jetty*.[36] What the group of American Indians portrayed in this image think about the *Spiral Jetty* is not the subject of the work. Rather, Tansey critiques the distorted modernist perceptions through his technique of setting up multiple views, simultaneously, a ploy very similar to that of Woody Crumbo. The work does not have a single meaning, but really poses a question about artistic canons. According to Tansey, there are three functions to this picture: first, it is a painting, and the oil on canvas medium is part of the Western canon of aesthetics. Second, the photographic sense of the image alludes to the sepia-tone pigment of documentary photography or films of Native Americans (not by Native Americans), where these so-called "documentaries" have the same status as truth or fact. Third, the work is about illustrative subject matter, about the interpretation of things, particularly in the visual arts. Everything is brought together in a unified image.[37] Time is suspended then upset as what is so photographically rendered—simulating the sepia of early photography—is juxtaposed against a narrative that could not have happened. There is a clash with the modernist and romantic definition of the "primitive" and the postmodern construction of the work.

Neither Reichek nor Tansey traveled to create these images. They did not learn the language of the cultures represented. They do not collect objects or matériel from other cultures, nor do they do "fieldwork," visiting the sites of their subjects. They are not pretending to be Native. Rather, their imagery is derived from within their own cultural and artistic traditions and perceptions.

Jaune Quick-to-See Smith's (Flathead / Salish) *Paper Dolls for a Post Columbian World*, 1991 (Figure 7), were done a year

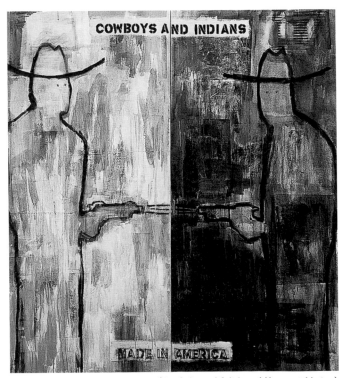

Figure 7. Jaune Quick-to-See Smith (Confederated Salish and Kootenai Nation), *Cowboys and Indians*, 1995, acrylic, mixed media on canvas, 80 x 72 inches. Courtesy of the Steinbaum Krauss Gallery, New York City.

Figure 8. Melanie Yazzie (Navajo), *She Keeps Silent*, 1993, collage, 56 x 43 inches. Collection of the Artist.

before the sesquicentennial "celebration." The concept of the paper doll is layered with multivalent meanings. Quick-to-See Smith has named her dolls Ken, Barbie and Bruce Plenty Horses. She has supplied them with several outfits ranging from a maids' uniform for Barbie to wear so she can clean "houses of white people" (after completing boarding school), to matching small pox suits for the entire Indian family. The work is double-edged, a caustic humor coupled with grief and a focused, intense anger only possible for survivors.

Quick-to-See Smith's *Cowboys and Indians* (1995) comment on the mythic construct of the American West. Like traveling abroad and seeing cowboy hats in Paris, Quick-to-See Smith's imagery makes us aware that, as stated by Joy Harjo, "the taking of the West is a construct that is very alive and continues to be used as a model."[38] This diptych presents two male figures wearing cowboy hats and shooting guns at each other. Each figure, portrayed in black outline only, fills one side of the diptych. Quick-to-See Smith has polarized the work in two ways. First is her use of text: she has literally split the text (Cowboys and Indians) that is stenciled at the top of the diptych between the a-nd. At the bottom of the image, Quick-to-See Smith has also split the text: "MADE IN AMERICA" is split between the "IN" and "AMERICA." Subsequently, the right side of the diptych, the darker side, contains the text "ND INDIANS, AMERICA." Could this be a reference to North Dakota American Indians? The work appears to be a commentary on polarities—dark / light, cowboys / Indians, right / wrong. However, Quick-to-See Smith engages the viewer and obfuscates narrative at the same time, for as one looks at the title—*Cowboys and Indians*, one is left to wonder "where are the Indians?" Is the presence of the Indian the absence of his silhouette, or is he wearing a cowboy hat and indistinguishable from an Anglo cowboy? Is this work a visual commentary about presence and absence?

Visual and verbal puns about sex and stereotypes that simultaneously refer to serious Native issues and history are central to the work of Ri-

Figure 9. Shelley Niro (Iroquois), from *The Border*, 1996, hand-tinted photograph, 30 x 40 inches. Courtesy of the Artist.

chard Glazer Danay (Mohawk). Glazer Danay, a former steelworker, is known for his series of hard-hat sculptures that allude to the many Iroquois steelworkers who were instrumental in the construction of inner-city skyscrapers. They often include texts such as "Bingo War Bonnet" that parody very real social constructions and stereotypes. The title of his *Indians are My Favorite Hobby* (1976),[39] an oil on canvas work, was taken from an actual letter written by a third-grader. Danay's painting thus becomes an original derived from an original. The irony is further pronounced when one considers that Glazer Danay's text-based works, works that are time-consuming to produce and meticulously-constructed, are contrived from products of material culture that were never intended to have permanence.[40]

Melanie Yazzie's (Navajo) collage *She Keeps Silent*, 1993 (Figure 8) and Shelley Niro's (Iroquois) *The Border*, 1996 (Figure 9) address the role of women in society. Yazzie's *She Keeps Silent* is a personal reference since she has placed an image of herself, with mouth covered, over a map of the Navajo reservation. The work references home, place and conditions of livelihood.

Niro's *The Border*, was part of an installation consisting of plywood, steel and horse-hair in conjunction with three 30 x 40" hand-tinted photographs. The work was created as part of a collective exhibition called "Crossing Borders" that explored various boundaries, such as those between nations, cultures or genders.[41] Niro places the profile of a Native American woman over the North American continent. Niro has literally placed her there to

Figure 10. Marcus Amerman (Choctaw), *Hopi Snake Priest*, 1995, glass beads, 10 x 10 inches. Courtesy of the Artist.

address the lack of presence of Native women in positions of authority in North American society. This is particularly ironic because women have always been strong individuals in Native communities. Indeed, the work *The Border* was ultimately inspired by the life and death of a strong woman—that of Anna Mae Aquash "a young Native American woman living in Nova Scotia, Canada, . . .[who] joined the United States-based American Indian Movement (AIM)."[42]

Niro's photographs are often trimmed with patterns and motifs that recall beadwork. In so doing, Niro alludes to a very traditional process—beading—while constructing a very contemporary narrative. Different responses to the traditional arts can be seen in works like *Hopi Snake Priest*, (1995) by Marcus Amerman (Choctaw); Colleen Cutschall's (Oglala-Sicangu / Lakota) *Beads and Boat People* (1995) and Sara Bates's (Cherokee) installations are examples of works by contemporary Native artists who have taken either a "traditional" material (such as the beads in Amerman's work, or the natural materials in Bates's), or a "traditional" style (e.g., Cutschall's work emulates bead-work). The work of these artists using "traditional" media or processes can also be read as specific histories or commentaries on current political

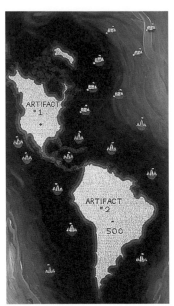

Figure 11. Colleen Cutschall (Oglala-Sicangu / Lakota), *Beads and Boat People*, 1995, acrylic on canvas, 72 x 40 inches. Collection of the Artist.

dialogues.[43] These works can reference a type of cultural text (much like quilting, for example) in which stories or history can be told through their imagery. In other words, the processes—beading, or the arrangement of objects—is a form of knowledge, writing, or knowing.

Amerman has created a wide range of works ranging from images in popular culture (such as Janet Jackson) to a dialogue with the icons of Western art. In *Hopi Snake Priest,* 1995 (Figure 10), Amerman uses an image by Edward Curtis; the artist spends hundreds of hours looking at the image while meticulously beading it.[44] In so doing, Amerman is critiquing long-accepted views of the visually-constructed vanishing American Indian. Curtis, who passionately photographed the "vanishing" American is being erased from his own imagery by a very much alive Native American. In this sense, Amerman's reconfiguration is again a reclamation of Native rights to control archetypical and individual identity.

Amerman exchanges Curtis's sepia photographs for brilliantly-colored tapestries of color, a contradiction of late nineteenth-century expectations. While it is the opposite application (adding color instead of being unable to provide it, thus denying it), the work has similar effects to Tansey's *Purity Test.* There is also a sense of tradition implied by this image. Amerman, out of respect for Hopi customs, sought out permission to use the image—not from the Smithsonian Institution, which holds copyright, but from Hopi relatives.

The adoption of glass beads by indigenous American peoples (one of the earliest trade goods with non-Indian cultures) has come to be identified with so-called "traditional" Native arts. Colleen Cutschall in *Beads and Boat People* (Figure 11) refers to beadwork, but it is the broader implications of the bead and its use as trade material that she asks the viewer to consider. She draws attention to the fact that an object as small as a bead really does carry the weight of a history of centuries of colonization.[45] Cutschall's acrylic on canvas "faux-bead" painting maps out the American continent. North and South America are labeled "artifact 1" and "artifact 2," respectively. Approaching the continent are "beaded" boats.

Sara Bates's work is uniquely contemporary in form and very traditional in spirit. Bates does not respond to the postmodernist notion that everything is produced socially or culturally through discourse. Her "honorings" (Figure 12) are a blending of personal and religious ritual. Her process is intricate and laborious as she

creates circles ranging from three and four feet to over twelve feet in diameter. Her materials carry personal meanings and she frequently adds or adjusts materials and patterns with each installation, yet the process remains the same. While her works have been compared to Navajo sandpaintings, and they may be similar in the sense of process, she does not consider herself a holy person, but an artist, committed to making her art. Unlike sandpaintings that are for healing purposes, Bates's *honorings* are an extension of the natural cycles of life. Though her work presents an awareness of multiple cultures, she responds to the Cherokee world view that recognizes mutual dependence with the natural world.[46] Bates's circular forms and materials are also rooted in Cherokee cosmology, but her creations "are not extensions of any fixed notion of Cherokee religion."[47] They are typically divided into equal quadrants—each quadrant representative of one of the four directions.[48] How Bates constructs each quadrant depends on the nature or "personality" of the direction it represents. For instance, East (red) is the place of fire, blood, success, and enlightenment; West (black) is the place of the ancestors and transformation, where the spirit moves on; South (white) is the place of peace and harmony; North (blue) is the place of worry or trouble.[49]

All of the artists represented in this portion of the exhibition are aware of and participate in contemporary critical discourses, presenting their artwork within the museum or gallery space. This "contact zone" presents a forum for dialogue with viewers and other artists. It is from within the context of the museum that these art works engage the viewer to think about issues of history, modernism, and authenticity. These artists are ultimately critiquing issues of identity and its relationship to anthropological history, tourism, art and art-making processes. In other words, issues of contact—how what is seen is interpreted and, subsequently, reframed or defined as history.

Figure 12. Sara Bates (Cherokee), *Honoring,* 1994, c. 136 inches diameter. Installation photo courtesy of the Artist.

This article is the result of many thought provoking discussions. I would like to thank Pat Andrews at the Indian Arts and Crafts Board, Sara Bates (Cherokee), Richard Glazer Danay (Mohawk), Rick Hill (Tuscarora), James Luna (Luiseño), Dr. J. Anthony Paredes, Dr. Ruth Phillips, Elaine Reichek, Hilary Scothorn, Dr. Jehanne Teilhet-Fisk, and Hulleah Tsinhnahjinnie (Seminole / Creek / Diné) for their patience and insightful comments.

1 Lucy R. Lippard, "Turning the Mirrors Around—The Pre-Face," in *American Art* (Winter/Spring 1991): 33.

2 See, for instance, Ivan Karp and Steven Lavine, eds. *Exhibiting Cultures* (Smithsonian Institution Press: Washington, D.C., 1991) and Maria Trogovenick's *Gone Primitive: Savage Intellects, Modern Lives* (Chicago: UP, 1990). For an excellent discussion on the problems of collecting Native art, see Janet Catherine Berlo and Ruth B. Phillips "Our (Museum) World Turned Upside Down: Re-positioning Native American Arts" in "The Problematics of Collecting and Display, Part I" *Art Bulletin* 77. 1 (March 1995): 6-10.

3 See also James Clifford's "Museums as Contact Zones" in *Routes: Travel and Translation in the Late Twentieth Century* (Cambridge: Harvard UP, 1997), 188-219.

4 For information on cultural brokers, see Margaret Connell Szasz, *Between Two Worlds: Cultural Broker* (Norman: U of Oklahoma P, 1994).

5 Zig Jackson, "Entering Zig's Indian Reservation," Artist Statement, courtesy of the American Indian Contemporary Arts, San Francisco, 1997.

6 Gill Perry, "Primitivism and the Modern," in *Primitivism, Cubism, Abstraction: The Early Twentieth Century*, Charles Harrison, Francis Frascina, and Gill Perry (New Haven: Yale UP, in association with Open University Press, 1993) 5.

7 Kroeber was an anthropologist who studied under Franz Boas at Columbia University in New York. He was also a linguist and very much interested in documenting Ishi's language and culture.

8 This refers to a photograph of Ishi in which he sits, dressed in a suit and tie, in front of a Yahi dwelling that he constructed as a demonstration in the back of the Museum. The accompanying sign says "Yahi house made by Ishi." Ishi's experiences are well chronicled in two publications: *Ishi in Two Worlds: A Biography of the Last Wild Indian in North America*, Theodora Kroeber (Berkeley: U of California P, 1989) and *Ishi the Last Yahi: A Documentary History*, Robert Heizer and Theodora Kroeber, eds. (Berkeley: U of California P, 1979). See also Alfred Kroeber's *Handbook of the Indians of California* (Berkeley: California Book Co., 1953) A documentary film, *Ishi the Last Yahi*, was produced and directed by Jed Riffe and Pamela Roberts in 1994.

9 Historically, museums and world's fairs represented the agendas of the dominant culture. This has been well documented in the writings of Annie Coombes, Ivan Karp, and Robert Rydell, for instance.

10 "Borderline" is a term used by Homi K. Bhabha to refer to the artist who is performing between two cultures. See "Beyond the Pale: Art in the Age of Multicultural Translation," in *Kunst and Museumjournaal* 5.4 (1994):15.

11 Andrea Liss, *The Art of James Luna: Postmodernism with Pathos* (Los Angeles: U of California P, 1992) 7. Naturally, as with any performance, different meanings depend on who makes up the audience. For an account of performances for a Native American audience, see Beverly Hanly, "Indian Tails," *News from Native California* 7.2 (Spring 1993); see also Nisha Supaman "Absurd Magic" in *News from Native California*, 9.3 (Spring 1996): 42. For accounts of non-Native audiences, see Liss. Note that these are not comparisons of the same performances but of comments on particular performances.

12 From Artist's Statement in *Encuento: Invasion of the Americas and the Making of the Mestizo* (Los Angeles: Social and Public Art Resource Center, 1991) n.p.

13 Scholars have discussed that the [Western] colonial perspective gave little consideration to multiple perspectives. There are a few early exceptions such as Julius E. Lips' *The Savage Hits Back*, with an introduction by Bronislaw Malinowski. First published in 1937, this work looks at how African artists depicted contact with the "White Man."

14 For further readings on Native humor in art see the exhibition catalogue *Indian Humor* curated by Sara Bates (Cherokee), essays by Jolene Rickard (Tuscarora) and Paul Chaat Smith (Comanche) (San Francisco, CA: American Indian Contemporary Arts, 1995); and Allan J. Ryan "Postmodern Parody: A political strategy in Contemporary Canadian Art" in *Art Journal* 51 (Fall 1991): 59-65

15 For an excellent discussion of tourism and its impact on the Southwest, see Leah Dilworth's *Imaging Indians in the Southwest: Persistent Visions of a Primitive Past* (Washington, D.C.: Smithsonian Institution, 1996).

16 For a discussion of the different perspectives involved in tourism, see Deirdre Evans-Pritchard, "How 'THEY' see 'US'–Native American Images of Tourists," *Annals of Tourism Research*, 16: 89-105.

17 This image also recalls the popular photographs of non-Natives with Natives. Luna has commented on how some Native Americans have had to "sell their red ass" to survive: his performance *Take Your Picture with an American Indian* parodies this tradition.

18 Leah Dilworth offers an excellent description of this work in *Imaging Indians in the Southwest*, see n. 14.

19 This is also a comparison to James Luna's *I wish I were an American Indian*, reprinted in *Art Journal* 51 (Fall 1991): 18-27.

20 Evans-Pritchard, 90.

21 See, for instance, Jackson Rushing *Native American Artists and the New York Avant Garde: A History of Cultural Primitivism* (Austin: U of Texas P, 1994).

22 See Marie Watkins "August Macke and Native American Imagery" in *Athanor XIII* (Tallahassee, FL: Florida State University Museum Press, 1995): 71-77; see also Christian Feest, ed. *Indians and Europe: An Interdisciplinary Collection of Essays* (Aachen: Edition Herodot, Rader Verlag, 1987).

23 For a full description of this performance, see Heiner Stachelhaus, *Joseph Beuys*, trans. by David Britt (New York: Abbeville Publishers, 1991) 173-176. For a discussion of the contemporary artist as a shaman, see Mark Levy "The Shaman Is a Gifted Artist: Yves Klein, Joseph Beuys, Mary Beth Edelson, Karen Finley) *High Performance* 43 (Fall 1988): 54-61

24 Stachelhaus 174.

25 For an excellent description of the work, see Anne Rorimer, "Lothar Baumgarten in Pittsburgh: Tongue of the Cherokee," in *Parachute* 58 (1989): 4-9.

26 For a discussion by Native artists and scholars of Lothar Baumgarten's permanent installation *Monument to the Native People of Ontario* (1984-1985) at the Ontario Gallery of Art in Toronto, see Robert Houle (Saulteaux) "The Spiritual Legacy of the Ancient Ones," in *Land Spirit Power: First Nations at the National Gallery of Canada*, Diana Nemiroff, Robert Houle, Charlotte Townsend-Gault (Ottawa, 1992) 49-52. Houle's excellent essay addresses issues of Naming. For an account of Baumgarten working with Indian populations in Venezuela and issues of naming, see also Craig Owens "Improper Names," *Art in America* 74 (October 1986):126-135.

27   Durham is / has been embroiled in issues of cultural identity that is beyond the scope of this paper. He is not a registered member of any tribe, but is very much aware of tribal issues. Durham proceeds on his rigorously individualistic path and he both includes and excludes the viewer (in works such as *Not Lothar Baumgarten's Cherokee*).

28   Quoted to author by Ann Beckett, publisher at A:shiwi A:wan Museum and Heritage Center, on November, 7, 1997 via telephone.

29   Hughte's drawings of Cushing may be found in his book *A Zuni Artist Looks at Frank Hamilton Cushing* (Zuni, NM: A:shiwi A:wan Museum and Heritage Center, 1996). For an essay of depictions of Frank Hamilton Cushing by Thomas Eakins, and comparative photographs, see William Truettner's article "Dressing the Part: Thomas Eakins' Portrait of Frank Hamilton Cushing," *The American Art Journal* (Spring 1985): 49-72.

30   Hughte 94.

31   Written comment by fellow Smithsonian expedition researcher Matilda Coxe Stevenson on back of the photograph among the Cushing Papers at the Southwest Museum. See Hughte, 94.

32   See Malcom Brenner's "Zuni Cartoonist Hughte Dead," in *Gallup Independent*, Wednesday, April 30, 1997.

33   Hulleah J. Tsinhnahjinnie, *Photographic Memoirs of An Aboriginal Savant*, exhibition brochure. CN Gorman Museum, UC Davis (November 13 - December 22, 1994) 4. In this brochure, Tsinhnahjinnie has constructed a conversation between herself and Kroeber.

34   Jimmie Durham, "Elaine Reichek: Unraveling the Social Fabric" reprinted in *A Certain Lack of Coherence: Writings on Art and Cultural Politics*, Jean Fisher, ed. (London: Kala Press, 1993) 234-235.

35   See, Therese Lichtenstein, "Elaine Reichek" *Journal of Contemporary Art* 6.2 (1993): 95.

36   In describing his reasons for selecting the site and shape of *Spiral Jetty*, Smithson recalls Jackson Pollock and other Abstract Expressionist views on the primordial seas. See "Spiral Jetty" by Robert Smithson, reprinted in *Theories of Contemporary Art: A Sourcebook of Artists Writings*, Kristine Stiles and Peter Selz, eds. (Berkeley: U of California P, 1996) 533.

37   Mark Tansey to the author, November 9, 1997.

38   Joy Harjo, "Creation Story: The Jaune Quick-to-See Survey" in *Subversions / Affirmations: Jaune Quick-to-See Smith, A Survey* (Jersey City, NJ: Jersey City Museum, 1996) 66. Harjo was referring specifically to places like New Guinea, Australia, and South Africa.

39   This work was originally conceived as one work but is now framed and juxtaposed with another letter, one to the artist's Aunt Viola (1976). In this letter, Glazer Danay discusses the difficulty of being a Native artist.

40   For examples of other letters, see Gerhard Hoffman, "Frames of Reference: Native American Art in the Context of Modern and Postmodern Art," in *Art of the North American Indian: Native Traditions in Evolution*, Edwin Wade, ed. (New York: Hudson Hills Press in association with Philbrook Art Center, Tulsa, 1986) 279.

41   See Shelley Niro, "Artist's Statement" in *The Border: The Contemporary Native American Photoart of Shelley Niro* (Hamilton, New York: Longyear Museum of Anthropology, Colgate University, 1997) 8-10.

42   Niro 8.

43   Clifford 188-219.

44   From an unpublished interview between Marcus Amerman and Hilary Scothorn, August 30, 1995. I would like to thank Hilary for her generous assistance and the sharing of her enthusiasm about Marcus' work.

45   Janet Clark, *Basket, Bead and Quill* (Thunder Bay, Ontario: Thunder Bay Art Gallery) 8.

46   See Grayson B. Noley, "Processing the Natural," in *Migrations of Meaning: A Source Book* (New York: Intar Gallery, 1992) 41.

47   Quoted in a lecture given at Florida State University, Museum of Fine Arts on November 6, 1997. The Cherokee belief system has undergone significant change over the last 300 years. See Lee Irwin, "Cherokee Healing: Myth, Dreams, and Medicine," *American Indian Quarterly* (Spring 1992): 237-257.

48   The recognition of the four directions are common throughout most Native American cultures, and other artists have addressed or made reference to this notion (the work of James Luna, for instance).

49   Jean Robertson, "Sara Bates: Honoring Connections with the Natural World," *Surface Design Journal*, 21. 4 (Summer 1997): 12.

Plains Indian child in "fancy dress" at Taos Powwow, New Mexico, 1990. (Photo: J. Teilhet-Fisk)

VI. REGIONAL AND PAN-NATIVE AMERICAN ART

"Pan-Indian Art"
An Aesthetic Phenomenon

Blue Sau-Pa Pahdocony
Comanche

What is Indian Art? In the Philbrook Art Center's 1986 *The Arts of the North American Indian*, Edwin L. Wade suggested that "The question is vast, involving whole societies as well as individual people, their values and beliefs, their imaginations, and their personal talents."[1] He added, though, that as with all individual artists "creation itself is justification."[2] John Anson Warner, Jamake Highwater, Gerhard Hoffman and others undertook to examine many questions in the Philbrook collection of essays, questions that Edwin Wade posed in the introduction:

> What are the messages or symbolic contents of American Indian art? What does tradition mean in the context of Native American artworks? What did, or do, they mean to their makers? What is the aesthetics of native art? How do we establish criteria for degrees of quality in native work? What is the place of creative individuality in native traditions? How has American Indian art generated controversy in our century?. . . What are some possible scenarios for the future of Native American art? Is its tribal, ethnic, or individual aesthetics still viable? Is the concept "ethnic" any longer an acceptable social identifier in the twentieth century?[3]

John Anson Warner has declared that "Human beings are by nature social. They learn, via the socialization process the attitudes and behavior of a distinct social milieu. Because of this, what it means to be an individual is always a question of what society one grew up in. Further, it is a question of where one's society is placed in history, and what relationships it sustains

with other cultures."[4] To me, this has particular significance as a factor in art recognized as pan-Indian. Pan-Indian art is produced by Native Americans who feel themselves no longer exclusively bound to the values and customs of their original tribal societies.[5] They work in the art market of the dominant "White" society and consequently regard themselves as global artists. While still drawing on the experience of their specific cultural backgrounds, their style is no longer unique to a tribe, but is largely shaped by white expectations about "Indian style."

In 1962 Paul Wingert wrote that "The fundamental way in which an art tradition is manifested, through its forms and designs, is a singular development, and because this is true it is possible to isolate and to characterize the distinctive artistic features of a specific geographical area."[6] This treats tradition as style, which isolates into formal components what Indians consider to be an all-encompassing whole. In my experience, Native artists may talk about technique, methods, quality—but they never mention style. When their art is pan-Indian art (because artists from widely different tribes produce remarkably similar works), it is considered ethnic art because it is based on white definitions of ethnic boundaries.

Although many tend to think of Native Americans as a single people, they are, in fact, as diverse as the various nationals of Europe. The Tlingits, for example, were as different from the Sioux as the Greeks are from Danes. As the people spread over the North American continent, more than 200 languages and dialects developed. Any two were no more alike than Russian and Spanish. Because of tribal diversities many exquisitely delicate creations and sophisticated abilities in craftsmanship have surfaced, resulting in the recognition of the artistic value of Native American art.

The '60s and '70s both brought about many changes and new and highly controversial things. As discussed by Wade *et al*, traditional and modernist points of view are temporal philosophies: in the attempts by some artists to fuse the two positions, a new wave of Indian art was formed. From the outset, this focus was repudiated and scorned by the art community who felt the fusion was an extremely limited expression. Both Indians and non-Indians shared this opinion. Although controversial, a broader range of techniques and imagery was the result of the Native artist's own recognition of contradictions in his / her world. Many viewers resisted these developments, partly because they could not grasp the intent of the artists, and partly because of their loyalty to traditional forms.

Blue Sau-Pa Pahdocony, Comanche, is committed to the preservation and perpetuation of Native American history and culture. He has been an educator developing and teaching programs for the Department of Natural Resources for students from elementary school through college, and he is a decorated veteran of the Vietnam conflict, serving two tours of duty—for which he was awarded two purple hearts, two silver stars and two bronze stars. He has a degree in Medical Science and Human Behavior from the University of California, Santa Barbara, and currently resides in southern Georgia, where he is President / Historian of Four Horses Native American Productions. Since March of 1997, he has served as an advisor on the Dimensions of Native America *project.*

Several artworks serve as examples of the evolving interests of Native American artists. In his 1973 painting *Laughing Indian*, Fritz Scholder's figure "counters the stereotypic idea of primitive stoicism."[7] Scholder (Luiseño) earned his MFA at the University of Arizona in 1964, and later taught at the Institute of American Indian Art (IAIA). "Scholder enjoyed introducing contradictory visual elements such as ice cream cones, beer bottles, and other artifacts of white culture into traditional Indian imagery,"[8] and he has been characterized by Jamake Highwater as "an artist and teacher who understood the modernist impulse,"[9] so that "Scholder's work found its way into the mainstream art market at the very moment" of change.[10] In drawing an international comparison, Highwater notes that in 1964 concerned "Indian traditionalists were demonstrating in front of Southwestern galleries against Scholder's 'grotesque and shameful' depiction of Indians—a reaction. . .almost identical to that of the European demonstrators at the turn of the century who had cried out against the debasement of academic art by Kandinsky, Picasso, and Matisse."[11]

Given this depiction of Indian individualists as rebels and heretics, let us recall that none of these artists is repudiating the validity of the Indian world or attempting to escape into some other world. To the contrary, as their statements and works often declare, they are highly traditional people, and their work focuses upon vital aspects of Indian culture. They often consider the inspiration for their paintings and sculptures to be visions, revelations, and the cumulative heritage of their people. They are among the most outspoken critics of the unthinking public display and commercialization of Indian ceremonial objects. They are among those Native Americans who are becoming increasingly vocal and resistant to the desecration of Indian religious life. In short, many of the new generation of artists are animated by a sense of spirituality and a deep involvement in their cultures, histories, religions, and symbols of power.[12]

T.C. Cannon (Caddo), 1946-1978, *Collector #5*, or *Osage with Van Gogh*, 1980, woodblock print on rice paper, 17 3/4 x 15 inches. Collecton of the University of Tulsa, Oklahoma.

The painting *You Can't Rollerskate in a Buffalo Herd Even if You Have All The Medicine* (1979-1980, acrylic on cloth), by artist George C. Longfish, Seneca / Tuscarora (Northeast Woodlands), who was "trained at the Art Institute of Chicago, has a remarkable ability to combine European technique with Indian images and themes"—to which Edwin Wade adds—"He opens a visionary door through symbol in his large, unframed canvases."[13] The third artwork to represent the expansion of imagery and approach is *Collector #5*, or "*Osage with Van Gogh*" (1980) by T.C. Cannon; this work

is among the most widely reproduced Indian works of the last decade. . . . This image, which exists as a painting, poster, and woodcut, shows a finely-dressed Osage, sitting in his wicker chair between a Navajo rug and Vincent van Gogh's painting, *Wheatfield*, thus incorporating the worlds of mainstream and Indian art. Through the confident and smiling Osage, Cannon is saying that the modern Indian makes his own culture and his own art, drawing from both worlds.[14]

Acknowledging two worlds and negotiating their borders is not without stress. Gerhard Hoffman perceptively points out that:

These tensions caused an alienation of the artist from a realistically conceived outside world, from society, and even from the self, and led to the perception of the artist's life as tragic. Gauguin, Van Gogh, Edward Munch, and Ernst Ludwig Kirchner stand as examples of this view new art forms developed, based on the need for a new kind of psychic and spiritual expressiveness, which could depict the "really real" beneath the outer surface.[15]

Hoffman suggests that from "the outer surface of reality to the aesthetic distillation of the spiritual form embedded in the material; or. . .from the urges and the hallucinatory pictures of the innermost soul to their incorporation in external images, distorted in the process by psychic energy. . . . the alienation of the subject from the world, from society and from reason results in a new spiritual quest."[16] Hoffman believes that the "postmodern world, with its breakdown of ideologies and social utopias, of dogmatic nationalism and aestheticism, is again on the path to the irrational and the imaginative"[17] and that "Indian art and postmodern art go hand in hand in trying to remain open to this potential. If in the course of detraditionalization and despiritualization, we are not to lose the possibility of a diversity of relationships and meanings, then perhaps artistic fictions are necessary"[18] for the possibilities of dialogues, experiences, and the imaginations of the Native American artists.

[1]   Edwin L. Wade, ed., *The Arts of the North American Indian: Native Traditions in Evolution* (New York: Hudson Hills Press, 1986) 17.

[2]   Wade 17.

[3]   Wade 17.

[4]   John Anson Warner, "The Individual in Native American Art: A Sociological View," *The Arts of the North American Indian: Native Traditions in Evolution*, Edwin L. Wade, ed. (New York: Hudson Hills Press, 1986) 171.

[5]   The definition of "Pan-Indianism" provided by Wade, et al, in *The Arts of the North American Indian: Native Traditions in Evolution*, 310, is: "A modern style of music, dance, art, and philosophy that transcends tribal and regional styles. Its elements are drawn from many tribes and regions and from the non-Indian world. In some cases the style serves as a unifying basis for national Indian political action."

[6]   Paul Wingert, *Primitive Art: Its Tradition and Styles* (New York: Oxford UP, 1962).

[7]   Jamake Highwater, "Controversy in Native American Art," *The Arts of the North American Indian: Native Traditions in Evolution*, Edwin L. Wade, ed. (New York: Hudson Hills Press, 1986) 239.

[8]   Highwater 239.

[9]   Highwater 238.

[10]   Highwater 238.

[11]   Highwater 238-239.

[12]   Highwater 241-242.

[13]   Wade (caption 265) 297.

[14]   Wade (caption 232) 267.

[15]   Gerhard Hoffman, "Frames of Reference: Native American Art in the Context of Modern and Postmodern Art," *The Arts of the North American Indian: Native Traditions in Evolution*, Edwin L. Wade, ed. (New York: Hudson Hills Press, 1986) 267.

[16]   Hoffman 267.

[17]   Hoffman 275.

[18]   Hoffman 281.

Florida Indian Youth Program Poetry

A PLACE WE CALL HOME

THE EVERGLADES IS A PLACE WE CALL HOME, IT'S BEEN
HERE FOR US SINCE THE BEGINNING OF TIME. IT'S FULL OF
LIFE—THE KIND YOU WOULD DREAM OF. THE BIRDS SING,
SPREADING THEIR WINGS TO FLY. THE FROGS CROAKING,
MAKING THE SOUND FOR RAIN. THE ALLIGATORS GLIDING
IN THE WATER, LOOKING FOR SOME PREY. THE TURTLES
SITTING ON THE ROCKS IN THE SCORCHING SOUTH
FLORIDA SUN. THE SAWGRASS STANDS STILL UNTIL THE
WIND MAKES IT DANCE. THE HAMMOCKS FULL OF
GOD'S ANIMALS JUST WAITING TO BE DISCOVERED. THE
WATER LOOKS SO PEACEFUL, LIKE IT WAS BACK THEN. A
FAMILY OF INDIANS IN A HAND-CARVED CANOE, RIDING TO
THEIR CAMP . . .THE FATHER MOVING THE CANOE WITH THE
EXPERT TOUCH.
AS THEY GET CLOSER TO THE CAMP
THE ONLY THING ON THEIR MIND IS GETTING HOME,
THE EVERGLADES IS A PLACE THEY CALL HOME.

—Elizabeth Osceola and Ida F. Osceola

Osceola, Elizabeth and Ida F. Osceola. "A PLACE WE CALL HOME," *The Gathering of the Clans,* Florida Indian Youth Program, 1993, 4.

———————

TO MY GRANDPARENTS WITH LOVE:

HE'S AN EAGLE THAT FLIES HIGH IN THE SKY
SHE'S A PANTHER KEEN WITH ITS EYES
ONE FLIES UPON THE EVERGLADES
ONE ROAMS THROUGH THE SAWGRASS BLADES
BUT IN THE REAL MANNER, THEY ARE GREAT PEOPLE
IN MY LIFE
HE IS A GREAT MAN WITH THE WISDOM
SHE IS THE MOST BEAUTIFUL PERSON I HAVE EVER
    SEEN
THEY HAVE THE WISDOM AND BEAUTY I WISH I HAD
BUT THAT'S WHAT I ONLY DREAM OF
TO BE AS GOOD AS THEM
INSIDE AND OUT
THEY ARE MY GRANDPARENTS
SEMINOLE / MICCOSUKEE AND PROUD.

—Ida F. Osceola

Ida F. Osceola, "TO MY GRANDPARENTS WITH LOVE," from *The Gathering of the Clans,* Florida Indian Youth Program, 1993, 34.

TRADITION

This word may not seem
important but don't take it
for granted. Tradition is the
one thing that has kept Indians
going all these years. Through
wars and disease, we have
always had tradition on
our side. Some of us stray
and walk that narrow walk
and look for things that we
don't need. We cannot lose
our tradition and we cannot
forget it. For the generations
to come, let's not deprive
them of this way of life. For
the generations that have
passed, it would be like our
ancestors died for nothing.
Losing our traditions is like
burying Indians alive.

—Elizabeth Osceola

Elizabeth Osceola, "Tradition," *Collection of Young Indian Thoughts,* Florida Indian Youth Program and Leadership Academy, 1995.

———————

They're Indian. They love nature. They love each other.
Nothing would ever tear them apart. The thatched roof
would say they're very artistic and love to work with their
hands. The poles give a sense that they're strong and work
long hours to finish what they started. They really like to
live together and enjoy each other very much.

We are all great people, not only as a whole, but as each
individual. Nothing ever told us we had some boundaries
we couldn't cross. No one ever told us there were rules we
had to follow. It lives in me, it lives beside me, and it
belongs in me. They always come to me to say I can do it
all, but who was I when I was told I was nothing if I wasn't
one of them. Maybe I am still nothing, but I can always do
it all.

—Ida F. Osceola

Ida F. Osceola, *Unbreakable Voices,* Florida Indian Youth Program, 1996, 38.

CATALOGUE OF EXHIBITION

[Checklist compiled by Robin Franklin Nigh.]

CARVING

Argillite:

Figurine, possibly by William Collison (Haida), *c.* 1910, argillite, 3 x 7 1/4 inches high. Collections of the Anthropology Department of the Florida Museum of Natural History, Gainesville, Florida, cat. no. P758.

Platter, possibly by Tom Price (Haida), *c.* 1910-1925, argillite, abalone inlay, 20 1/16 x 2 1/4 inches high x 10 inches wide. Collections of the Anthropology Department of the Florida Museum of Natural History, Gainesville, Florida, cat. no. P1203.

Shaman Wearing Bear Headdress, Haida, 1865-1910, argillite, 12 inches high x 3 3/8 inches wide. Collections of the Anthropology Department of the Florida Museum of Natural History, Gainesville, Florida, cat. no. P752.

"Totem pole" (miniaturized), figures bottom to top—bear, human, eagle, bear, Haida, *c.* 1865-1910, argillite, 18 3/4 high, 2 1/2 inches maximum thickness. Collections of the Anthropology Department of the Florida Museum of Natural History, Gainesville, Florida, cat. no. P1006.

Wood:

Cecil Calnimptewa (Hopi), *Flower Kachina Doll,* 1993, wood, height 17 inches. Private Collection.

Cigar-store Indian, n.d., wood, height 5 feet 2 inches. Private Collection.

Neil David, Sr. (Hopi), *Black Bear Kachina Doll,* 1974, wood, height 19 inches. Private Collection.

Ronald Honyouti (Hopi), *Butterfly Maiden Kachina Doll,* 1978, wood, height 16 inches. Private Collection.

Alvin James (Hopi), *Eagle Kachina Doll,* 1972, wood, height 12 inches. Private Collection.

Kachina Doll, Hopi, *c.* 1940s, wood, height 8 1/8 inches. Collection of Sara W. Reeves and I.S.K. Reeves V.

Butterfly Kachina, Hopi, 1954, painted cottonwood and feathers. Made for the Arizona State Fair Arts and Crafts Competition, 1954. Collections of the Anthropology Department of the Florida Museum of Natural History, Gainesville, Florida, cat. no. E1114.

Kachina Doll ["Kachinoid"], Navajo, *c.* 1945-1946, wood, height 6 inches. Collection of Sara W. Reeves and I.S.K. Reeves V.

Kachina Doll, *Kokopelli Kachina,* Hopi, late twentieth century, wood, height 5 3/4 inches. Collection of Sara W. Reeves and I.S.K. Reeves V.

Kachina Doll, *Shalako Kachina,* Zuni, *c.* 1945, cottonwood, height 14 1/2 inches. Collection of Sara W. Reeves and I.S.K. Reeves V.

Kachina Doll, *Kohosorhoya Kachina,* Hopi, *c.* 1945-1950, wood, height 10 inches. Collection of Sara W. Reeves and I.S.K. Reeves V.

Bennett Rogers (Hopi), *Kachina Long-Haired Maiden,* 1993, cottonwood, height 7 inches. Star / Fire Collection—Sandra Starr-Tanner.

Manfried Susunkewa (Hopi, Second Mesa), Kachina Doll: *Kokosori Kachina,* late twentieth century, wood, height 11 inches. Collection of Sara W. Reeves and I.S.K. Reeves V.

Clark Tenakhongua (Hopi, First Mesa) Kachina Doll: *Tihu of a Skunk Kachina,* late twentieth century, wood, height 12 1/2 inches. Collection of Sara W. Reeves and I.S.K. Reeves V.

Bess Yanez (Hopi, First Mesa), Kachina paired miniatures on base, 1997, *Mudhead and Whipper,* wood, height 1 3/4 inches; *Black Buffalo,* wood, height 1 1/4 inches. Private Collection.

FIBERS

Baskets:

Linda Baletso (Seminole Tribe of Florida) Basket with Lid, 1992, applied bird design with feathers, 18 x 18 inches. Star / Fire Collection—Sandra Starr-Tanner.

Paul Billie (Seminole), Basket, 1993, applied dog forms, 8 1/2 x 9 1/2 inches. Star / Fire Collection—Sandra Starr-Tanner.

Doubleweave Swampcane Basket with Handle, Choctaw, *c.* 1993, 10 1/2 x 10 inches. Gift of Theo S. Vaughey, Lauren Rogers Museum of Art, Laurel, Mississippi.

Linda Farve (Choctaw), Swampcane Hamper with Cover, 1985, 26 x 14 inches. Lauren Rogers Museum of Art, Laurel, Mississippi.

Martha Jim (Choctaw), Basket, *c.* 1995-1997, swampcane, height 9 1/2 inches, diameter 8 inches. Collection of Mary Lyon.

Pictorial Basket, Hopi, *c.* 1910-1920, 7 3/4 x 11 inches. Collection of Sara W. Reeves and I.S.K. Reeves V.

Berdie Steve (Choctaw), Basket, *c.* 1995-97, swampcane, height 9 inches, diameter 7 1/2 inches. Collection of Mary Lyon.

Lela Soloman (Choctaw), Doubleweave Swampcane Basket, 1976, 13 x 10 1/2 inches. Lauren Rogers Museum of Art, Laurel, Mississippi.

Jeffrey Denson Solomon (Choctaw), Doubleweave Wastebasket, 1979-1980, swampcane, 12 1/2 x 10 inches. Lauren Rogers Museum of Art, Laurel, Mississippi.

Jeffrey Denson Solomon (Choctaw), Swampcane Burden Basket, 1979-1980, 16 x 19 inches. Lauren Rogers Museum of Art, Laurel, Mississippi.

Lonie Alec Wallace (Choctaw), Swampcane Elbow Basket with Handle, 1976, 14 x 11 inches. Lauren Rogers Museum of Art, Laurel, Mississippi.

Louise Wallace (Choctaw), Doubleweave Insideout Basket, *c.* 1995-1997, swampcane, height 10 1/2 inches, diameter 14 inches. Collection of Mary Lyon.

Louise Wallace (Choctaw), Rattlesnake Diamond Patterned Basket, *c.* 1995-1997, swampcane, height 12 inches, diameter 7 inches. Collection of Mary Lyon.

Beadwork:

Beaded Bag, Plateau, early twentieth century, glass beads, cotton thread, 10 3/4 x 6 inches. Collection of Sara W. Reeves and I.S.K. Reeves V.

Beaded Bag, Micmac, *c.* 1890, glass beads, cotton thread on fabric, 6 1/4 x 7 inches. Collection of Sara W. Reeves and I.S.K. Reeves V.

Flower Belt, possibly Cree from the Turtle Mt. Reservation, *c.* 1890, leather, cotton cloth backing, glass seed beads, shell, 35 1/2 long x 2 1/2 inches wide. Collections of the Anthropology Department of the Florida Museum of Natural History, Gainesville, Florida, cat. no. P379.

Beaded Snake, Plains, *c.* 1880s, glass seed beads, length 19 inches. Collection of Sara W. Reeves and I.S.K. Reeves V.

Loomed Beadwork Strap, Seminole, c. 1890, glass beads, cotton string, 4 inches wide, 28 inches long. Historical Society of Martin County, The Elliot Museum, Stuart, Florida.

Tourist Wall Pocket (Eastern Sioux, Yankton or Sisseton), c. 1880, buckskin, seed beads, muslin-covered cardboard back, silk ribbon, 49 x 19 1/2 cm. Collections of the Anthropology Department of the Florida Museum of Natural History, Gainesville, Florida, cat. no. 91983.

Seminole Patchwork and Fibers:

Finger-woven Sash, Seminole, c. 1825-1840, wool yarn and "pony beads," length with tassels 142 5/8 inches. Collection of Sara W. Reeves and I.S.K. Reeves V.

Woman's Skirt, Seminole, c. 1954, patchwork. Collection of former First Lady of Florida, Mrs. Leroy Collins.

Man's Jacket, Seminole, c. 1954, patchwork. Collection of former First Lady of Florida, Mrs. Leroy Collins.

Man's Jacket, Seminole, c. 1954, patchwork. Collection of former First Lady of Florida, Mrs. Leroy Collins.

Man's Big Shirt, Seminole, c. 1925, patchwork, length 43 1/2 inches. Collection of Sara W. Reeves and I.S.K. Reeves V.

Man's Jacket, Seminole, c. 1935, patchwork, length 37 inches. Collection of Sara W. Reeves and I.S.K. Reeves V.

Man's Turban with Beaded Fobs, Seminole, c. 1890, wool, 5 1/2 high 15 inches in diameter. Historical Society of Martin County, The Elliot Museum, Stuart, Florida.

Young Man's Big Shirt, Seminole, c. 1925, patchwork, length 36 inches. Collection of Sara W. Reeves and I.S.K. Reeves V.

Quilts:

Nancy Blackhawk (Sioux), Tepees 'Round the Lake, c. 1970-75, Morningstar pattern quilt, 87 x 73 inches. Star / Fire Collection—Sandra Starr-Tanner.

Elaine Brave Bull (Sioux), Morningstar Quilt, c. 1992, Morningstar pattern quilt, 74 x 88 inches. Star / Fire Collection—Sandra Starr-Tanner.

Regina Brave Bull (Hunkpapa Sioux), Patchwork Eagle Star, c. 1970-1975, Morningstar pattern quilt, 86 x 66 inches. Star / Fire Collection—Sandra Starr-Tanner.

Artie Crazy Bull (Oglala Sioux), Star and Arrows, 1970-1975, Morningstar pattern quilt, 68 x 83 inches. Star / Fire Collection—Sandra Starr-Tanner.

Elsie Holland and Alice McGhee (Poarch Creek), Big Star Quilt, 1972, cotton, c. 70 x 86 inches. Collection of J. Anthony Paredes.

Becky E. Masayesoa (Hopi), Child's Quilt, 1989, 4 x 3 feet. Collection of the School of American Research, Santa Fe, New Mexico.

Navajo blanket-styled quilt, 1988, cotton, 43 x 55 inches. Private Collection.

Quilt, Poarch Creek, 1980s, commercial fabric, c. 70 x 86 inches. Collection of J. Anthony Paredes.

Quillwork:

Pine Ridge Sioux, Washabaugh Co., South Dakota, Quill Bag, n.d., leather (rawhide), seed beads, dyed quillwork, feathers, tin, 28 1/2 x 8 1/4 inches. Collections of the Anthropology Department of the Florida Museum of Natural History, Gainesville, Florida, cat. no. P239.

Navajo [Diné] Rugs:

Chief's Blanket, Navajo, c. 1895, wool, 73 x 51 inches. Collection of Sara W. Reeves and I.S.K. Reeves V.

Germantown "Eye Dazzler" Rug, Navajo, c. 1880-1890, wool, 59 x 35 inches. Collection of Sara W. Reeves and I.S.K. Reeves V.

Louise Nez, Dinosaur Scene, Navajo pictorial rug, 1991, 43 x 49 inches, Museum of Northern Arizona, Flagstaff (E9622).

Pictorial Tapestry, Navajo, 1960, length 153 cm. Collection of the School of American Research, Santa Fe, New Mexico.

Rug, American Flag, Navajo, n.d., wool, 28 x 27 inches. Private Collection.

Rug, Home Sweet Home, Country Road, Navajo, n.d., wool, 31 1/4 x 20 1/2 inches. Private Collection.

Yei (Yé'ii) Rug, Navajo, early twentieth century, wool, 54 X 37 inches. Private Collection.

INSTALLATION AND PERFORMANCE

Sara Bates (Cherokee), Honoring, 1998, mixed media installation, c. 12 feet diameter.

James Luna (Luiseño), Our Indians, 1998, mixed media installation and performance, dimensions variable.

Blue Sau-Pa Pahdocony (Comanche) and Joe Quetone (Kiowa): installation of artworks and artifacts of particular signficance in the region.

METALWORK AND METALS WITH MIXED MEDIA

Bandolier Pouch, Navajo, c. 1910-1920, leather with cast silver, 8 x 5 3/4 inches. Collection of Sara W. Reeves and I.S.K. Reeves V.

Bracelet, Navajo, c. 1930s, silver and turquoise, width 2 1/2 inches. Collection of Sara W. Reeves and I.S.K. Reeves V.

Bracelet, Zuni, c. 1930s, silver and turquoise, width 2 1/2 inches. Collection of Sara W. Reeves and I.S.K. Reeves V.

Bracelet, Zuni, c. 1940s, silver and turquoise, width 2 1/4 inches. Collection of Sara W. Reeves and I.S.K. Reeves V.

Child's Bracelet, Navajo, c. 1950s, silver and turquoise, width 1 5/8 inches. Collection of Sara W. Reeves and I.S.K. Reeves V.

Cluster Style Bracelet, Navajo, 1940s, silver and turquoise. Star / Fire Collection—Sandra Starr-Tanner.

Concha Medallion Belt, Navajo, c. 1940, silver. Star / Fire Collection—Sandra Starr-Tanner.

Concha Medallion Belt, Navajo, signed AO, c. 1970-1980, silver, c. 30 inches, conchas 3 1/4 x 2 1/2 inches each. Star / Fire Collection—Sandra Starr-Tanner.

Coral Necklace, Navajo, c. 1930s, coral, silver and turquoise, length 17 inches. Collection of Sara W. Reeves and I.S.K. Reeves V.

Daniel Sunshine Reeves (Navajo), Small Bowl with Lid, 1997, silver, 2 1/4 inches high x 3 inches wide. Star / Fire Collection—Sandra Starr-Tanner.

Edith Martza (Zuni), Bracelet, 1970, silver with turquoise, 6 x 2 1/2 cm. Collection of the School of American Research, Santa Fe, New Mexico.

Fetish Necklace (Zuni), c. 1960, ten strands, turquoise, abalone, jet catlinite and shell, 14 1/2 x 10 1/2 inches. Star / Fire Collection—Sandra Starr-Tanner.

Filigree Brooch, late nineteenth / early twentieth century, gold filagree, paste jewels, 7 1/2 x 9 1/2 cm. Collections of the International Folk Art Foundation, Museum of International Folk Art, Santa Fe, New Mexico.

Holy Water Container, early nineteenth century, silver plated, height 19 1/2 cm., diameter 28 cm. Collections of the International Folk Art Foundation, Museum of International Folk Art, Santa Fe.

Horse Headstall, Navajo, c. 1890-1900, silver, 15 1/4 x 16 3/4 inches. Collection of Sara W. Reeves and I.S.K. Reeves V.

Man's Squash Blossom Necklace, Navajo, c. 1960-1970, silver and turquoise, 17 inches. Star / Fire Collection—Sandra Starr-Tanner.

Multiple Row Work Needlepoint Bracelet, probably Zuni, c. 1940-1950, silver and turquoise, 2 3/4 inches diameter x 2 1/4 inches high. Star / Fire Collection—Sandra Starr-Tanner.

Necklace, Santo Domingo, c. 1900, shell and turquoise, height 3 1/2 inches, width 3 3/4 inches. Collection of Sara W. Reeves and I.S.K. Reeves V.

Pin, Zuni, c. 1960, silver, coral, jet, turquoise, abalone, white shell, channel inlay, 1 7/8 x 7/8 inches. Collection of the School of American Research, Santa Fe, NM.

Sandcast Bracelet, Navajo, c. 1930-1940, silver and turquoise, 2 inches diameter, band 1 3/4 inches wide. Star / Fire Collection—Sandra Starr-Tanner.

Squash Blossom Necklace, Navajo, c. 1920, silver and sandcast naja, length 17 1/2 inches. Collection of Sara W. Reeves and I.S.K. Reeves V.

Squash Blossom Necklace, Navajo, c. 1930-1940, silver and turquoise with pomegranate blossom beads, 11 inches. Star / Fire Collection—Sandra Starr-Tanner.

Tobacco Container, Navajo, c. 1910-1920, silver, 4 x 3 inches. Collection of Sara W. Reeves and I.S.K. Reeves V.

Denise Wallace (Inuit), King Island Dancer I, 1989, pin of silver and fossil ivory, 14K with mask, 1 5/8 x 1 3/4 inches. Collection of Sara W. Reeves and I.S.K. Reeves V.

POTTERY

Canteen, Zuni, late nineteenth / early twentieth century, ceramic, leather strap (may not be original to canteen) 6 7/8 x 7 inches wide. Collections of the Anthropology Department of the Florida Museum of Natural History, Gainesville, Florida, cat. no. P1869.

Dough Bowl, possibly Santo Domingo, late nineteenth / early twentieth century, ceramic, 4 7/8 x 8 7/8 inches maximum diameter. Collections of the Anthropology Department of the Florida Museum of Natural History, Gainesville, Florida, cat. no. 26310.

Martin J. Haythorn, Pedestaled Duck Effigy Miniature, 1997, ceramic, height 3 inches. Collection of the Artist (GA-204).

Martin J. Haythorn, Flattened Globular Bowl, 1996-1997, ceramic, height 4 inches. Collection of the Artist (FL-1300).

Martin J. Haythorn, Derived Effigy Vessel Miniature, 1997, ceramic, height 3 inches. Collection of the Artist (FL-1342).

Martin J. Haythorn, Derived Effigy Bowl, 1996-1997, ceramic, height 5 inches. Collection of the Artist (FL-2901).

Martin J. Haythorn, Pedestaled Bird Effigy, 1996-1997, ceramic, height 9 inches.

Collection of the Artist (FL-1832).

Martin J. Haythorn, Flattened Globular Bowl, 1996-1997, ceramic, diameter 8 inches. Collection of the Artist (FL-1300).

Martin J. Haythorn, Owl Effigy Vessel, 1996-1997, ceramic, height 6 inches. Collection of the Artist (FL-1810).

Martin J. Haythorn, Pedestaled Owl Effigy Miniature, 1997, ceramic, height 3 inches. Collection of the Artist (FL-1371).

Lucy Lewis (Acoma), Polychrome Jar, 1965, height 13.4 cm., diameter 16 cm. Collection of the School of American Research, Santa Fe, New Mexico.

María and Julián Martínez, (San Idlefonso), Bowl, black on black pottery, c. 1930s, 2 7/8 x 6 1/4 maximum diameter. Given to Dr. James A. Ford for an Indian Arts Show in Atlanta, Georgia, 1936. Collections of the Anthropology Department of the Florida Museum of Natural History, Gainesville, Florida, cat. no. E252.

María and Julián Martínez, (San Ildefonso), Vase, c. 1920s, black on black pottery, height 11 1/4, width at shoulder 8 1/2 inches. Collection of Sara W. Reeves and I.S.K. Reeves V.

Fanny Nampeyo (Hopi-Tewa), Bowl, c. 1936-1940, ceramic, 4 1/2 x 7 3/4 inches. Donor purchase from Navajo Reservation at Windowrock, 1936-1940. Gift of Mrs. Solon T. (Hannah) Kimball. Collections of the Anthropology Department of the Florida Museum of Natural History, Gainesville, Florida, cat. no. E828.

Fanny Nampeyo (Hopi-Tewa), Ceramic Bowl, 1905-1907, height 7.8 cm., diameter 24.1 cm. Collection of the School of American Research, Santa Fe, NM.

Michael Stuckey, Bat Effigy Rattle Bowl, 1996, ceramic, height 3 inches, diameter 6 inches. Collection of the Artist.

Michael Stuckey, Owl Effigy, 1998, ceramic, height 12 1/2 inches, diameter 13 inches. Collection of the Artist.

Owl Head Sherd, Southeast Ceremonial Complex, Choctawhatchee Beach Cemetery Site, Walton Co., Florida, c. 1350-1500, ceramic, 2 x 3 inches, Indian Temple Mound Museum, Ft. Walton Beach, Florida (#1415).

Pelican Head Sherd, Southeast Ceremonial Complex, Choctawhatchee Beach Cemetery Site, Walton Co., Florida, c. 1350-1500, ceramic, 2 x 3 inches. Indian Temple Mound Museum, Ft. Walton Beach, Florida (#1089).

Marriage Bowl, Southeast Ceremonial Complex, Pickens-Pencak Ceremonial Site, Walton Co., Florida, c. 1350-1500, ceramic, 4 x 8 inches. Indian Temple Mound Museum, Ft. Walton Beach, Florida (#1253).

Pottery Jar, Zía (also identified as San Ildefonso), n.d., ceramic, 31 x 31 cm. maximum diameter. Collections of the Anthropology Department of the Florida Museum of Natural History, Gainesville, Florida, cat. no. P1894.

Sikyatki Revival Bowl: Corn Maiden, Hopi, c. 1895-1900, ceramic, diameter 10 1/2 inches. Collection of Sara W. Reeves and I.S.K. Reeves V.

Turkey Vulture Effigy Incense Burner, McKeithen Site, Columbia County, Florida, c. 250-700, ceramic, 27 x 30 x 23 cm. Collections of the Anthropology Department of the Florida Museum of Natural History, Gainesville, Florida, cat. no. A-20086.

Water Jar, Acoma, c. 1880-1900, ceramic, diameter 12 3/4 inches. Collection of Sara W. Reeves and I.S.K. Reeves V.

Water Jar, Zía, c. 1900, ceramic, diameter at greatest width 10 1/2 inches. Collection of Sara W. Reeves and I.S.K. Reeves V.

Water Jar, Zuni, n.d., ceramic, 10 1/4 x 13 1/8 inches in diameter. Collections of the Anthropology Department of the Florida Museum of Natural History, Gainesville, Florida, cat. no. P1861.

Water Jar, Zuni (also identified as Acoma), n.d., ceramic, 11 x 13 1/8 inches maximum diameter. Collections of the Anthropology Department of the Florida Museum of Natural History, Gainesville, Florida, cat. no. P1859.

Water Jar, Zuni, 1910-1915, ceramic, height 25.4 cm., diameter 33 cm. Collection of the School of American Research, Santa Fe, New Mexico.

PHOTOGRAPHY

Edward Sheriff Curtis, *Chief Garfield*, 1904, photogravure (re-strike), 12 x 15 inches. Star / Fire Collection—Sandra Starr-Tanner.

Gertrude Käsebier, *Iron Tail*, 1898, reprint from Department of Photographic History, National Museum of American History, Smithsonian Institution, Washington, D.C. Photo no. 81-9567.

Gertrude Käsebier, *Willie Spotted Horse*, c. 1901, reprint from Department of Photographic History, National Museum of American History, Smithsonian Institution, Washington, D.C. Photo no. 83-903.

Gertrude Käsebier, *Zitkala-Sa*, c. 1898, reprint from Department of Photographic History, National Museum of American History, Smithsonian Institution, Washington, D.C. Photo no. 85-7209.

Gertrude Käsebier, *Profile of Iron Tail*, 1898, reprint from Department of Photographic History, National Museum of American History, Smithsonian Institution, Washington, D.C. Photo no. 89-13428.

PAINTING, DRAWING, AND MIXED MEDIA

Marcus Amerman (Choctaw), *Jicarilla Girl*, c. 1995, cut glass beads, 12 x 10 inches. Sandy Green, Glenn Green Galleries, Santa Fe, New Mexico.

Karl Bodmer, *Mato-tope, a Mandan Chief*, drawn c. 1822-1834, printed c. 1840-1843, engraver Hurlimann, etching and aquatint (hand-colored), 25 1/2 x 18 7/8 inches. Buffalo Bill Historical Center, Cody, Wyoming. Gift of Clara S. Peck.

Buffalo Meat (Cheyenne), Ledger Art, c. 1875-1877, colored pencil drawing, 15 1/2 x 10 1/2 inches. Collection of Sara W. Reeves and I.S.K. Reeves V.

George Catlin, *Osceola, Chief of the Seminoles*, 1838, oil on board, 29 x 24 3/4 inches. American Museum of Natural History, New York.

Pop Chalee (Taos), *Black Forest*, n.d., 49.5 x 64.8 cm. Collection of the School of American Research, Santa Fe, New Mexico.

Colleen Cutschall (Oglala-Sicangu / Lakota), *Beads and Boat People*, 1995, acrylic on canvas, 72 x 40 inches. Collection of the Artist.

Richard Glazer Danay (Mohawk), *Indians Are My Favorite Hobby*, 1976, oil on canvas, 36 x 24 inches. Collection of George Longfish.

Jimmie Durham (Cherokee descent), *Not Lothar Baumgarten's Cherokee*, 1990, mixed media on paper, 17 x 20 1/4 inches. Collection of the Whitney Museum of American Art, New York.

Howling Wolf (Cheyenne), Ledger Drawing, c. 1875-1877, colored pencil, 24 1/2 x 22 3/8 inches. Collection of Sara W. Reeves and I.S.K. Reeves V.

Phil Hughte (Zuni), Images from *A Zuni Artist Looks at Frank Hamilton Cushing*, published in Zuni, New Mexico, by A:shiwi Publishing, 1994.

Shelley Niro (Iroquois), *Taste of Heaven*, 1998, hand-tinted photograph, 3 panels at 4' x 5' each. Collection of the Artist.

Elaine Reichek, *Sampler: (The Country Was Made)*, 1992, embroidery on linen, 24 x 21 inches. Collection of Elaine Reichek, New York.

Elaine Reichek, *Painted Blackfoot*, 1990, oil on photo and wool, 79 x 73 inches. Collection of Elaine Reichek, New York.

Elaine Reichek, *Sampler: (Wagon Image)*, 1992, embroidery on linen, 21 1/2 x 18 1/2 inches. Collection of Elaine Reichek, New York.

Elaine Reichek, *Sign of the Cross*, 1991, photocollage, 47 x 60 inches. Collection of Elaine Reichek, New York.

Abel Sanchez (San Ildefonso), Painting, 1930-1935, 27.9 x 35.6 cm. Collection of the School of American Research, Santa Fe, New Mexico.

Joseph Henry Sharp, *Wolf Ear*, c. 1900, oil on canvas, 14 x 10 inches. Butler Institute of American Art, Youngstown, Ohio.

Joseph Henry Sharp, *Chief Two Moons*, c. 1899, oil on canvas, 14 x 10 inches. Butler Institute of American Art, Youngstown, Ohio.

Joseph Henry Sharp, *Sun Feather (Pueblo)*, 1898, oil on canvas, 13 x 10 inches. Butler Institute of American Art, Youngstown, Ohio.

Jaune Quick-to-See Smith (Confederated Salish and Kootenai Nation), *Paper Dolls for a Post-Columbian World. . .with ensembles donated by the U.S. Government*, 1991, watercolor and pencil, photocopy on paper, 13 pieces, each 17 x 11 inches. Courtesy of the Steinbaum Krauss Gallery, New York City.

Jaune Quick-to-See Smith (Confederated Salish and Kootenai Nation), *Cowboys and Indians*, 1995, diptych, acrylic and mixed media on canvas, 80 x 72 inches. Courtesy of the Steinbaum Krauss Gallery, New York City.

Mark Tansey, Study for *Purity Test*, 1982, oil on canvas, 24 x 30 inches. Collection of the Artist.

Andrew Van Tsihnahjinnie (Diné), *Male Sand Painting*, c. 1954, oil on board, 28 x 21 7/8 inches (sheet). The Philbrook Museum of Art, Tulsa, Oklahoma.

Hulleah Tsinhnahjinnie (Seminole / Creek / Diné), *Diné 007-A* (from Creative Native Series), 1983, silverprint, 40 x 30 inches. Collection of the Artist.

Hulleah Tsinhnahjinnie (Seminole / Creek / Diné), *Racially Pure* (from Creative Native Series), 1983, silverprint, 40 x 30 inches. Collection of the Artist.

Hulleah Tsinhnahjinnie (Seminole / Creek / Diné), *Ishi and Me*, 1996, photocollage, 40 x 30 inches. Collection of the Artist.

Hulleah Tsinhnahjinnie (Seminole / Creek / Diné), *Native Motion*, 1997, photocollage, 20 x 24 inches. Collection of the Artist.

Hulleah Tsinhnahjinnie (Seminole / Creek / Diné), *When Did Dreams of White Buffalo Turn to Dreams of White Women?*, 1990, photocollage, 20 x 24 inches. Collection of the Artist.

Awa Tsireh (Alfonso Roybal—San Ildefonso), *Deer Dance*, 1918-1919, 28 x 10 1/2 inches. Collection of the School of American Research, Santa Fe, New Mexico.

Romando Vigil (San Ildefonso), *Thunderbird and Deer*, c. 1930, watercolor on board, 21 5/8 x 28 3/8 inches (sheet). The Philbrook Museum of Art, Tulsa, Oklahoma.

Melanie Yazzie (Navajo / Diné), *She Keeps Silent*, 1993, collage, 56 x 43 inches. Collection of the Artist.

Melanie Yazzie (Navajo / Diné), *Our History Can Be Seen in the Navajo Times*, 1986, mixed media, 22 x 18 inches. Collection of the Artist.

The Curators

• **Jehanne Teilhet-Fisk**, co-curator, editor of research and content, and contributing catalogue author for *Dimensions of Native America: the Contact Zone* received her Ph.D from the University of California, Los Angeles, in 1975. Since the Fall of 1995, Dr. Teilhet-Fisk has been a Professor of Art History at Florida State University. From 1968-1994, she was Professor of Art History at the University of California in San Diego, where she now has Emeritus status. In 1967-68, Dr. Teilhet-Fisk worked as an Assistant Curator in the Department of Antiquities at the Jos Museum in Nigeria. Dr. Teilhet-Fisk has curated several exhibitions including *Dimensions of Black* held at the La Jolla Museum of Contemporary Art in 1970; and *Dimensions of Polynesia* held at the San Diego Museum of Fine Arts in 1973. In addition to many articles on Polynesian art and culture, Dr. Teilhet-Fisk's publications include her book *Paradise Reviewed: An Interpretation of Gauguin's Polynesian Symbolism* (1988).

• **Robin Franklin Nigh**, co-curator and contributing catalogue author of *Dimensions of Native America: the Contact Zone* received her M.A. from the School of the Art Institute of Chicago in 1991 and is currently a Ph. D. candidate in the Department of Art History at Florida State University. Ms. Nigh serves as Special Projects Coordinator in the Museum and directs the Art in State Buildings Program for the University. From 1994-1996, Ms. Nigh taught Art History as part of an Appleton teaching scholarship. From 1991-1994, she was the instructor for various Art History courses at Palm Beach Community College and Florida International University. Ms. Nigh has also served as the Director of Art in Public Places for Palm Beach County and as Associate Curator for the Norton Gallery of Art in West Palm Beach, Florida. In February, 1998, she will present a paper at the College Art Association meeting in Toronto on the use of time in the works of James Luna.

Florida State University

Talbot D'Alemberte, President
Lawrence G. Abele, Provost & VP for Academic Affairs
J.L. Draper, Dean, School of Visual Arts & Dance

Museum of Fine Arts Steering Committee

Ray Burggraf, Associate Professor of Art
Charles Dykes, Assistant Chair, Interior Design
Paula Gerson, Chair, Art History
Janice Hartwell, Professor of Art
Ed Love, Professor of Art
Sally McRorie, Chair, Art Education
Roald Nasgaard, Chair, Department of Art
Sandra Talarico, Director, Appleton Museum of Art
Jehanne Teilhet-Fisk, Professor of Art History
Patricia Young, Associate Professor of Dance

Museum of Fine Arts Staff

Allys Palladino-Craig, Director
Viki D. Thompson Wylder, Registrar & Education Curator
Julienne T. Mason, Graphic Design & Fiscal Officer
Jean D. Young, Appleton / Museum of Fine Arts Projects
Mark Fletcher, Preparator
Robin F. Nigh, Special Projects
William Walmsley, Professor Emeritus, Special Projects Advisor
Alyssa Whittle and Mary Spadafora, Volunteer Coordinators, 1997-1998 Season
Harry Bleattler, Graduate Assistant
Jeanette Balchunis, Graduate Assistant
Kevin Sandridge, Graduate Assistant
Ya-Mei Su, Graduate Assistant
William J. Woolf, Graduate Assistant

Florida State University Volunteers and Interns

Yamilett Abejon	Vicki Mariner
Kimberly Baker	Keith S. Mason
Jackie Beaulieu	Alix Miczulski
Hillary Crawford	Jackie Miller
Kelly Dorn	Shelly Mudgett
Beth Durbin	Karen Peterson
Lenee Essig	Dawn Rosa
Shelley Goldsby	Stacey Rosenberg
Sherill Gross	Melody Samples
Faye Hunt	Loren Sparling
Cynthia Killingsworth	Kathy Williamson
Esther Lee	J. Thomas Wylder